An Introduction to European Foreign Policy

An Introduction to European Foreign Policy provides a concise introduction to European foreign policy and its role in world politics. Written by a consummate Brussels insider, the book assesses the external issues and priorities facing the EU in the twenty-first century. By examining the origins, workings and priorities of European foreign policy, Fraser Cameron argues that the European Union (EU) has become a new and increasingly influential superpower.

The book reviews the evolution of the EU's international role over the past two decades and illustrates the growing influence of the EU in traditional areas such as trade and development, as well as in new areas such as the environment and global governance. The development of the EU's military capabilities is also assessed, as is the EU's wide range of relationships with key actors (the US, China, Russia) and regions (the Mediterranean, the Middle East, Africa) around the globe. The book covers the institutional arrangements for the Common Foreign and Security Policy and explains what was planned to strengthen the EU's external role in the constitutional treaty – an EU foreign minister and an EU diplomatic service.

With clearly illustrated up-to-date case studies, covering major issues such as Iraq and Iran, each chapter includes key questions and suggestions for further reading. As such, *An Introduction to European Foreign Policy* will be of great interest to students of European and international politics and for those who wish to become involved in the external relations of the EU.

Fraser Cameron is one of the foremost experts on the external relations of the EU and has published widely on all aspects of European foreign policy. A former British diplomat and EU official, he is Director of EuroFocus-Brussels, a senior advisor to the European Policy Centre and Director of the EU–Russia Centre.

An Introduction to European Foreign Policy

Fraser Cameron

LONDON AND NEW YORK

First published 2007
by Routledge
2 Park Square, Milton Park, Abingdon, Oxon OX14 4RN

Simultaneously published in the USA and Canada
by Routledge
270 Madison Ave, New York, NY 10016

Routledge is an imprint of the Taylor & Francis Group, an informa business

© 2007 Fraser Cameron

Typeset in Times New Roman by
Keystroke, 28 High Street, Tettenhall, Wolverhampton
Printed and bound in Great Britain by
Antony Rowe Ltd, Chippenham, Wiltshire

British Library Cataloguing in Publication Data
A catalogue record for this book is available from the British Library

Library of Congress Cataloging in Publication Data
Cameron, Fraser, 1947–
An introduction to European foreign policy / by Fraser Cameron.
p. cm.
Includes bibliographical references.
1. European Union–Foreign relations. I. Title.
D2025.C36 2007
341.3094–dc22   2006028482

ISBN 10: 0–415–40767–2 (hbk)
ISBN 10: 0–415–40768–0 (pbk)
ISBN 10: 0–203–96464–0 (ebk)

ISBN 13: 978–0–415–40767–0 (hbk)
ISBN 13: 978–0–415–40768–7 (pbk)
ISBN 13: 978–0–203–96464–4 (ebk)

Contents

The EU as a model 215
Conclusion 216

Illustrations

Figures

Map

Boxes

Case studies

Preface

With nearly 500 million citizens and the world's largest internal market, the European Union (EU) represents a quarter of the world's economic output and a fifth of global trade. With its unique range of policy instruments, trade, aid, political dialogue and crisis-management capacity, the EU is well placed to play a major role as a global actor; but despite its economic superpower status the EU is only slowly becoming a political player. The 1992 Treaty on European Union (TEU) states boldly that the EU is 'to assert its identity on the international scene, in particular through the implementation of a common foreign and security policy'. This ambitious aim is shared by an overwhelming majority of Europeans who, according to numerous polls, want the EU to play a more coherent and effective role on the world stage. A clear majority also think that the EU should be able to look after its own security. But how realistic is this after the open disarray of the Europeans over the Iraq war? Will the EU ever – as some believe it should – have its own seat on the United Nations Security Council (UNSC)?

There are very different views on the external relations of the EU and on the Common Foreign and Security Policy (CFSP) in particular. Some argue that it will never work, or at most will affect only the margins of foreign-policy making. Others argue that the CFSP has been in existence for scarcely a decade and yet has some credible achievements. Still others argue that the prism of the CFSP is too narrow to judge the EU's external performance and that one has to assess all the other policy areas such as enlargement, trade, the environment, agriculture, fisheries, development, finance, customs, energy, transport, terrorism and asylum that impact on foreign policy. Taking this wider perspective, it may be argued that the EU is already a global actor. The EU is the world's leading trade power and the largest provider of development assistance, while the euro is the second most important global currency. Even in crisis management terms the EU is becoming a global player. In 2006 it was active in areas as far apart as Aceh in Indonesia, the Sudan and Congo in Africa, Rafah in the Middle East, Bosnia and Macedonia in the Balkans, and Georgia and Moldova in eastern Europe.

What is foreign policy anyway? It is usually defined as the external actions of a state. But the EU is not a state, although it has some trappings of statehood such as a flag, an anthem and a currency. It was also planned to have an EU foreign minister and an EU diplomatic service to give more coherence and visibility to EU foreign policy, but these proposals are on ice after the 'no' votes in the French and Dutch referendums on the EU constitutional treaty in the first half of 2005. If the EU is not a state, what is it? It is perhaps best defined as a *sui generis* political actor, a unique institution that has developed a shared sovereignty in an increasing number of areas over the past fifty years. For the purposes of this book, I propose to consider foreign policy as all external actions that are undertaken by the actor, in this case the EU. This broad definition is contrary to how many traditionalists in the member states view foreign policy (see Further Reading at the end of Chapter 1). As a result of this limited view, and since the Maastricht Treaty, the EU has developed an unnecessary and complicated pillar system which attempts to separate 'foreign and security policy' from other policy areas. This pillar system is confusing both to insiders and to outsiders and a major structural weakness for the Union. It is likely to continue, however, for some considerable time.

This textbook aims to introduce readers to the EU's role in world politics. It examines the gradual rise of the EU as an international actor and considers the implications of that role for the EU and for the wider world. The book considers the interplay between internal and external developments, examining the impact of the internal market and the common commercial policy (CCP) on external policy. It examines some of the main theoretical approaches to foreign policy, but the stress is on the impact that the EU has on international affairs. This general aim leads to more specific objectives, including an assessment of the development of the CFSP and the European Security and Defence Policy (ESDP). It examines the difficult birth of these policies in the immediate after-math of the end of the Cold War and the break-up of the former Yugoslavia, and then explains the institutional structures that underpin the CFSP and the ESDP. There is an assessment of the interplay between the EU member states and the EU institutions. The dispute over Iraq is used as a case study, as is the EU3 model in dealing with Iran. The book then assesses the EU's relation-ships with major partners such as the USA and Asia as well as with its principal neighbours, including Russia and Ukraine, the states in the Balkans, the Mediterranean and the Middle East. There is an evaluation of the role played by the EU in the broader development of world order, including development policy, conflict prevention and crisis management. The EU's reaction to the global terrorist threat is also considered, while a final chapter considers future prospects.

In writing this book I have drawn on past experience in a national diplomatic administration and the European Commission. Over the years I have also had many discussions on foreign policy with EU officials and friends in the think-tank and policy communities on both sides of the Atlantic and elsewhere. I was also able to test some of my views with various student audiences and I remain confident that the next generation will be firmly committed to the idea of 'more Europe' in foreign policy. If this book sheds some light on European foreign policy and encourages some readers to become involved in the external relations of the EU, I shall feel a sense of achievement. Finally, I wish to thank my wife, Margaret, for her patience and help in completing this project.

Fraser Cameron
Brussels, December 2006

Abbreviations

ACPs	African, Caribbean and Pacific countries
AMM	Aceh Monitoring Mission
APEC	Asia-Pacific Economic Forum
APF	Africa Peace Facility
ARF	Asian Regional Forum
ASEAN	Association of South-East Asian Nations
ASEM	Asia–Europe Meeting
AU	African Union
BSEC	Black Sea Economic Co-operation
CAP	common agricultural policy
CARDS	Community Assistance for Reconstruction, Development and Stabilisation
CCP	common commercial policy
CEECs	countries of Central and Eastern Europe
CEPOL	European Police College
CFSP	Common Foreign and Security Policy
CIS	Commonwealth of Independent States
COPS	Comité politique et securité
Coreper	Committee of Permanent Representatives
COREU	Correspondant Européen (CFSP communications network)
CPA	Comprehensive Peace Agreement
CSCE	Conference on Security and Co-operation in Europe
CTBT	Comprehensive Test Ban Treaty
DCI	Defence Capabilities Initiative
DG	Directorate General
EBA	European Business Association
EC	European Communities
ECAP	European Capability Action Plan
ECB	European Central Bank
ECHO	European Commission Humanitarian Aid Office
ECJ	European Court of Justice
ECOFIN	Economic and Finance Council
ECOSOC	Economic and Social Committee (UN)

ECOWAS	Economic Community of West African States
ECSC	European Coal and Steel Community
EDA	European Defence Agency
EDC	European Defence Community
EDF	European Development Fund
EEA	European Economic Area
EEAS	European External Action Service
EEC	European Economic Community
EFTA	European Free Trade Area
EIB	European Investment Bank
EITI	Extractive Industries Transparency Initiative
EMU	European Monetary Union
ENP	European Neighbourhood Policy
ENPI	European Neighbourhood and Partnership Instrument
EP	European Parliament
EPAs	Economic Partnership Agreements
EPC	European Political Co-operation
ESDP	European Security and Defence Policy
ESS	European Security Strategy
EU	European Union
EUMC	European Union Military Committee
EUMM	European Union Monitoring Mission
EUMS	European Union Military Staff
EUPAT	European Union Police Advisory Team
EUPM	European Union Police Mission
Euratom	European Atomic Energy Community
Eurojust	European network of judicial authorities
Europol	European Police Office
EUSC	European Union Satellite Centre
EUSR	European Union Special and Personal Representatives
FAC	Foreign Affairs Council
FAO	Food and Agriculture Organisation
FATF	Financial Action Task Force
FDI	Foreign Direct Investment
FTA	Free Trade Agreement
FYROM	Former Yugoslav Republic of Macedonia
G8	Group of 8
GAC	General Affairs Council
GAERC	General Affairs and External Relations Council
GATS	General Agreement on Trade in Services
GATT	General Agreement on Tariffs and Trade
GCC	Gulf Co-operation Council
GDP	gross domestic product
GMOs	genetically modified organisms
GNP	gross national product

GSP	Generalised System Preferences
HHGs	Helsinki Headline Goals
HR	High Representative
IAEA	International Atomic Energy Agency
IBRD	International Bank for Reconstruction and Development (World Bank)
ICAO	International Civil Aviation Organisation
ICC	International Criminal Court
ICTY	International Criminal Tribunal for Yugoslavia
IFIs	international financial institutions
IFOR	Implementation Force (in Bosnia-Herzegovina)
IGC	Inter-governmental Conference
ILSA	Iran–Libya Sanction Act
IMF	International Monetary Fund
IR	international relations
JHA	justice and home affairs
KEDO	Korean Peninsula Energy Development Organisation
LDCs	least-developed countries
MDGs	Millennium Development Goals
MEDA	Mediterranean assistance programme
MEP	Member of the European Parliament
Mercosur	Common Market of the Southern Cone
MFA	Ministry of Foreign Affairs
MFN	most-favoured nation
MoU	memorandum of understanding
NATO	North Atlantic Treaty Organisation
NEPAD	New Economic Partnership for Africa's Development
NGO	non-governmental organisation
NPT	Non-Proliferation Treaty
NTA	New Transatlantic Agenda
OAS	Organisation of American States
ODA	Official Development Assistance
ODIHR	Office of Democratic Institutions and Human Rights
OECD	Organisation for Economic Co-operation and Development
OEEC	Organisation for European Economic Co-operation
OSCE	Organisation for Security and Co-operation in Europe
PCA	Partnership and Co-operation Agreement
Phare	Pologne–Hongrie aide à la reconstruction économique
POLMIL	Political Military
PPEWU	Policy Planning and Early Warning Unit
PSC	Political and Security Committee
PPP	purchasing power parity
QMV	qualified majority voting
RRF	Rapid Reaction Force
RRM	Rapid Reaction Mechanism

SAAs	Stabilisation and Association Agreements
SAARC	South Asian Association for Regional Co-operation
SACEUR	Supreme Allied Commander Europe
SADC	Southern African Development Community
SAP	Stabilisation and Association Process (in the Balkans)
SARS	Severe Acute Respiratory Syndrome
SCIFA	Strategic Committee on Immigration, Frontiers and Asylum
SEA	Single European Act
SFOR	Stabilisation Force in Bosnia-Herzegovina
SG/HR	Secretary General/High Representative
SHAPE	Supreme Headquarters Allied Powers Europe
SIS	Schengen Information System
SITCEN	Joint Situation Centre
SMEs	small and medium-sized enterprises
TABD	Transatlantic Business Dialogue
TACD	Transatlantic Consumer Dialogue
Tacis	Technical Aid to the Commonwealth of Independent States
TAED	Transatlantic Environmental Dialogue
TALD	Transatlantic Legislators Dialogue
TEP	Transatlantic Economic Partnership
TEU	Treaty on European Union
TREVI	Terrorism, Radicalisme, Extrémisme, Violence, Internationale
TRIPs	Trade Related Aspects of Intellectual Property Rights
TRNC	Turkish Republic of Northern Cyprus
UN	United Nations
UNCAC	United Nations Convention Against Corruption
UNCTAD	United Nations Conference on Trade and Development
UNEP	United Nations Environment Programme
UNESCO	United Nations Educational, Scientific and Cultural Organisation
UNGA	United Nations General Assembly
UNMIK	United Nations Interim Administration Mission in Kosovo
UNSC	United Nations Security Council
US/USA	United States (of America)
USTR	United States Trade Representative
WEU	Western European Union
WMD	weapons of mass destruction
WTO	World Trade Organisation

Map The European Union. Country names in own language

Source: European Commission

1 A strange superpower

SUMMARY

The European Union (EU) has become an increasingly important global actor but only in some areas. It is an economic superpower with its own currency (the euro) and plays a key role in international trade negotiations. It also plays an important role in many other areas such as the environment and development policy. It is the largest provider of development assistance and the largest contributor to the United Nations (UN) budget. It increasingly sends peace-keeping missions to far-flung regions of the world but it has nothing like the power-projection capabilities of the United States (US). Internal developments have often had an impact on external relations, and similarly the EU has had to respond to external events such as the end of the Cold War and 9/11. The EU's external representation is absurdly complicated and baffling to outsiders. Given its special nature, scholars find it difficult to agree on a theoretical label for the Union.

THE CHANGING GEO-STRATEGIC ENVIRONMENT

Between 1949 and 1989 the Cold War was the dominant security paradigm for Europe. The US and the Soviet Union were the two global superpowers vying for power and influence around the world. In these circumstances Europe was unable to assert itself as a global actor. European integration developed under the security umbrella of the US, which from the beginning was a strong supporter of a more cohesive Europe. In many ways the integration process was about abolishing traditional foreign policy. Indeed, the process of integration was largely about developing a new form of security, based on sharing sovereignty, that was unique in world history. The success of the integration process and the growing economic power of the EU were important factors in propelling the EU to be a more forceful global actor. The move towards globalisation in the 1980s and 1990s also blurred the lines between traditional foreign policy and other aspects of external relations. But it was the collapse of communism and the resulting unification of Germany that were the main factors in moves to establish a common foreign and security policy (CFSP).

The failure of the EU to prevent the conflict in the Balkans was a reality check on the more ambitious advocates of the CFSP. But the Balkans disaster propelled the Union to build up its crisis-management tools, including a robust military peace-keeping capability. The terrorist attacks of 11 September 2001 brought another profound shift in attitudes to international relations. This was not a state attacking another state but a global terrorist network striking at the heart of the world's only superpower. The subsequent terrorist attacks in Madrid and in London brought home to Europeans the threat to their own cities. The last decade has also witnessed a developing global consensus on the main security threats, even if there are differences in approach to tackling these threats. These include failed states, terrorism, regional and ethnic conflicts. But citizens are also concerned about transnational threats including health pandemics (Asian flu), environmental disasters (tsunami) and illegal migration. It is evident that no one state, no matter how powerful, can tackle these threats on its own. It is equally evident that the military instrument alone is inadequate to deal with these threats. This is where the EU has a certain advantage in that it can bring to the table an impressive array of civilian and military instruments to tackle these problems. It can engage in political dialogue, impose sanctions, offer trade concessions, lift visa restrictions, provide technical assistance, and send monitoring missions and even troops if required. This growing capability in crisis management is one of the defining features of the EU's growing global role.

THE EU AS AN ACTOR

The British prime minister, Tony Blair, once said that the EU should be a super-power but not a superstate. Some might regard the EU already as a superpower in some areas such as trade policy. Clearly it is not a military superpower like the US and has no ambitions to develop in that direction. But what kind of actor is the EU? There are many kinds of actor on the world stage. The vast majority are nation states (189 at the last count), of which the US is the most prominent. Former Secretary of State Madeleine Albright once described the US as 'the indispensable nation', meaning that it was involved in almost every major security issue around the world. It is certainly true that the US is in a class of its own in terms of the ability to project military power, but military power alone is rarely sufficient to resolve sensitive political problems. The war in Iraq was a sobering experience for many in the US who believed in the supremacy of the military machine. Nearer to home the US has not been able to secure a peaceful, democratic Haiti, nor has it been able to impose its will on countries it regards as 'difficult' such as Cuba or Venezuela in Latin America.

The other permanent members of the United Nations Security Council (UNSC) – Russia, China, Britain and France – are also important nation-state actors, but none has the global reach of the US. Russia, the largest country in the world, remains in a weak state fifteen years after the collapse of communism. It is not regarded as a model by any other country. But it has vast reserves of oil and gas, and if it were to resolve its internal problems, such as Chechnya, and diversify its economy it could become a more important global actor. China has increased its global presence significantly in the past decade as a result of its very high growth rates, but it also has major internal problems such as environmental damage and uneven regional development to overcome. It is nevertheless widely predicted to become a global superpower within the next two or three decades. Some predict that it may even surpass the US in gross domestic product by the middle of the century. India and Brazil are also important regional powers and both have been growing rapidly; but they, too, have huge internal problems including widespread poverty. Size is not everything. Small states such as Switzerland, Israel, Norway or Singapore can play a disproportionate role owing to their skilled population and technological prowess. Some states such as Iran or North Korea have also become important because of their desire to acquire nuclear technology. Others such as Saudi Arabia and Nigeria are important because of their possession of vast quantities of oil or gas. In Europe, many new actors have appeared in the past twenty years as a result of the collapse of communism. The three Baltic states, Estonia, Latvia and Lithuania, were part of the Soviet Union until 1991. Slovenia used to be part of Yugoslavia until the same year. The Czechs and the Slovaks used to be one country until their 'velvet divorce' in 1993. All these states are now independent actors within the EU and the North Atlantic Treaty Organisation (NATO).

Britain and France are the only two EU member states that have permanent seats on the UNSC. This has given rise to some rivalry, with Germany arguing that it should also be a permanent member while others have pushed the case for an EU seat at the UN. These three countries (Britain, France and Germany) have formed an interesting grouping (EU3) to deal with the problem of Iran's attempts to acquire nuclear weapons technology. It is evident that Britain and France bring more to the table in terms of military capabilities than Malta or Estonia. Poland has more knowledge about and a greater interest in developments in Ukraine than Italy and aspires to play a regional leadership role. Similarly, Spain is more closely involved in Latin America than most other member states, and its views carry particular weight when the EU discusses that region. The same is true for Austria and Greece with respect to the Balkan region. Thus, within the EU there are different categories of actor depending on the country's size, military and diplomatic capabilities, experience and interests. How these differences are managed inside the Union is discussed later.

There are also many international institutions such as the UN or NATO that are actors in the global arena. The UN is of special importance in that it has a global membership and is the only international body that can authorise the use of force. It has many peace-keeping missions around the world from

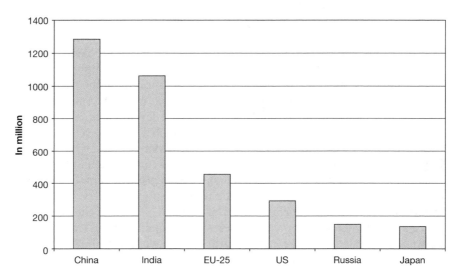

Figure 1.1 Population comparison
Source: European Commission

Cambodia to Cyprus, from Kashmir to Kosovo. Following the 2005 Millennium Summit, it is engaged in a thorough overhaul of its structures and operations. NATO, still searching for a role after the Cold War, has twenty-six member states, mostly European, and is engaged in peace-keeping operations in Afghanistan after playing a similar role in the Balkans. It has a number of countries wishing to join and engages in dialogues with many partner countries. These institutions are composed of member states that all have to agree if the organisation should become involved in a particular area; but once this happens the institution becomes the principal point of focus for public attention.

The international stage also contains many other kinds of actor. For example, there are major companies such as Shell or Microsoft, non-governmental organisations (NGOs) such as Amnesty or Greenpeace, and media organisations such as the BBC or Al Jazeera that also play a role in global politics. The large oil companies often play a significant role in the politics of oil-producing countries. One American company, Wal-Mart, with a turnover of $285 billion in 2005, enjoys greater revenues than the combined gross domestic products of Belgium, Austria and Greece. Large European companies such as Renault and Siemens also have higher revenues than several EU member states. Human rights and environmental organisations can hold governments to account and influence world public opinion. The land-mines treaty would probably not have been signed without pressure from NGOs. Animal rights organisations have had an impact on public perceptions of countries such as Canada and Japan which engage in the culling of seals and whale fishing. The presence of the world's media can influence whether a crisis receives the attention of politicians – the so-called 'CNN factor'.

There are thus many different kinds of actor in world politics, but how to define the role of the EU? Clearly it is not a state such as Britain or Italy. It has no prime minister to order troops into war, yet there are thousands of EU soldiers engaged in various peace-keeping and crisis-management operations around the world. The EU has no seat at the UN yet it is the strongest supporter of the UN system, and its member states increasingly vote together in New York. In other areas the EU is a direct actor. It is an economic giant, the largest supplier of development and technical assistance in the world. Its internal market is a magnet for foreign investors and for the EU's neighbours that desire access to a rich market of over 450 million citizens. It negotiates as one in international trade negotiations. It has taken a lead in the negotiations on climate change (Kyoto Protocol) and on the establishment of the International Criminal Court (ICC) in the face of strong opposition from the US. It seeks to expand its value system (e.g. promotion of democracy and human rights, abolition of the death penalty) and its own rules and norms in negotiations with third countries by imposing conditions on them. It also drew up a set of conditions (Copenhagen criteria) in 1993 that had to be met before new countries could join the EU. The EU is thus a strange animal, not quite a state but with more powers than many nation states in the international system. It is increasingly recognised as an actor by third parties, and this is important for its own prestige and ability to act. When President George W. Bush visited the European Commission in February 2005, and received the President of the Commission, José Manuel Barroso, in the White House in October 2005, this sent an important message to other actors in the international arena: the US was taking the EU seriously as a global player.

The economic superpower

Much of the EU's power derives from its economic strength. Its gross domestic product is roughly the same as that of the US, twice as big as Japan's, four times bigger than China's and ten times bigger than Russia's. With over 450 million citizens with high levels of spending power, its internal market is crucial for many countries around the world. The EU is the biggest exporter of both goods and services. The advent of the euro has also increased the EU's standing in the world. It is the second largest reserve currency in the world (with roughly 30 per cent of global reserves compared to the US dollar, roughly 60 per cent). More and more countries are using the euro either directly or indirectly, and with enlargement the eurozone could increase from twelve to twenty or thirty countries within a decade. There are also more European firms in the top 150 of the Fortune 500 than American. Airbus has become a global leader in aircraft design and sales, while European banks, insurance companies and telecom operators have carved out a global presence. BMW, Nokia, BP, Siemens and Hermès are just a few of the many European

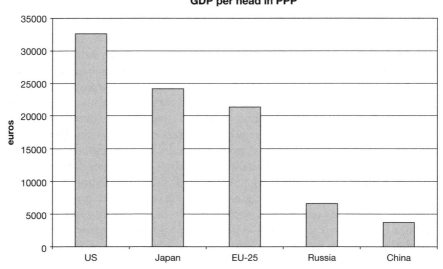

Figure 1.2 GDP comparison

Source: European Commission

global brands. Europe has also taken a lead in sustainable development, with far greater attention to energy efficiency and environmental issues than other major centres of economic power. But the EU cannot afford to rest on its laurels. Its productivity rates are considerably behind those of the US (although the figures are disputed), and it spends far less on research and development (R&D) than America. Its growth rates are way below those for China and India as well as the US. Its leading universities struggle to match those in the US. Overall, however, these economic achievements have contributed to the growing assertiveness of the EU as a major player in international economic and financial matters (Rifkin, 2004; Leonard, 2005).

THE EUROPEAN SECURITY STRATEGY (ESS)

> Europe has never been so prosperous, so secure nor so free. The violence of the first half of the 20th Century has given way to a period of peace and stability unprecedented in European history. The creation of the European Union has been central to this development. (ESS, December 2003)

For many years the EU was unable to agree on its security priorities. Every time such an attempt was made it ended in failure as each member state insisted that its priorities were also EU priorities. Strangely, it was the impact of the Iraq war, when the EU was hopelessly divided, that propelled the Union into agreeing a strategy document for the first time. France, Germany and the UK were the prime movers in giving a mandate to Javier Solana to produce a historic document entitled 'A Secure Europe in a Better World' (see Appendix 2). This was adopted by the December 2003 European Council and marked a major step forward for the EU in agreeing for the first time a strategic concept. The ESS has no illusions regarding the weakness of the EU as a military power. Indeed, the Union's lack of military capability is highlighted as a major weakness. The ESS stresses that tackling major threats (terrorism, proliferation of weapons of mass destruction, regional conflicts, state failure and organised crime) should be addressed through 'effective multilateralism', e.g. by supporting the UN system. These characteristics, along with an emphasis upon 'preventive engagement' rather than 'pre-emption', are generally acknowledged to make the ESS stand apart from the US national security strategy of September 2002. The ESS suggests that the EU has three key strategic objectives in applying its external instruments to meet contemporary security challenges: extending the zone of security on Europe's periphery; supporting the emergence of a stable and equitable international order; and seeking effective counter-measures to new and old threats. Whether applied to new or old threats, these counter-measures have certain common elements: recognising that the first line of defence lies beyond EU frontiers; acknowledging that inaction is not an option; understanding that a military response is not always appropriate but might form one element of a combined response. In this way, the EU can engage in the systematic political process of 'prevention'. Since its publication, the ESS has become a central point of reference for any discussion on EU foreign and security policy.

PUBLIC DIPLOMACY

How do you sell the EU? What is the EU brand? How do citizens both inside and outside the EU view this strange animal? Very few citizens could name the President of the European Commission or the President of the European Parliament. How do you distinguish between those things that are quintessentially European like the Eurovision Song Contest or the Champions League and national images, whether of Mozart or Picasso, French cheese or German cars, that equally are part of European culture and tradition? Only rarely does a European team take on other opponents. The biennial Ryder Cup between the best European and American golfers is a rare example of European identity in the sports arena. London and Paris were rivals for the 2012 Olympic bid, but increasingly there are consortia of two or more European countries bidding to host major sports events. The EU is certainly not an easy sell, mainly because of complicated structures and its image of grey men in suits engaged in endless rounds of negotiations. This does not make for good television; and, despite their qualities, neither the President of the Commission, José Maria Barroso, nor the High Representative for the CFSP, Javier Solana, perhaps the two most important EU public figures, is unlikely to attract large audiences. There is no doubt that the EU has to be sold in the first instance by member-state governments. The EU institutions and their leaders only have a supporting role to play. This has been the clear lesson of the various referendum campaigns that have been held in Europe over the years.

At the same time European culture and commerce are very appealing to global consumers. Polls conducted in July 2005 by the Pew Institute found that a majority of Americans had a favourable image of the EU, and ranked it fourth for influence in the world behind the US, Britain and China. The Union has major assets in the institutions and resources of the twenty-five member states – but too often these resources are competing to promote national interests. The UK has the British Council, the Germans the Goethe Institute, the French the Centre Culturelle to promote their language and culture. The EU, however, only has a tiny budget to promote knowledge of its activities. But budgets are only part of the problem. Actions speak louder than words, and the growing number of EU actions around the world is slowly but surely making an impact on global perceptions. In Asia, for example, a 2004 survey found that the respondents were aware of the Union's economic strength and soft-power approach to international relations (Chaban and Holland, 2005).

It might be easier to sell the EU if its structures were less complicated. But since the Treaty of Maastricht (1992) the EU has been based on three pillars. The first and most extensive pillar covers the traditional European Community (EC) policies such as trade, development and agriculture. The second pillar covers the CFSP. The third pillar covers justice and home affairs, issues such as immigration, asylum and borders. The first pillar is organised under the 'Community method', which gives a leading role to the European Commission; while the second and third pillars are organised on an inter-governmental basis,

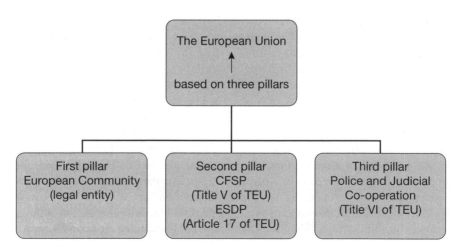

Figure 1.3 The pillar system of the EU

in which the member states play the decisive role. For most outsiders the system is overcomplicated and difficult to comprehend.

THE INTERNAL–EXTERNAL INTERPLAY

There has always been a close connection between EU internal and external developments. When the six founding states created the European Coal and Steel Community (ECSC) in 1952, this had an impact on global trade in these products. Similarly, as the EU developed common policies in other areas such as trade, environment, agriculture and fisheries, this impacted on third countries. In recent years the EU has made considerable strides forward in justice and home affairs; and, despite internal wrangling between foreign and interior ministries, this, again, has had an impact on external relations (e.g. visa and asylum policy, control of borders). The US Department of Homeland Security, for example, prefers the EU as a single interlocutor in tackling issues such as container security, border management, passenger data, rather than twenty-five member states (although it sometimes requests all member states to endorse what has been agreed at EU level). The following examples covering trade policy, air transport and the environment demonstrate the constant interplay between internal and external developments.

TRADE POLICY

The EU is perhaps best known as the world's leading trade power. It negotiates on a par with the US, China, Japan, Brazil and India in world trade negotiations such as the Doha round. It is regularly criticised in the media for failing to open up its protected agricultural market, a criticism that could also be levelled at other rich countries such as the US, Japan, Norway and Switzerland. The common commercial policy (CCP) is at the core of EU external relations and has been in place since the customs union was established in the late 1960s. The CCP results from European Community (EC) competence (or power) under the first pillar to regulate access to the EC market. Article 133 of the Treaty of Rome gives the EC, rather than the member states, authority to negotiate treaties on trade and tariffs. Negotiations, such as those for the Doha round, are conducted by the European Commission under the general oversight of the Article 133 Committee (composed of representatives of the member states). The results are then formally adopted by the Council, normally by qualified majority voting. The Directorate General (DG) Trade is the lead agency for trade negotiations, and many of the brightest and best Commission staff tend to work there as it is a DG that wields real power. Most agreements involve granting non-member states preferential access to the EU's internal market through an increase in or abolition of quotas, or a lowering of the common external tariff. EU rules dictate that most agreements must involve

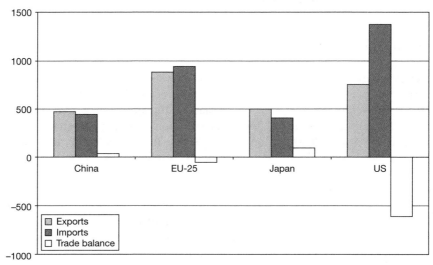

Figure 1.4 International trade

Source: European Commission

the creation of a free-trade area or a customs union within a reasonable period of time and cover substantially all goods. Traditionally, the CCP has covered mainly trade in goods, but with the Treaty of Nice the coverage of the CCP was extended to include trade in services.

Case study 1.1: The EU and the WTO

The EU is the most important player in the World Trade Organisation (WTO), which was established in January 1995 as the successor to the General Agreement on Tariffs and Trade (GATT). This was a body set up in the late 1940s with the aim of liberalising international trade by reducing the levels of tariffs. By the 1990s the international trade agenda had widened considerably to include protectionism, competition policy, social and environmental policy, and labour-market deregulation. GATT had been a useful body but was limited in its scope, and hence it was decided to establish a new organisation that became the WTO, which, in 2006, comprised 144 member countries. Based in Geneva, the Director General of the WTO is the Frenchman Pascal Lamy, who was the former EU Trade Commissioner. One of the important successes in recent years was the accession of China to the WTO. This meant that China had to open up its markets and play by the international rulebook. There are hopes that Russia, Ukraine and Saudi Arabia will also join the WTO in the next few years.

The WTO has a crucial role to play in ensuring, promoting and protecting trade liberalisation. Based on the consensus principle, it also serves as a forum to settle trade disputes and has established a dispute-settlement mechanism, which involves independent panels making judgements on cases brought to the WTO. The parties are expected to comply with the panel's rulings. In recent years these have involved many transatlantic disputes touching on issues as diverse as bananas, steel, tax policy and genetically modified organisms. Despite the logic of such an international forum to resolve trade disputes, the WTO has been the centre of sometimes violent demonstrations by anti-globalisation protesters. In 2003, WTO members launched the Doha development round of trade negotiations following the failure of summits in Seattle in 1999 and Cancún in 2002. The Doha round was supposed to conclude at a ministerial meeting in Hong Kong in December 2005; but the major trade powers, the EU, the US, Brazil and India, could not agree, and the negotiations were only partially successful. As of late 2006 the negotiations had still not been concluded.

The reason for the protracted negotiations was continuing distrust between the industrialised countries and the least-developed countries (LDCs). Among the main items under discussion in the Doha round were duty-free access from the fifty LDCs, 'aid for trade' and help for African cotton producers. The LDCs together account for less than 1 per cent of world trade, but the US wanted to exclude from the negotiations sugar, textiles and cotton; the Japanese rice and leather; and the EU some agricultural products. These exemptions would have significantly reduced the value of the offer. The EU, the US and other developed countries pledged $3 billion for trade-capacity building and another $10 billion for aid in infrastructure. West African cotton producers wanted rapid elimination of subsidies to US cotton farmers worth more than $4 billion in 2005, and creation of an emergency fund to compensate them for depressed world prices. Brazil and India wanted the EU and the US to open their agricultural markets if they were to allow the EU and the US to penetrate their markets in goods and services.

The EU member states have all recognised the benefits of being able to negotiate as a single entity vis-à-vis the US and other players. Their trade officials agree a mandate to the Trade Commissioner (currently Peter Mandelson), and he then negotiates on behalf of the 450-million-strong Union.

AIR TRANSPORT

As the EU moved in the 1990s to liberalise air transport, thus leading to a mushrooming of low-cost airlines such as Ryanair and EasyJet, this had a major impact on how the EU managed its external relations in this field. In November 2002 the European Court of Justice (ECJ), as it often does, played a key role in ruling on EU competence. The ECJ had consistently taken the view that, each time the EU adopts new rules, member states can no longer affect these rules or alter their scope. More specifically, the ECJ ruled in 1971 that where the EC has exercised an explicit internal competence it also has a parallel external competence, and that in such circumstances member states cannot act independently of the EC in entering into international agreements. In other words, when the Community develops exclusive powers (competence) for a policy area, it should also represent the EC in dealing with third countries. As regards air transport, the EU has progressively moved to harmonise sectors such as air fares, slot allocation and reservation systems. This has allowed greater competition and freedom for airlines of one member state to operate in another member state (a policy known as cabotage). The November 2002 ECJ ruling involved a case brought by the European Commission against eight member states regarding their bilateral air-service agreements with the US. The Court ruled that the member states had infringed the external competence of the Community as several elements of their bilateral agreements (air fares, slots, reservation systems) were areas of Community competence. The judgement did not declare that the EU had exclusive competence for air services but it did decide that jurisdiction was broadly shared and that the Commission could not be ignored.

In February 2003 the Commission returned to the Council seeking a mandate to negotiate with the US and third countries. The Commission then started negotiations with the US for an 'open skies' agreement that would establish a North Atlantic aviation area. As of late 2006 the negotiations were not completed, with the sticking-points being US reluctance to end the 'Fly America' policy (where all government employees have to fly with US carriers on official business) and to allow cabotage to European airlines. This would mean, for example, that Lufthansa or Air France could pick up and fly passengers from New York to Los Angeles. It may be that there will be a partial agreement pending resolution of these difficult issues. Meanwhile the Commission has also started similar negotiations with many other countries in its neighbourhood (Turkey, Russia) and further afield (Japan, Chile). The high fees that Russia charges EU airlines for over-flying Siberia en route to the Far East have become a major issue for EU–Russia relations. There was an agreement in November 2006 to phase out these changes by 2013. In short, the liberalisation of air services within the EU has had a far-reaching impact on third countries and on the EC's competence to negotiate as a single body in this area. EU aviation rules now apply to twenty-eight countries, and this number is set to increase. The increased EC competence in this field has not led, so far, to EC membership of the International Civil Aviation Organisation (ICAO), but this is probably only a matter of time.

ENVIRONMENTAL POLICY

The EU has also become an important actor in global environmental policy. In the 1970s environmental issues were largely internal, with the Green Party in Germany perhaps the most vocal and successful in raising issues such as clean air. In the 1980s and 1990s environmental issues became increasingly European and then global. Today there is widespread concern about the impact of climate change on glaciers, marine systems, terrestrial ecosystems and bio-diversity, agriculture and health. The major floods in Europe during the past few years caused huge economic losses. The EU adopted its first environmental policy in 1972 and since then has adopted several action programmes. It enshrined environmental policy in the Maastricht Treaty on European Union (TEU), committing the Union to a 'balanced and sustainable development'. The TEU then stated that environmental concerns must be taken into account in all Community policies such as agriculture and fisheries, transport, energy and industry. The environment has become a major area for EU legislation, with over 200 laws – mainly directives under the co-decision procedure involving the European Parliament – on the statute book. The Commission also has powers to institute infringement procedures against offenders. The EU also provides substantial funding for the environment, has introduced a voluntary system of labelling and a logo for organisations that improve their environmental performance on a continuous basis – the eco-management and audit scheme. The sixth environmental action programme (2002–12) has four priority areas: climate change, environmental health and quality of life, nature and biodiversity, natural resources and waste. The budget for this programme amounts to €7.1 billion per year.

The internal developments in the area of the environment have been accompanied by a growing EU presence and a drive to improve international standards. The EU was either directly involved in or followed up the recommendations of the 1972 Stockholm programme, the 1987 Brundtland report and the 1992 Rio conference on the environment and development. The EU played a major role in the establishment of the Kyoto Protocol, in the agreements on biological diversity, on the ozone layer and on hazardous waste. The EU (or, strictly speaking, the EC) is a contracting party to over forty conventions including the UN Framework Convention on Climate Change (1992) and the Kyoto Protocol (1997); the UN Convention on Biological Diversity (1992); the UN Environment Programme Vienna Convention for the Protection of the Ozone Layer (1985) and the Montreal Protocol (1987); and the Basel Convention on the control of trans-boundary movements of hazardous waste and its disposal (1989). It is perhaps with the Kyoto Protocol that the EU has taken a very prominent role, in the face of fierce American opposition, that has given the EU real leadership status in the eyes of the world.

In terms of external representation, the environment arena is an area of mixed competence between the EC and the member states, and there has been an ad hoc approach in recent years. This is mainly because the limitations of the six-monthly rotating Presidency have been exposed in international environmental negotiations, which usually last several years. In the negotiations on climate change and implementation of the Kyoto Protocol, it is the Presidency which negotiates on behalf of the EU, although the Commission plays an important role, in particular on issues which need to be co-ordinated and harmonised. In recent years, some informal arrangements have been put in place to maximise the EU's impact in international environmental negotiations, to facilitate preparations and to ensure continuity. Two specific ad hoc experiences deserve mention: first, the 'lead-country approach' in the Commission on Sustainable Development and, second, the 'EU-team' approach in the bio-safety negotiations. As in the CFSP domain, there are substantial differences in capacities between the member states and attitudes towards EU representation. Some favour giving the Commission a negotiating mandate, as in trade policy, but others are opposed to what they would regard as increased power to the Commission.

A complex animal

These examples covering trade, air services and the environment demonstrate the complexity of the EU's legal order. Rarely does the EU have exclusive competence in any field, but competence is often shared or 'mixed', and hence the necessity for the European Community to play, at a minimum, some co-ordinating role. In the early 1970s the EC participated, together with the member states, in the negotiations leading to the UN Convention on the Law of the Sea. There were difficulties in reaching common positions, but the member states all agreed that the Community should be a party to the Convention. The EC is also a party to many other bodies such as the World Trade Organisation (WTO) and the Food and Agriculture Organisation (FAO); but each case is different, with the EC often having to state exactly where it has competence in any subject under negotiation. The complexity of the EU's position in international organisations is discussed in more detail below, but this brief review has shown the interplay between internal and external policy developments.

WHO SPEAKS FOR THE EU?

To describe the EU's external representation as confusing would be a huge understatement. If it were an individual, the CFSP would have long been enclosed in a psychiatric ward with doctors assessing how it could have survived so long with such a deep split personality. Its schizophrenia was programmed in the pillar system set up at Maastricht and was further complicated by the addition at Amsterdam of the post of Secretary General/High Representative (SG/HR) for the CFSP. The EU's external representation currently varies between different policy areas: the CFSP, trade, financial, economic, environmental and development affairs. Every six months the US Secretary of State has a new European interlocutor. It is little wonder, therefore, that Condoleezza Rice and most of the media know the telephone number of the High Representative for the CFSP, Javier Solana, better than whoever of the twenty-five foreign ministers of the EU is currently holding the Presidency of the Council. Solana, by dint of his experience and contacts, has carved out an important role, even though his position as described in the treaties is mainly 'to assist the Presidency'. He is, for example, the EU's representative on the quartet dealing with the Middle East peace process (the others being the UN, the US and Russia). Although Condoleezza Rice has Solana's telephone number, she may need to call one of several commissioners such as Benita Ferrero-Waldner or Louis Michel or Olli Rehn dealing with different aspects of external relations. Washington may also wish to speak to one of the EU's many special representatives dealing with the Middle East, the southern Caucasus, Bosnia or other regions and issues. Depending on circumstances, the EU may be represented, therefore, by Solana or the Presidency alone, the Presidency and the Commission, or by all three. If the US, with its lengthy history of close co-operation with the EU, finds the situation baffling, other partners are even more perplexed.

The EU troika is one of the main formats for external representation but baffling to outsiders. The word 'troika' would suggest just three members, but the EU has never fewer than four participants at political dialogue meetings: the Presidency, the future Presidency, the Council Secretariat and the Commission. It is often the case that there is more negotiating with the host country over seats for the EU delegation than over the substance of the agenda. Significantly, the only permanent members on the EU side of the table at Brussels-based troikas are the Commission and the Council Secretariat. As to representation abroad, the embassies of EU member states and the delegations of the European Commission are also encouraged (as well as enjoined by the treaty) to co-operate locally and present a united front to their host country or international organisation. In practice, this co-operation varies considerably from country to country and is often dependent on local personalities. In addition, in many capitals there is no resident Presidency representative, which somewhat complicates matters. The troika is also a misnomer abroad as the Council Secretariat is never present, except in the two cities where it keeps an office – New York and Geneva – for reasons of multilateral as opposed to bilateral diplomacy. Thus, the Commission delegation is actually the only permanent part of the troika abroad. Presidency ambassadors with little personal experience of the Brussels machinery often tend to go it alone or invent procedures. More than one member-state ambassador has had to be formally reminded that the Commission is a permanent part of the troika. In important posts such as Washington and Moscow there is a further problem in that the larger member states in particular often prefer to plough their own furrow rather than maintain EU solidarity. In Washington there are sometimes visits by four or five foreign ministers from member states within a two-week period. These visits are rarely co-ordinated and are hardly a good advertisement for EU coherence. Some statistics are revealing here. The European Commission delegation in Washington, DC, has about twenty Brussels-based staff. The British, French and German embassies there have over 200 staff each from London, Paris and Berlin. Even though trade policy is an EU competence, most member states have more officials dealing with trade policy than the EC delegation. The scope for confusion, not to mention unnecessary duplication, is enormous. There is thus considerable scope for member states and Commission delegations to co-operate more effectively in third countries. In terms of numbers, the EU disposes by far the largest diplomatic network in the world. More than 40,000 officials work in the foreign ministries of the member states and the approximately 1,500 diplomatic missions abroad. Each member state maintains between forty and 160 diplomatic missions, while the Commission has a network of over 120 delegations around the world. In comparison, the US has about one-third of the human resources that the EU devotes to diplomacy and one-fifth of the diplomatic missions. However, as Solana once remarked, it was not apparent that the US was less effective than the EU in pursuing its policy objectives.

The UN poses a special problem for the EU. The EU has 40 per cent of the permanent members of the UNSC and 33 per cent of all members. But it simply does not punch its weight owing to the lack of political will. The two permanent members of the UNSC, Britain and France, are supposed to inform and take into account the views of the Union as a whole. Although co-ordination between member states at the UN has improved in recent years, there is still some criticism of Britain and France pursuing national as opposed to EU interests in the UNSC. In January 2003, Spain and Germany joined the UNSC, but even with four major European states on this supreme international body it was difficult to produce a coherent European voice as these four states took divergent positions in the Iraq crisis. Although both London and Paris favour reform of the UNSC, the proposed changes would more likely add members to the UNSC than lead towards a single EU seat. Germany's demand for a permanent seat on the UNSC has sparked opposition from Italy, Spain and others. There is co-ordination of EU positions in the UN General Assembly (UNGA) and six main committees; plus the Economic and Social Committee (ECOSOC) and functional commissions dealing with transnational issues such as terrorism, crime and drugs – but only member states are members of these bodies. EU co-ordinating meetings are chaired by the Presidency, which also prepares statements on behalf of the EU. Increasingly the EU votes together on UNGA resolutions, but the main actor in the UN system, the US, tends to ignore this body. With the G7 able to muster over 100 votes in the UNGA – and its resolutions are non-binding – the US (with one vote) sees little point in trying to exert influence on it.

With regard to the Organisation for Security and Co-operation in Europe (OSCE), it is the Presidency that speaks for the EU when there is an agreed political position. On economic issues, it is the Commission that takes the floor. But, as member states often exercise their right to speak at OSCE meetings, this tends to dilute any EU message. There is also an element of duplication in some EU and OSCE activities, e.g. election monitoring, that leads to a feeling of competition rather than of co-operation between the two bodies. The position of the EU in the Council of Europe is equally weak. The confused external representation of the EU in the CFSP is mirrored in many other policy areas. The one notable exception is trade policy, which has been an area of EC competence for some time. In international trade negotiations it is the Commissioner for Trade who represents and speaks for the EU. The advantages of this approach for all member states have been proved in many trade negotiations, from the Kennedy round to the Doha development agenda. The approach is simple. The Council agrees a mandate, which the Commission then uses as the basis for its negotiations with third parties. After agreement is reached, the Commission presents the results to the Council for approval. Such an approach could usefully be used in the foreign and international economic policy fields.

Despite the introduction of the euro, the EU continues to punch below its weight in international financial institutions (IFIs). With the shift, in eurozone countries, of monetary policy sovereignty from national level to the European Central Bank (ECB), the EU's role in international economic and financial governance has increased significantly, although there are still problems stemming from the non-membership of some member states in the eurozone and jealousies surrounding participation in G8 meetings. The G8 does little to help EU coherence and visibility. In recent years there has been mounting criticism of the G8 for its lengthy communiqués, lack of follow-through, lack of transparency and its restricted membership. Given the lack of substance of G8 meetings, it is not surprising that there have been calls, not just from anti-globalisation protesters, to abolish the G8. Abolition is unlikely, but an alternative might be to transform the G8 into a G20 to allow for greater representation from the south (India, Brazil, China, etc.). Despite this pressure, it is unlikely that the current members will agree to change the status quo as it suits their vested interests. As in any international grouping, there is often a trade-off between increased size, and thus greater legitimacy, and reduced size, and allegedly greater efficiency. But the current arrangements whereby Britain, France, Germany and Italy occupy four seats is scarcely defensible. Many consider that there should be just one EU seat.

In 1998 the European Council agreed rather complicated guidelines on the Union's external representation in financial forums. Some member states have begun to realise, however, that these ad hoc solutions are not the best way for the Community's voice to be heard internationally. There is also increasing pressure from emerging markets and non-European G8 countries for streamlining EU representation in bodies such as the International Monetary Fund (IMF) and the World Bank. In the IMF, procedurally, the euro-area dimension has been taken into account by the twice-yearly consultation of the euro-area economic policies in addition to the traditional EU national consultation process. Institutionally, however, less progress has been made. The 1945 IMF Articles of Agreement confer on countries the right to become members. This is difficult to reconcile with the specific nature of the EU and the European Monetary Union (EMU). Furthermore, the IMF decision-taking process, with countries grouped in mixed EU/non-EU constituencies, can sometimes be at odds with the EU's need to respect EU treaty requirements on position-taking and representation.

The above situation is highly confusing and clearly weakens the EU position in international forums. During a debate in the European Parliament on 11 June 2005 the Commissioner for Economic and Monetary Affairs, Joaquin Almunia, deplored the disparity between the EU's political and economic weight and its participation in the governance of international financial institutions. The aim, he said, should be single EU representation in the Bretton Woods institutions. Speaking in the same debate, the Luxembourg European Affairs Minister, Nicolas Schmit, pointed out that the twenty-five member states held 28 per cent of the votes at the World Bank compared to 18 per cent for the US, but that the influence of the US was far greater as it spoke with one voice. Members of the European Parliament (MEPs) in the debate were unanimous in calling for greater EU co-ordination in the IFIs as a prelude to single representation. But how to achieve a single EU seat in the IFIs? There are those who argue for a gradual approach, placing the emphasis on improved co-ordination *sur place* in Washington. Others suggest that, as issues concerning EU competence increasingly dominate the IMF agenda, the EU should play a more prominent role through the EU Economic and Finance Council (ECOFIN). This would mean ECOFIN discussing IMF issues at its regular meetings and adopting common positions. A further complicating issue is Britain's self-exclusion from the eurozone. This may be overcome if and when Britain joins the euro, but until then only piecemeal reform is likely. The constitutional treaty did, however, provide for the possibility of the eurozone members agreeing on their own external representation. A step towards this goal might be a joint Franco-German seat, as these two countries have traditionally been pioneers in European integration.

THE THEORETICAL DEBATE

Political scientists find it difficult to pin a theoretical label on the EU. For most scholars, a theory is simply an explanation of an event or pattern of behaviour in the 'real' world. This is otherwise known as *empirical theory*. A theory explains such patterns by elaborating on why they take place. There is a considerable variety of empirical theory in the study of international relations. For example, there is a big difference between a theory that tries to explain single events like the US invasion of Iraq in 2003, a theory that tries to account for the variation of patterns of war and peace among the great powers during the last two hundred years, and a theory that attempts to explain why war itself takes place. Second, there is *normative theory*, which is concerned to elaborate the ethical standards used to judge international conduct. Today, there exists a large body of normative theory concerned with the use of force (just war theory) and distributive justice in international relations. When is it right or appropriate to use military force? Is the present distribution of global wealth and income fair? These are the kinds of question that normative theory seeks to answer. Third, the term is sometimes used in a constitutive sense. Unlike empirical or normative theory, this use of the term is perhaps best expressed through other concepts, such as *paradigm*, *worldview* or *framework of analysis*. Some of the terms, such as *realism*, *critical theory* and *liberal interventionism*, are examples of *constitutive theory* in the study of international relations.

One of the traditional clashes in international relations theory is between the *realist school* and the *liberal-institutionalist school*. The former focuses exclusively on the state and power as the main determinants and dismisses institutions as playing no major role in foreign policy. The latter, of which Professor Robert Keohane of Princeton University is the foremost guru, accepts the primacy of the state but argues that economic interdependence and institutions can and do have an impact on the foreign-policy process. The debate about the EU has often been explained in terms of federalism or functionalism. A *federal system* of government is characterised by a division of powers between the centre and the component states. The US is a classic federal system, with some powers taken at national level in Washington, DC, and other powers reserved for the states of the Union. In Europe, Germany is an advanced federal state with powers divided between Berlin (the Bund) and the states (Länder) such as Bavaria or Hamburg. France, in contrast, is a centralist state with nearly all decisions taken at national level in Paris. But, whatever the system, it is nearly always the case that foreign and security policy is reserved for the national or federal level. The European federalists, often traced back to the founding fathers of the EU, statesmen such as Robert Schuman and Konrad Adenauer, hoped that the EU would evolve into a federal system whereby there would be a European government based on the member states agreeing to share sovereignty and the centre would deal with foreign and security policy among other matters. There is, however, little prospect of a 'European, federal, super-state' emerging in the near future. Indeed, many consider that the failure to secure ratification of the constitutional treaty in 2005 dealt a deathblow to hopes of an 'ever closer union'.

Functionalism is the idea that international co-operation should begin by dealing with specific transnational problems (such as health or the environment) where there is some prospect of applying specialised technical knowledge and where the success of ad hoc functional arrangements will hopefully lead to further efforts to replicate the experience in an ever-widening process. Co-operation leading to integration (e.g. the EU's internal market) thus increases the benefits to the population. In the early years after the Second World War, this expectation was raised by the recognition that governments faced a growing responsibility to provide welfare for their citizens, a responsibility that they could not fulfil in isolation. Functionalism is also based on the hope that, if governments begin to transfer functional responsibilities to international agencies with specific mandates to deal with issues over which there is a wide consensus regarding the need for co-operation, over time the principle of territorial and legal sovereignty will weaken. In the 1960s and 1970s, what became known as the *neo-functionalist school* argued that the spill-over effect of co-operation would lead to a growing sense of European identity. Neo-functionalism is associated with the work of Ernst Haas, who acknowledged that the process of functionalism was easier to achieve in a regional context such as Western Europe, particularly in light of its history and shared democratic values in the post-1945 era. He accepted that it would be difficult to avoid conflicts between states if the gains from co-operation were unequally distributed among them. Consequently, it was crucial to establish formal supranational institutions that could impose and uphold agreements made by states. Neo-functionalists have also paid a great deal of attention to the mechanics of and obstacles to spill-over, examining issues such as socialisation and collaborative learning among political elites. Although many scholars of functionalism and neo-functionalism have become somewhat disenchanted with the project as progress towards integration in Western Europe slowed down considerably in the 1980s and 1990s, many of the ideas and theories associated with these concepts remain pertinent in the study of international collaboration.

Constructivism is a distinctive approach to international relations that emphasises the social dimension of world politics. Constructivists insist that international relations cannot be reduced to rational action or a system of institutional constraints. For constructivists, state interaction is not among fixed national interests, but must be understood as a pattern of action that shapes and is shaped by identities over time. In contrast to other theoretical approaches, social constructivism presents a model of international interaction that explores the normative influence of fundamental institutional structures and the connection between normative changes and state identity and interests. At the same time, however, institutions themselves are constantly reproduced and, potentially, changed by the activities of states and other actors. Institutions and actors are mutually conditioning entities. According to constructivists, international institutions have both regulative and constitutive functions. Regulative norms set basic rules for standards of conduct by prescribing or proscribing certain behaviours. Constitutive norms define behaviour and assign meanings to that behaviour. Without constitutive norms, actions would be unintelligible. The familiar analogy that constructivists use to explain constitutive norms is that of the rules of a game, such as chess. Constitutive norms enable the actors to play the game and provide the actors with the knowledge necessary to respond to each other's moves in a meaningful way. Constructivism also highlights the power of ideology and beliefs in international politics. As the traditional left–right split in politics has diminished there has been a rise in religious influence, including Islamic fundamentalism and the Christian right in America. Europe is much more secular than the US, but there is also a question over the future of multiculturalism in Europe. What kind of society do we wish to create and what will be the implications of our own internal societal developments for the rest of the world? The image of Europe can have important foreign policy implications, as was seen in the reactions to the cartoons depicting Muhammad published in the Danish press in 2005. For many in the Islamic world all European countries were guilty by association with Denmark.

CONCLUSION

The EU has developed steadily as an actor in international affairs and today is widely recognised as playing an important role in many different policy areas. More and more governments and media organisations are demanding 'the EU view' on international issues rather than the views of twenty-five member states. Indeed, the enlargement of the EU has increased these demands, and where appropriate there is an EU view, usually put forward by Javier Solana, officially called the EU's High Representative for the CFSP but more often described as 'EU foreign policy chief'. But the EU still has many problems to overcome if it wants to be a more coherent, more visible and more influential global actor.

The EU stands for strengthening the institutions of global governance through its aim of 'effective multilateralism'. But this is not so easy to implement when there are rivalries and jealousies between the member states, especially in how the EU and member states seek to represent themselves in international bodies. There is little likelihood of the EU having its own seat on the UNSC in the near future, but there is much the EU can do to support the UN. Following enlargement to twenty-five member states there is growing pressure from third countries for the EU to reduce its seats in various bodies or to speak with one voice. But it is not only foreign ministries that are involved in such decisions; prime ministers and finance ministers also want their say. Meanwhile, theorists will continue to argue over various models to interpret EU behaviour for some time to come.

KEY QUESTIONS

What is an actor in the global system?
Explain how internal EU policies affect EU foreign relations.
What theory best explains the EU as an actor?
How would you assess the EU's ability to sell itself around the world?
What are the obstacles to the EU having its own seat on the UNSC, the IMF
    and the World Bank?
How would you define 'effective multilateralism'?

FURTHER READING

For the EU's role in foreign policy, see Whitman (1998), Ginsberg (2001), Hill and Smith (2005). The second edition of Bretherton and Vogler (2006) looks at the EU as a global actor and is more up-to-date than Piening (1997) or Buchan (1993). For an analysis of the ESS, see Biscop (2005). Rifkin (2004) and Leonard (2005) argue that the twenty-first century will belong to Europe as a result of its soft power. Elsig (2002) examines the EU as a trading power. On the theoretical aspects, see Keohane (1983), Deutsch (1968) and Haas (1958).

2   From EPC to CFSP

SUMMARY

Despite the setback of the failure to ratify the European Defence Community in 1954 the EU never gave up the aim of a common foreign and security policy. The first hesitant steps occurred during the 1970s, and then the pace quickened with the development of European Political Co-operation (EPC), given treaty status in the 1987 Single European Act (SEA). This was an inter-governmental method of co-operation different from the traditional Community way of making decisions. The end of the Cold War paved the way for the 1992 Maastricht Treaty that saw the establishment of the CFSP. But the CFSP could not have been set up at a worse time, with the break-up of the former Yugoslavia. The first decade of the CFSP was very difficult, with little agreement over aims and objectives. The EU's failure in the Balkans in the 1990s, however, was the catalyst for the development of the EU's military capabilities and the creation of the European Security and Defence Policy (ESDP). Further changes were agreed in the Treaties of Amsterdam (1997) and Nice (2001) which helped strengthen the CFSP and the ESDP.

EUROPEAN POLITICAL CO-OPERATION (EPC)

The founding fathers of the EU always considered that there should be a security dimension to their unique undertaking. Their thinking was motivated by the three catastrophic wars which had been fought in Europe between 1871 and 1945, all involving Germany and France fighting each other. By the end of the Second World War it was clear that the US and the Soviet Union would play the dominant roles in European security. London, Paris and Rome had all lost influence while Berlin was divided between the major powers. The founding fathers recognised that Europe could only regain international influence by working together. The idea for a supra-national EU in which states would share sovereignty was thus a major contribution in itself to creating a security community (Deutsch, 1968). Soon after the successful launching of the European Coal and Steel Community (ECSC) there was an ambitious proposal to establish a common European army within the framework of a European Defence Community (EDC). This would have pooled the armed forces of the six founding member states (France, Germany, Italy, Belgium, the Netherlands and Luxembourg), and the plan was strongly supported by the US, which considered it would provide a more effective European force in standing up to the Soviet Union at the height of the Cold War. But the proposal fell at the last hurdle, the ratification in the French senate. A majority of French politicians baulked at the idea of a revived German army. Yet the end result was to speed Germany's membership of NATO and the Western European Union (WEU), a defence organisation that predated NATO and which provided a security guarantee for its members.

The French decision meant an end for some time to European ambitions in the security field and a concentration of effort in the economic domain. The next three decades were dominated by the Cold War and the nuclear super-power rivalry between the US and the Soviet Union. Europe was divided by the Iron Curtain and played only a secondary role in world politics. But there was always the recognition that the European project would be incomplete without a foreign and security policy dimension. In the 1970s, as the European Economic Community (EEC) developed and changed to the European Community (EC), there were renewed efforts to establish some co-ordination mechanism for foreign and security policy. The reasons for this renewed attempt to forge greater unity in foreign policy were partly the desire for the 'economic giant' to punch its political weight in the world, and partly owing to the emerging changes in the geopolitics of Europe. In 1970 ministers adopted the Luxembourg Report that proposed the establishment of a structured form of foreign policy co-ordination called European Political Co-operation (EPC). This involved a process outside the traditional Community pillar where the Commission enjoyed a monopoly right of initiative. Member states did not want the Commission to enjoy the same rights in foreign policy, and hence the EPC was established on a separate inter-governmental basis. This led to some absurd situations such as when EU foreign ministers finished a meeting on general affairs in Brussels in the morning and then boarded a plane to Copenhagen, capital of the then rotating Presidency, to continue their meeting there in the afternoon albeit in the EPC format.

EPC established regular ministerial meetings to discuss foreign policy. These were prepared by the Political Committee, a body of senior officials from the foreign offices of member states who were assisted by a more junior grouping of European correspondents. They exchanged diplomatic messages under a telegraphic system known as COREU, for 'Correspondant Européen'. There were only two working languages, French and English, with no interpretation. A small secretariat was created in the Council that was responsible for keeping records and sending out agendas in accord with the Presidency. EPC was an important first step in establishing the machinery that came to run EU foreign policy. The sensitivities of member states were preserved, and all decisions were taken by unanimity. EPC was essentially declaratory, with the EU condemning this action, expressing concern over another and occasionally welcoming another. But it also developed the habit of co-operation between officials from the ministries of foreign affairs (MFAs) of member states and inculcated a feeling of European identity that played a role alongside the stronger feelings of national identity. It was, as one insider remarked, akin to 'a private club operated by diplomats, for diplomats' (Nuttall, 2000).

In 1987, EPC was given a treaty base, Article 30 of the Single European Act (SEA), which codified procedures that had been established for several years. Under the treaty, the members undertook 'to inform and consult each other on any foreign policy matters of general interest so as to ensure that their combined influence is exercised as effectively as possible through co-ordination, the convergence of their positions and implementation of joint action'. The parties were, as far as possible, 'to refrain from impeding the formation of a consensus'. EPC could discuss the political and economic aspects of security, but military issues remained out of bounds. The European Commission was 'fully associated' with EPC while the European Parliament (EP) was to be 'regularly informed' about EPC and its views 'taken into consideration'. Both the Presidency and the Commission had special responsibility to ensure consistency in external relations. The question of 'consistency' in external affairs was to raise its head many times over the years.

Box 2.1: Single European Act (SEA), Title III

Treaty Provisions on European Co-operation in the Sphere of Foreign Policy

Article 30. European Co-operation in the sphere of foreign policy shall be governed by the following provisions:

1. The High Contracting Parties, being members of the European Communities, shall endeavour jointly to formulate and implement a European foreign policy.
2. (a) The High Contracting Parties undertake to inform and consult each other on any foreign policy matters of general interest so as to ensure that their combined influence is exercised as effectively as possible through coordination, the convergence of their positions and the implementation of joint action.
   (b) Consultations shall take place before the High Contracting Parties decide on their final position.
   (c) In adopting its positions and in its national measures each High Contracting Party shall take full account of the positions of the other partners and shall give due consideration to the desirability of adopting and implementing common European positions.

continued

(d) The High Contracting Parties shall endeavour to avoid any action or position which impairs their effectiveness as a cohesive force in international relations or within international organisations.

3. (a) The Ministers for Foreign Affairs and a member of the Commission shall meet at least four times a year within the framework of European Political Co-operation.

(b) The Commission shall be fully associated with the proceedings of Political Co-operation.

(c) In order to ensure the swift adoption of common positions and the implementation of joint action, the High Contracting Parties shall, as far as possible, refrain from impeding the formation of a consensus and the joint action which this could produce.

4. The High Contracting Parties shall ensure that the European Parliament is closely associated with European Political Co-operation. To that end the Presidency shall regularly inform the European Parliament of the foreign policy issues which are being examined within the framework of Political Co-operation and shall ensure that the views of the European Parliament are duly taken into consideration.

5. The external policies of the European Community and the policies agreed in European Political Co-operation must be consistent. The Presidency and the Commission, each within its own sphere of competence, shall have special responsibility for ensuring that such consistency is sought and maintained.

6. (a) The High Contracting Parties consider that closer co-operation on questions of European security would contribute in an essential way to the development of a European identity in external policy matters. They are ready to co-ordinate their positions more closely on the political and economic aspects of security.

(b) The High Contracting Parties are determined to maintain the technological and industrial conditions necessary for their security. They shall work to that end both at national level and, where appropriate, within the framework of the competent institutions and bodies.

(c) Nothing in this Title shall impede closer co-operation in the field of security between certain of the High Contracting Parties within the framework of the Western European Union or the Atlantic Alliance.

7. (a) In international institutions and at international conferences which they attend, the High Contracting Parties shall endeavour

to adopt common positions on the subjects covered by this Title.

(b) In international institutions and at international conferences in which not all the High Contracting Parties participate, those who do participate shall take full account of positions agreed in European Political Co-operation.

8. The High Contracting Parties shall organise a political dialogue with third countries and regional groupings whenever they deem it necessary.

9. The High Contracting Parties, and the Commission through mutual assistance and information, shall intensify co-operation between their representations accredited to third countries and to international organisations.

10. (a) The Presidency of European Political Co-operation shall be held by the High Contracting Party which holds the Presidency of the Council of the European Communities.

(b) The Presidency shall be responsible for initiating action and co-ordinating and representing the positions of the Member States in relations with third countries in respect of European Political Co-operation activities. It shall also be responsible for the management of Political Co-operation and in particular for drawing up the timetable of meetings and for convening and organising meetings.

(c) The Political Directors shall meet regularly in the Political Committee in order to give the necessary impetus, maintain the continuity of European Political Co-operation and prepare Ministers' discussions.

(d) The Political Committee or, if necessary, a ministerial meeting shall convene within forty-eight hours at the request of at least three Member States.

(e) The European Correspondents' Group shall be responsible, under the direction of the Political Committee, for monitoring the implementation of European Political Co-operation and for studying general organisational problems.

(f) Working Groups shall meet as directed by the Political Committee.

(g) A Secretariat based in Brussels shall assist the Presidency in preparing and implementing the activities of European Political Co-operation and in administrative matters. It shall carry out its duties under the authority of the Presidency.

Assessment

EPC was useful in co-ordinating the positions of member states on issues such as the Middle East and the 1975 Helsinki conference on security and co-operation in Europe (CSCE, later OSCE). Gradually EPC also began to develop synergy with the EC that allowed it to use Community instruments for foreign policy purposes. Some examples included the imposition of sanctions after the Soviet invasion of Afghanistan in 1979; similarly on Poland after the declaration of martial law in 1981 and then on Iraq after Saddam Hussein's invasion of Kuwait in 1990. The member states also developed the habit of working together and began to consult each other in advance of meetings to try to reach a common position. But EPC was handicapped by the consensus rule, and thus the common position was often the lowest common denominator. The inability to discuss defence matters was another serious problem. All issues with military implications were taboo. Third countries also found EPC difficult to understand but gradually began to take notice. Although broadly welcomed by the US, Washington was also critical of the EPC in the 1980s for opposing US policy in Central America and Libya.

THE CFSP

Even the improvements made as a result of the treaty base for EPC could not cope with the dramatic changes in European and international affairs as a result of the sudden collapse of communism in central and eastern Europe in 1989, of which the fall of the Berlin Wall was the most dramatic symbol. President George Bush (father of George W. Bush) proposed at the G7 meeting in Paris that year that the European Commission, under Jacques Delors, should be given the task of co-ordinating assistance to the states of central and eastern Europe. This arrangement was to have significant consequences for the Commission as it propelled it into a completely new and rapidly growing policy area. In 1990 the Commission had fewer than ten officials dealing with the communist countries. Less than a decade later it had over a thousand officials involved in the region, and Commission delegations had been opened in nearly all countries there.

The dramatic changes in 1989, opening up the prospect of German unification a year later, were the backdrop to the establishment of the CFSP. France and Germany both agreed that the completion of the internal market and the drive towards economic and monetary union required corresponding moves towards political union, of which the CFSP was a central element. With the end of the Cold War, Europe was expected to use its increased weight to achieve more political influence and ensure stability around its borders. The limitations of EPC had been reached, and it was necessary to establish stronger structures for foreign and security policy. The reasons for launching the CFSP were variously ascribed to the need for the EU, as the major actor in global trade and development assistance, to punch its weight in the world, to shoulder more of the transatlantic burden and to develop externally apace with internal developments (single market, single currency, enlargement). The CFSP was also a popular endeavour. Opinion polls revealed (and continue to reveal, according to Eurobarometer polls) a high level of public support across the EU in favour of closer co-operation in foreign and security policy. In a widely quoted article, one analyst suggested that there was a substantial 'capability–expectations gap' in terms of what the public expected the EU to deliver and the capabilities it had developed in this area. Looked at from the perspective of the early 1990s, the EU 'was not an effective international actor in terms both of its capacity to produce collective decisions and its impact on events' (Hill, 1993).

The negotiations to establish the CFSP were not easy and reflected the fundamental differences between those who wished to move towards a more integrated EU and those who wished to ensure that decision-making remained in the hands of the member states. The other main dispute was whether the EU should develop a defence capability or whether defence should be left to NATO. In the end a hybrid pillar structure was established involving EC affairs under the first pillar, the CFSP under the second pillar, and justice and home affairs under the third pillar. The three pillars together were called the European Union (see Chapter 1).

Assessment

The text of the CFSP part of the treaty was very ambitious (see Appendix 1). It stated that 'the Union shall define and implement a CFSP covering all areas of foreign and security policy'. The text further stated that 'the CFSP shall include all questions related to the security of the Union, including the eventual framing of a defence policy, which might in time lead to a common defence'. This was the first official reference to defence as an EU policy objective, even though it was hedged with various qualifications. Despite the grand aims, the actual changes made under the CFSP compared to EPC were modest. The structures largely reflected EPC procedures. Joint Actions and Common Positions were new features of the CFSP. Joint Actions meant that the member states would act together to achieve a particular object. Common Positions were when the member states agreed on a policy stance and also agreed to promote the stance as an EU position. There was a lengthy delay in ratifying the treaty, which meant that the CFSP did not start until November 1993.

The CFSP machinery created at Maastricht was based largely on the previous EPC structures. The second, or inter-governmental, 'pillar' for the CFSP remained, which did little to promote coherence and led to frequent squabbling between the Commission and the Council over issues of competence. Another problem was the sheer number of actors involved in the CFSP: the member states, the Council, the High Representative, the special representatives, the Commission, the Parliament, each with their bureaucracies, interests and ambitions. There were some member states, notably the Benelux, that wished to go further at Maastricht and place the CFSP under the first pillar, but there was no consensus to do so. The heads of state and government agreed, however, to review the operation of the CFSP five years after Maastricht – hence the 1997 Amsterdam Inter-governmental Conference (IGC). The Amsterdam IGC did not lead to any fundamental changes in the inter-governmental nature of the CFSP. But some modest improvements were made, notably the decision to create a High Representative and a Policy Planning and Early Warning Unit. At Nice, while the political oversight via the European Council and the renamed General Affairs and External Relations Council (GAERC) remained unchanged, the motor running the CFSP was greatly enhanced by the establishment of the Brussels-based Political and Security Committee (PSC), known more frequently by its French acronym (COPS). The Nice IGC also agreed to establish a Military Committee and a Military Staff.

THE CFSP IN ACTION

The CFSP could not have started at a worse time, with the break-up of Yugoslavia. Many expected the EU to stop the conflict, but the EU did not have the resources for this (neither did NATO) and had to look on from the sidelines while the Balkans erupted in bloody warfare. Despite this failure the CFSP did have a number of modest successes in the early years. One of the most important was the first Stability Pact, or Balladur Plan, named after the French prime minister at the time who launched the plan. The Stability Pact Joint Action was a mechanism whereby the EU organised a number of conferences and round tables to deal with outstanding border and ethnic issues in central and eastern Europe. With some well-targeted technical and financial assistance, the Union was able to make an impact on the problems of the Hungarian minorities living outside Hungary (mainly in Romania and Slovakia) and the substantial Russian minorities living in the Baltic states (mainly Latvia and Lithuania). This assistance provided *inter alia* for language training and help in drafting legislation to protect minorities, an essential prerequisite for later membership of the EU.

Another useful CFSP Joint Action was administering the city of Mostar, which had been devastated during the early stages of the Balkan conflict. Before the conflict it had been a good example of a multicultural society, with Croats and Bosnian Muslims living peacefully together. But there had been fierce inter-ethnic fighting during the war and considerable destruction. When the EU took over the city administration in July 2004 the population had shrunk to 60,000 from a prewar figure of 127,000. The EU chief administrator was Hans Koschnik, a former mayor of Bremen, who led a team of policemen, engineers and local government administrators that helped rebuild the city. The EU team carried out their tasks with only limited co-operation from the local parties, but within two years the city had been largely rebuilt and the mission declared a success.

A third Joint Action was the EU lobbying together for an extension of the Non-Proliferation Treaty (NPT) in 1995. This was a sensitive issue, especially for the two nuclear weapons states, Britain and France, who feared they might be pressed to adopt positions against their national interests. The idea for a Joint Action came from the Belgian Presidency in October 1993 and was taken forward by the Greeks during the next Presidency. At the June 1994 European Council in Corfu, EU leaders agreed on a Joint Action to strengthen the non-proliferation system by agreeing to an unconditional and indefinite extension of the NPT. The EU then prepared *démarches* (diplomatic notes) to press third states, especially doubters such as Ukraine, Algeria, Argentina and Chile, to align themselves with the EU position. This work was divided up between the member states in the second half of 1994 under the German Presidency and into the first half of 1995 under the French Presidency. The EU efforts were quietly successful in contributing to a positive outcome of the 1995 NPT review conference.

These three examples were typical of the low-key diplomacy in the early years of the CFSP. These Joint Actions received little media attention but nevertheless made a useful contribution to the resolution of some difficult and sensitive issues. The EU was able to secure a consensus on each issue and then follow up with a mix of diplomatic effort and technical and financial resources. But these quiet diplomatic achievements were overshadowed by the continued fighting in the former Yugoslavia and the widespread public perception that the EU was still not bringing its collective weight to bear decisively on foreign and security policy issues.

INSTRUMENTS

The CFSP has only three instruments. The first is Joint Actions, of which there were twenty-nine in 2003 and twenty-five in 2004. These can be used for various purposes ranging from election monitoring to the appointment of special representatives. The second is Common Positions, of which there were twenty-one in 2003 and twenty-three in 2004. These are designed to align the member states' policies towards third countries or on functional issues like non-proliferation. Finally, there are Common Strategies, of which there have only been three: Russia in June 1999, Ukraine in December 1999 and the Mediterranean in June 2000. These normally last four years and are efforts to ensure that the EU and the member states adopt a consistent line in dealing with these countries and regions. In addition the EU is good at issuing statements about currents and issues of concern. There were 143 statements issued in 2003 and 141 issued in 2004. The Union also makes regular use of *démarches* to third countries. There were 157 in 2003 and 179 in 2004. The effectiveness of these instruments leaves much to be desired. The Joint Actions have rather more substance and enjoy greater loyalty from the member states; but the Common Positions and the Common Strategies are often loosely interpreted by the member states. A good example is the Common Strategy towards Russia. All the large member states have pursued their own policy towards Russia, with scarcely a reference to the EU Common Strategy.

Case study 2.1: The EU and the Iraq crisis

The Iraq crisis of 2002–3 was a nightmare for the EU, exposing deep differences between the member states on the principle of war against Iraq, the role of the UN and the weapons inspectors, and support for the American policy of pre-emption. EU policy had been fully supportive of the American military engagement to defeat the Taliban regime in Afghanistan. However, with President Bush's focus shifting from the war against Afghanistan towards Iraq, one of the three states mentioned in his January 2002 'axis of evil' speech, the differences among member states became wider. At the same time, there was an increasing tendency to sideline EU institutions in preference for a 'directoire' approach. This first became evident when the Big Three (France, Germany, the UK) held a mini-summit to discuss the situation in Afghanistan ahead of the meeting of EU leaders in Ghent in October 2001. This move was met with much criticism from smaller member states and Commission President Romano Prodi, who stated that 'it is a shame that some are going and some are not'. A month later Tony Blair held an invitation-only dinner at Downing Street which comprised the leaders of the five EU countries who had offered military assistance. This meeting, gate-crashed by Solana, also caused considerable concern and resentment.

The debates during and following Germany's September 2002 election campaign highlighted Europe's differing positions towards Iraq. In the final weeks of the election campaign, Chancellor Schroeder emphasised his strong opposition to war, calling Bush's policy towards Iraq an 'adventure'. This stance helped him secure a narrow and unexpected election victory but it visibly angered the US administration. President Bush refused to congratulate Schroeder on his victory or take any telephone calls from him for over a year. US Defense Secretary Donald Rumsfeld complained that Schroeder had 'poisoned' US–German relations and further poured oil on troubled waters by describing Germany and France as 'old Europe' while Britain and others who supported the war were 'new Europe'.

Meanwhile, in the absence of an agreed position, the EU was hiding behind the UN. In November 2002 the GAERC stated that 'the Council welcomes the unanimous adoption of UNSC resolution 1441 which paves the way for weapons inspectors to return to Iraq on the basis of a strengthened inspection regime. The European Union's policy towards Iraq has a clear objective – disarmament of Iraq's weapons of mass destruction, in accordance with UNSC resolutions.' Germany and France were also co-ordinating their positions. On the occasion of the 40th anniversary of the Elysée friendship treaty on 22 January 2003, Chancellor Schroeder and President Chirac pledged to deepen their co-operation against a US-led war in the region. Chirac stated that 'Germany and France have the same judgement on this crisis', and that 'war is not inevitable'. On 30 January 2003 a serious dispute within the inner circles of the EU was triggered when eight European leaders (the gang of eight) signed an open letter backing US policy towards Iraq without consulting France or Germany or the Greek Presidency. The letter was seen as direct retaliation for the anti-war positions adopted by France and Germany. The declaration was initiated by the Spanish prime minister, José Aznar, and signed by the UK, Italy, Portugal, Denmark, the Czech Republic, Hungary and Poland. The declaration was criticised by the Greek prime minister, Costas Simitis, who stated that 'the way in which the initiative was expressed does not contribute to a common approach to the problem. The EU aims to have a common foreign policy, so on Iraq there is a need for co-ordination.'

On 7 February 2003, shortly after the famous UNSC meeting addressed by US Secretary of State Colin Powell, the Vilnius group, composed of Slovakia, Lithuania, Bulgaria, Estonia, Latvia, Romania, Slovenia, Albania, Croatia and Macedonia, pledged in a joint letter to support the United States position on Iraq. The letter, published in the *Wall Street Journal*, stated that:

the US presented compelling evidence detailing Iraq's weapons of mass destruction programs, its active efforts to deceive UN inspectors, and its links to international terrorism. Our countries understand the dangers posed by tyranny and the special responsibility of democracies to defend our shared values. The trans-Atlantic community, of which we are a part, must stand together to face the threat posed by the nexus of terrorism and dictators with weapons of mass destruction. Iraq is in material breach of UN Security Council Resolutions, including Resolution 1441. We are prepared to contribute to an international coalition to enforce its provisions and the disarmament of Iraq.

France and Germany meanwhile had secured Russian support for their position. In a joint declaration issued by France, Germany and Russia on 10 February 2003, the three leaders stated that 'there is an alternative to war' and called for more time for the weapons inspectors to complete their work. On 17 February 2003 the European Council held an extraordinary meeting to discuss the crisis over Iraq. A proposal put forward by France, the UK and Belgium served as a basis for the compromise statement promoting a peaceful resolution to the crisis. Member states reiterated their 'full support for the on-going work of the UN inspectors. They must be given the time and resources that the Security Council believes they need. However, inspections can not continue indefinitely in the absence of full Iraqi co-operation . . . Iraq has a final opportunity to resolve the crisis peacefully.' Following the emergency summit, Chirac attacked the candidate countries that had signed the two public letters. He called their behaviour 'childish and dangerous' and said 'they missed a great opportunity to shut up'. He warned that their behaviour could have an impact on their hopes of joining the EU. On 20 March 2003 at the spring European Council, leaders focused their attention on the humanitarian situation in Iraq rather than on the disputed merits of war. A common statement on humanitarian aid and the continued importance of the UN was agreed upon. Referring to a 'new situation' after the beginning of military conflict in Iraq, the statement underlined the 'central role during and after the current crisis' for the UN.

During the entire crisis Javier Solana kept an extremely low profile. He recognised that the splits between the member states were so deep that he could not perform any mediating function. The crisis was a severe blow to the CFSP and the transatlantic alliance. It demonstrated the fragility of the CFSP when issues of war and peace were on the table. Relations between several member states (and the US) reached freezing point, but at no stage did any major figure suggest that there should be a complete rupture in transatlantic relations. At the same time, the crisis also paved the way for significant new advances in the CFSP and the ESDP. These included the agreement on the ESS, provisions in the draft constitutional treaty for an EU foreign minister and 'structured co-operation' in defence, and new arrangements between the EU and NATO.

THE PROBLEM OF COHERENCE

One of the central problems of the EU is that it is an unidentified political object, with the member states having different visions about its future. Some would like a tight federal structure with more powers for the institutions in foreign and security policy while others prefer a loose system with most powers reserved for the member states. These differences have made it very difficult for the EU to act coherently and consistently in international affairs. The problem was recognised in the Treaty on European Union (TEU), which stated 'the Union shall in particular ensure the consistency of its external activities as a whole in the context of its external relations, security, economic and development policies'. But the TEU was silent on how this consistency was to be achieved. The member states agreed to support the CFSP 'actively and unreservedly in a spirit of loyalty and mutual solidarity'. They further agreed 'to refrain from any action contrary to the interests of the Union or likely to impair its effectiveness as a cohesive force in international relations'.

These fine phrases did not amount to much in 2003 when the member states engaged in an undignified public dispute over the Iraq war. Some argued that as the EU had no common position on Iraq the member states were free to go their own way. This may technically be true, but it gave a very bad impression to the outside world. A plethora of different legal bases for external action in the CFSP, development, trade and monetary fields further complicates the picture, as does the fact that the EU itself has no clear legal personality. It means, for example, that the EU as such cannot join an international organisation. The EC can sign international agreements, but not the EU as such. Only the EC has legal personality, which means that third-country ambassadors dealing with the EU are accredited to the EC and not to the EU. Most international agreements are mixed, i.e. they have to be ratified by the EC and all twenty-five member states. Sometimes, when the EU wishes to act as one, it runs into problems. It wanted to sign a number of criminal justice issues with the US (data protection, mutual assistance, etc.) but the US insisted on all twenty-five member states signing and ratifying. As noted in Chapter 1, there are external relations competences in all three pillars. Many first-pillar issues, e.g. trade conflicts over beef, bananas, hormones, steel, have high political overtones, as do third-pillar issues such as border controls and asylum seekers.

The external representation of the EU is also fragmented. The EC is still the most important actor in terms of both representation and negotiation of international agreements, but in the CFSP it is the Presidency that takes on the lead responsibility for representation and negotiation. These different systems have different voting procedures with qualified majority voting (QMV) available in pillar one but not in pillar two. The role of the European Parliament (EP) is also different, more restricted under pillars two and three. In terms of judicial control the European Court of Justice (ECJ) is excluded from the CFSP (Article 46 TEU). This was a conscious decision of the member states to prevent any judicial activism that had occurred under the EC. The ECJ therefore only has a limited role ensuring the compatibility of the CFSP with Community measures. In cases of cross-pillar issues, with differing legal instruments at play, there is a recipe for confusion with regard to legal effects and the possibilities for legal protection. In terms of visa bans, individuals cannot take the EU to court unless their own member state allows it.

In framing the TEU the negotiators recognised the problem of coherence and called on the Commission and the Council, each in its respective field, to ensure consistency in EU external relations. It has proved easier to agree such an article than to ensure its operation. In practice there have often been dual legal regimes operating. The 1996 Joint Action in which the EU agreed to protest about the US attempts to impose sanctions on EU companies operating in Cuba, Iran and Libya was done on the basis of Articles J3 and K3 in the TEU as well as an EC regulation. The 2001–3 Council Common Positions on combating terrorism were also based on EU and EC treaty articles. When we consider the question of sanctions we rapidly see the absurdity of the current situation. Sanctions may be imposed on the basis of a Commission proposal with the possibility thereafter of using QMV under article 301 of the EC or unanimity under article 23 (1) of the TEU. Sanctions could also be imposed under pillar one direct (e.g. many sanctions based on UNSC resolutions) or under pillar two (e.g. arms embargoes). The first and second pillars have a continuing influence on each other. CFSP decisions to organise election monitoring in Russia or Ukraine, to support the KEDO initiative in North Korea, to restrict the export of dual-use technology have to be financed from the EC budget. The EC's involvement in pillar IV of the UN Interim Administration Mission in Kosovo (UNMIK) also has consequences for the CFSP, as does its human rights and democracy promotion efforts around the world. Under the proposed constitutional treaty it was intended to merge the EC and EU personalities into one legal personality of the Union. Common Strategies, Joint Actions and Common Positions were to have made way for 'European decisions'.

VOTING

On a number of occasions there have been attempts to introduce some form of voting into the CFSP. The most that was achieved was the agreement to allow qualified majority voting (QMV) when implementing Joint Actions. Even this modest provision has rarely been used. When asked by the author what QMV the UK might be able to accept in implementing the Joint Action on Mostar, the British diplomat replied that London might allow voting on the colour of the Land-rovers for the mission! Most member states seem content to retain unanimity in what is considered a sensitive domain. No one has proposed any form of voting for defence questions as it is recognised that decisions in this area must remain the preserve of national governments.

BUDGETS

It is impossible to conduct foreign policy without a budget. The EU budget is approximately €100 billion a year, of which two-thirds is spent on agriculture and structural funds including regional policy. This does not leave much for other activities, including external affairs. In 2005 the budget for external affairs was €4,500 million, but the sum devoted to the CFSP was a paltry €30 million. In 2006 this was increased to €102.6 million (not including a possible operation in Kosovo). At the Hampton Court European Council in October 2005 there was a broad agreement that the CFSP budget should be increased to around €300 million per annum. Solana outlined the problems of CFSP funding in a paper presented to the December European Council three months later. He pointed to the difficulties of current funding of CFSP and ESDP operations, especially as there were different mechanisms for civilian and military operations. This had led to delays in establishing operations. He called for member states to agree on adequate funding for the CFSP in the next Financial Perspectives and the annual budget process.

Solana's paper was timely as it was drafted just before agreement was reached on the budget for the period 2007–13 at the December 2005 European Council. This amounted to just 1.045 per cent of the EU's GDP, which was considerably lower than the 1.23 per cent that the European Commission had proposed in light of enlargement and new policy commitments. The Commission proposed a modest increase in the budget for external affairs from €6.28 billion (9.3 per cent of the EU budget in 2006) to €8.07 billion (9.9 per cent in 2013). The Commission also proposed to simplify and rationalise the financial instruments through which the EU delivers its policies, condensing over thirty legislative instruments into just six, of which four are new. The new instruments are: the Development Co-operation and Economic Co-operation Instrument, for the drive to raise living conditions worldwide; the European Neighbourhood and Partnership Instrument (ENPI), to build closer relations with the EU's nearest neighbours (including Russia); the Pre-Accession Instrument, assisting EU candidate countries (Turkey and Croatia) and potential candidates on the road towards membership; and the Instrument for Stability, a new mechanism to tackle crisis and instability in third countries. Two existing instruments – Humanitarian Aid and Macro Financial Assistance – will continue as before.

In the early years of the CFSP, debates on policy were too often over-shadowed by ideological arguments over whether an action was to be funded by member states or by the Community budget. The usual result was to use the Community budget for CFSP actions, a move that inevitably brought complaints from the Commission. Such disputes remain a handicap to the efficient operation of the CFSP (as does the woefully inadequate budget) but they also explain the enduring co-existence of a CFSP mentality and a first-pillar mentality amongst Commission staff. The management of the Commission's input has been plagued with the vagaries and intricacies of the three-pillar system. There are regular battles as to whether an action should be financed from the first- or second-pillar budget with all the consequent competence questions. The co-operation programme between the EU and Russia in the field of non-proliferation and disarmament (managed by the security unit in the CFSP directorate of the Commission) is a case in point. It is difficult to reconcile the rather modest budget for external affairs with the EU's stated ambition to be a global actor. The UK Presidency actually presented a budget to the December 2005 European Council that would have reduced assistance to the western Balkans exactly when those countries most needed aid to carry out their reform policies.

CONCLUSION

The move from EPC to CFSP was a recognition that the growing economic power of the EU needed a political dimension. The changed geopolitical circumstances of 1989–91 provided the catalyst for the introduction of the CFSP, which largely built on the structures of EPC. There were major divisions between the member states on how the CFSP should be organised and on whether it should have its own defence capability. Furthermore, the new, ambitious policy could hardly have been launched at a less auspicious moment. As the negotiations on the CFSP continued in the second half of 1991, Yugoslavia disintegrated into civil war. The Luxembourg foreign minister, Jacques Poos, proudly forecast that 'the hour of Europe' had arrived. But, far from the EU being regarded as the strong actor that could bang heads together and bring peace to the warring factions in Yugoslavia, it was regarded as weak and divided, both in the Balkans and in Washington. The experience in Yugoslavia did have some positive results. First, it demonstrated to member states the futility of trying to pursue diplomacy without some military capability. Second, it led to greater efforts to produce more integrated policy-making, albeit with mixed success. Third, the EU learned to use a judicious mix of carrots and sticks to ensure the spread of its norms, whether political or economic, throughout the continent and now has an extensive web of agreements covering practically all its neighbours from Morocco to Russia. The EU, however, has not been able to build a consensus in all areas. There have been disputes, for example, over how to respond to violations of human rights in third countries and how to deal with Iraq. But the overall trend has been towards greater EU cohesion in its external policies towards the rest of the world. These developments have led to the EU playing an important leadership role on many global issues. Many third countries also perceive the EU as an alternative kind of power to that of the US. Its 'soft' power and its unique model of governance are increasingly cited as attractive concepts by other countries and regions.

KEY QUESTIONS

How successful was European Political Co-operation?
Why did the EU establish the CFSP?
What did the EU achieve in the first decade of the CFSP?
How significant is the problem of coherence in EU external relations?
Is the budget for foreign affairs sufficient for the EU's ambitions in this field?

FURTHER READING

EPC and the CFSP are described in detail by Nuttall (2000). For an assessment of the early years of the CFSP, see Holland (2002). Other assessments are provided by Pappas and Vanhoonacker (1996), Smith, M. E. (2003), while Hill and Smith, K. E. (2000) provide a useful collection of key documents on EU foreign policy. See also Hill's 1993 article. The annual publication of core documents on EU security and defence by the EU Institute for Security Studies is also essential reading.

3 The EU foreign policy machinery

SUMMARY

The machinery of EU external relations is highly complicated owing to the existence of different systems or pillars for different aspects of external policy (foreign and security policy, trade, development, etc.). During the 1990s and early 2000 there was a strengthening of the institutional system in Brussels that included the creation of the position of High Representative for the CFSP, a political and security committee plus a military staff and committee. There were further attempts to deepen the machinery in the constitutional treaty, but the treaty is in abeyance after the double rejection by French and Dutch voters in 2005. Nevertheless, some of the provisions in the treaty are likely to reappear, including the position of an EU foreign minister and an EU diplomatic service. The reactions of member states to these ideas are mixed. Foreign and security policy remains a very sensitive area.

INTRODUCTION

It is a fact of life that bureaucracies spend much time on internal power struggles. With regard to EU foreign policy there are constant turf wars within and between the Commission and the Council. Within the Commission there are struggles over who should control which directorate generals (DGs) and budget lines. Within the Council there are struggles for the ear of Solana. Between the Commission and the Council there are struggles for power and influence. At the same time the member states play their own game, sometimes supportive of the EU institutions and sometimes preferring to plough their own furrow. Most member states have been reluctant to grant the Commission increased powers over what they consider to be foreign and security policy. Yet, as we have seen in Chapter 1, this depends on the definition of foreign policy. The Commission is very much in the driving seat when it comes to trade policy, enlargement and development policy; but it is the Council, representing the member states, that leads on political–security issues. It is not always apparent, however, where the dividing line rests, and this has led to continuing turf wars between the Commission and the Council which are detrimental to the aim of a more coherent foreign policy and which are confusing to the outside world. In one case the Commission actually took the Council to court over who had competence to implement a programme aimed at preventing the spread of small arms in West Africa (21 February 2005, Case C-91/05).

One of the main changes as a result of the Treaty of Amsterdam, coinciding with the start of the Romano Prodi Commission, was the appointment of Javier Solana as the first Secretary General/High Representative (SG/HR) for the CFSP. Solana had a distinguished background as Spain's foreign minister and as Secretary General of NATO. At the same time, Chris Patten was appointed as Commissioner for External Affairs. He also had a distinguished background as a former British cabinet minister and as the last governor of Hong Kong. Their respective appointments gave rise to much speculation about how they would work together and how the Council–Commission bureaucracies would cope with what seemed to be the inevitable turf wars. Patten and Solana enjoyed a good relationship with each other, but their respective staffs were often engaged in disputes for control of foreign policy. This took place against the background of a growing number of political and bureaucratic structures dealing with the CFSP – a process that is sometimes referred to as the 'Brusselisation' of European foreign policy.

THE EUROPEAN COUNCIL

The European Council, composed of the heads of state and government of the twenty-five member states, is the highest decision-making body in the EU but spends little time on external affairs. It devotes most of its time to negotiating difficult issues such as the budget or new treaties and, as regards foreign policy, it usually rubber-stamps decisions and declarations that have been prepared at lower levels. One of the criticisms of the European Council is that it spends so much time on other issues that it rarely finds time to debate strategic issues. It agrees Common Strategies towards countries such as Russia and China without ever having a real exchange of views on the strategy.

THE GENERAL AFFAIRS AND EXTERNAL RELATIONS COUNCIL (GAERC)

The GAERC meets every four to six weeks and is attended also by the SG/HR and Commission representatives. The Presidency foreign minister chairs the meetings, and the agenda is prepared by the Presidency in co-operation with the Council secretariat. Items are usually discussed before, and often agreed, in Coreper. The agenda for the GAERC meetings is usually divided into general affairs and external relations. If ministers cannot attend personally, they usually send their deputy or the Coreper ambassador. Occasionally defence ministers

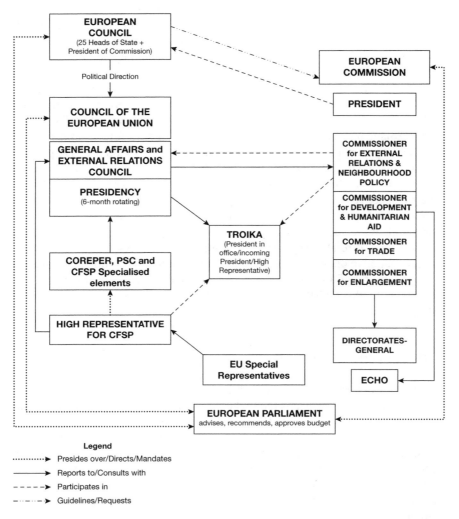

Figure 3.1 CFSP structures

accompany them. The GAERC may issue declarations or agree on Joint Actions and Common Positions. Again, there is little time for strategic debate. Indeed, foreign ministers from major member states sometimes just appear for the lunch, which is usually held in a more restricted setting. At meetings of the GAERC there can be over a hundred people in the room, which hardly makes for intimate discussions. A recent trend is for the Big Three (France, Germany, the UK) to discuss issues informally outside the meeting room and then try to convince the other member states after they have reached a consensus. The influence of the GAERC has declined in recent years, owing partly to the tendency for prime ministers to keep the major decisions for themselves and partly to the increasingly influential role played by the Economic and Finance Council (ECOFIN) in EU affairs.

Box 3.1: *Typical agenda of the GAERC*

2691st Council meeting General Affairs and External Relations, External Relations Brussels, 21–22 November 2005, Presidents Mr Jack Straw Secretary of State for Foreign and Commonwealth Affairs, Mr Douglas Alexander, Minister of State for Europe, of the United Kingdom

Main results of the Council

On the basis of the agreement on movement and access between Israel and the Palestinian Authority, which it welcomed as a major break-through, the Council agreed that the EU should undertake the third party role proposed in the agreement and decided to launch, as a matter of urgency, an ESDP mission to monitor the operations of the Rafah border crossing point. The Council also endorsed the appointment of Major General Pietro Pistolese as head of mission, approved a Concept of Operations for this mission and looked forward to the early deployment of an initial team of monitors to allow operations at Rafah to begin as soon as possible.

On the tenth anniversary of the Dayton/Paris peace agreement, the Council warmly welcomed progress made by Bosnia and Herzegovina and authorised the Commission to open negotiations on a stabilisation and association agreement at the earliest opportunity. The Council also:

- agreed to establish a follow-on mission to the EU Police Mission in BiH (EUPM) with a mandate refocused on supporting the fight against organised crime in a more proactive way and implementation of police reform;
- reviewed the EU military operation, Althea, on completion of its successful first year and approved high representative Javier Solana's recommendation that force levels should remain broadly unchanged for the coming year;
- agreed to strengthen the EUSR's role in co-ordinating all its instruments in Bosnia and Herzegovina.

Ahead of the WTO ministerial conference in Hong Kong, the Council reconfirmed the objective of a comprehensive, balanced and ambitious trade agreement with an ambitious development perspective. It examined

---

continued

a package of 'aid for trade' measures that could enable developing countries to gain from the agreement.

The Council also agreed on adjustments to the framework of the EU's development policy in order to take account of changes both within the EU and internationally over the last few years.

In its six-monthly review of developments in the European security and defence policy, in the presence of defence ministers, the Council noted progress in military capabilities, including on EU battle groups and in the work of the European Defence Agency (EDA).

In the margins of the Council:

- The EDA steering board agreed a voluntary code of conduct for defence procurement in order to encourage competition in the European defence equipment market, which will take effect from July 2006.
- At a civilian capabilities improvement conference, ministers emphasised the growing role of civilian crisis-management in the EU's support for international peace and security and reiterated their commitment to the further development of civilian crisis-management.

COREPER

The Committee of Permanent Representatives (Coreper) occupies a pivotal point in EU decision-making and consists formally of the heads of the delegation, or permanent representatives, that each member state maintains in Brussels; but the term Coreper is also used to refer to the totality of the delegations and their various committees and subcommittees. The members of Coreper have senior ambassadorial status, and their main task is to prepare the agenda for Council meetings. If Coreper is able to reach unanimous agreement on a particular issue, the proposal is given an 'A' category on the Council agenda, which means that the proposal is approved by the Council without discussion. Ministers then focus on the more contentious items, or 'B' points. The ambassadors cover the full spectrum of EU business and prepare the dossiers for all Council meetings. Since they are very senior national officials with the confidence of their government, they have considerable negotiating flexibility and can inform their political masters if a position cannot be maintained. Coreper meets at least once a week, so the ambassadors have a good idea of what is possible. Much of the daily routine is handled by the deputy heads of mission, who meet as Coreper I, while the ambassadors' committee is known as Coreper II. By tradition, Coreper does not discuss agricultural questions: these are the province of the special committee on agriculture.

Although Coreper is formally above the Political and Security Committee (PSC) in hierarchy, it rarely has time for detailed discussions on foreign and security policy matters and hence tends to accept the recommendations from the PSC.

THE POLITICAL AND SECURITY COMMITTEE (PSC)

The PSC, known more by its French acronym, COPS, has a remit to cover all aspects of the CFSP including defence issues. Established by the 2001 Nice Treaty, the PSC has a mandate to:

> monitor the international situation in the areas covered by the common foreign and security policy and contribute to the definition of policies by delivering opinions to the Council at the request of the Council or on its own initiative. It shall also monitor the implementation of agreed policies, without prejudice to the responsibility of the Presidency and the Commission. Within the scope of this Title, this Committee shall exercise, under the responsibility of the Council, political control and strategic direction of crisis-management operations.

The PSC is the hub around which the CFSP revolves, and since its creation there has been a greater urgency and an improved capacity to respond swiftly to crisis situations. Unlike the old political committee, composed of senior officials who travelled to Brussels once a month for meetings, the PSC comprises ambassadors in Brussels and is active on a daily basis. It meets formally on Tuesdays and Fridays, but there are informal discussions almost every day. It often invites international personalities or EU special representatives to brief the committee. In theory it reports to ministers via the more senior committee of EU ambassadors (Coreper), with which there is a certain rivalry, but in reality they enjoy a large measure of autonomy partly because of the specialised nature of their discussions and partly because of the usually overloaded agendas for Coreper meetings. The PSC is, however, seen as junior to Coreper and is still developing a sense of institutional corporate identity. Like Coreper, much of its effectiveness has depended on the standing of its members with their governments and on an intimate work atmosphere that encourages compromise. The PSC has developed a key role in the planning and oversight of crisis-management operations.

  The PSC and the Council Secretariat are further supported by a variety of structures including a network of European Correspondents in all the MFAs of member states and the Commission that co-ordinates daily CFSP business. They maintain daily contact via the Correspondant Européen (COREU) telex network that allows exchange of encrypted messages. In addition there is a group of Relex Counsellors (including the Commission) who draft CFSP legislation and ensure consistency, and CFSP working groups composed of national diplomats and DG Relex officials, divided along geographical and thematic lines. There are over thirty working groups in the CFSP process that meet at regular intervals in Brussels to discuss the latest developments in either regional, country or thematic issues. Their members are usually the desk officers from the MFAs of member states plus representatives from the Council and the Commission. It is the job of the Council Secretariat to take notes of the meetings, circulate agendas and follow up points of action.

Box 3.2: CFSP working groups

1. Working Party of Foreign Relations Counsellors
   (a) Sanctions
2. Working Party on Public International Law
   (a) International Criminal Court
3. Working Party on the Law of the Sea
4. United Nations Working Party
5. Working Party on OSCE and the Council of Europe
6. Working Party on Human Rights
7. Working Party on Transatlantic Relations
8. Working Party on Central and Southeast Europe
9. Working Party on Eastern Europe and Central Asia
10. Working Party on EFTA
11. Working Party on the Western Balkans Region
12. Ad hoc Working Party on the Middle East Peace Process
13. Middle East/Gulf Working Party
14. Mashreq/Maghreb Working Party
15. Africa Working Party
16. ACP Working Party
17. Asia–Oceania Working Party
18. Working Party on Latin America
19. Working Party on Terrorism (International Aspects)
20. Working Party on Non-Proliferation
21. Working Party on Conventional Arms Exports
22. Working Party on Global Disarmament and Arms Control
23. Working Party on Dual-Use Goods
24. Working Party on European Arms Policy
25. Politico-Military Working Party
26. Military Committee Working Group (EUMCWG)
27. Working Party on Trade Questions
28. Working Party on the Generalised System of Preferences
29. Export Credits Group
30. Working Party on Development Co-operation
31. Working Party on Preparation for International Development Conferences

---

32. Working Party on Food Aid
33. Working Party on Commodities
34. Working Party on Consular Affairs
35. Working Party on CFSP Administrative Affairs and Protocol
36. Nicolaidis Group

THE PRESIDENCY

The six-monthly rotating Presidency chairs CFSP meetings, helps set the agenda and represents the EU to the outside world. There is concern that too often Presidencies set their own (national) priorities. The Finns may pay more attention to the Nordic dimension, the Belgians to Africa, Spain to Latin America, and so on. It is good that Presidencies find the energy to organise meetings on these 'priority' issues; but, then, there are serious problems concerning lack of continuity and the resources now required to run the Presidency. When the Presidency was established it was never intended that it should have an external representational role; rather its role was seen as organising and chairing meetings. Now it is a huge burden on each member state, and the smaller ones are fully stretched to meet the requirements. There has been much debate about ending the rotating Presidency, partly because of the increased burdens. At the beginning and end of each Presidency the prime minister of the country holding the Presidency reports to the European Parliament on what he hopes to achieve and the results of his six months at the helm of the EU.

Box 3.3: Future EU Presidencies

2007	Germany, Portugal
2008	Slovenia, France
2009	Czech Republic, Sweden
2010	Spain, Belgium
2011	Hungary, Poland
2012	Denmark, Cyprus
2013	Ireland, Lithuania
2014	Greece, Italy
2015	Latvia, Luxembourg
2016	Netherlands, Slovakia
2017	Malta, UK
2018	Estonia

THE COUNCIL SECRETARIAT AND HIGH
REPRESENTATIVE (MR CFSP)

The Council of the EU is supported by a Secretariat headed by the SG/HR. The Secretariat's main function is to prepare meetings of the Council in its many formations and its preparatory bodies, such as Coreper and the PSC. The Secretariat is divided into nine Directorates General, one of which deals with External Relations and is further divided into nine directorates for geographic and functional areas. Since Amsterdam, the Council's role has increased, with Javier Solana becoming an increasingly visible figure of European diplomacy. The treaty was deliberately vague on the responsibilities of the SG/HR. It stated that he 'shall assist the Presidency', and inevitably in such a situation much depends on the personality of the office-holder. Some Presidencies like more assistance than others. The EU was certainly fortunate in having someone with Mr Solana's experience and standing as the first Mr CFSP. He is regularly on television and in the press commenting on EU foreign policy. He also chairs the military committee and the defence agency. Despite his limited mandate and resources, Solana has become a key player, representing the Union in the quartet (the UN, the US, Russia and the EU) dealing with the Middle East peace process, and playing important mediation roles in the Balkans and elsewhere. Solana has two other hats. He is the Secretary General of the Council, which means he controls a bureaucracy of some 3,000 officials (the Commission has about 25,000 officials and the EP about 2,000), and he is also Secretary General of the WEU, a largely defunct defence organisation. While the choice of a politician as opposed to a senior official for the HR post was by no means a foregone conclusion, such is the political role that Solana has carved out that it would now be unthinkable to replace him with a bureaucrat. In 2004, Solana was re-appointed for a further five years.

Although he is also Secretary General of the Council, Solana has been able to leave the traditional functions of Council administration to his deputy, Pierre de Boissieu, previously French Permanent Representative to the EU. The lack of clarity in the treaty about the HR made relations between the HR and successive Presidencies more crucial than ever. It is fair to say that these relations have varied. All Presidencies, whether large or small member states, have little desire to share the limelight. Some Presidencies have sought to define a complementary role for Solana, some have attempted to ignore him and others have attempted to promote him. He has spent a great deal of time travelling, notably to the Balkans and the Middle East. The Council has also sent him on delicate missions as far afield as Cairo, Turkey, Iran and East Timor. Solana has also sought to carve out a niche for himself in the ESDP, constantly pressing member states to fulfil their commitments to improve EU military capabilities. Another Solana triumph has been to gain admittance to G8 deliberations, albeit at foreign-minister and not head-of-government level, and notwithstanding the formal presence of the Commission at all levels of G8 business.

THE POLICY UNIT

Another new creation at Amsterdam was the establishment of a Policy Planning and Early Warning Unit (PPEWU), known more commonly as the Policy Unit, composed largely of representatives from the member states, plus Commission and Council representatives, with a mandate to provide policy advice to Mr Solana. The first head of the Policy Unit, Christoph Heusgen, became Angela Merkel's foreign policy adviser in November 2005. Another German, Helga Schmid, previously head of Joschka Fischer's private office, took over as head of the Policy Unit in January 2006. The Policy Unit is divided into eight taskforces: European Security and Defence Policy, Western Balkans/Central Europe; Early Warning/Conflict Prevention/Terrorism; Horizontal Questions; Latin America; Russia/Ukraine/Transatlantic/Baltic States; Asia; Mediterranean/Middle East/Africa; and Administration/Security and Situation Centre/Crisis Cell. The Policy Unit is Solana's eyes and ears, providing him with daily policy guidance, and has become an extended personal cabinet with an early-warning function. Its ability to perform this task is assisted by access to the political reporting from Commission delegations worldwide, member states and open sources. But one of the problems of the rigid division between the pillars is the lack of input and experience in the Policy Unit on first-pillar matters such as trade and aid.

THE JOINT SITUATION CENTRE (SITCEN)

The Policy Unit also oversaw the establishment of a Joint Situation Centre (SITCEN), which joined the (civilian) Policy Unit and the military Situation Centre. The SITCEN opened on 1 January 2003, to coincide with the start of the EU's police mission (EUPM) in Bosnia. It has recruited intelligence officers to facilitate information exchange with member states and put secure communications networks into place. It combines early warning, situation monitoring and assessment; provides facilities for a crisis taskforce; and serves as an operational point of contact for the SG/HR. Its tasks include risk assessment, ad hoc intelligence briefings, and urgent reports in the wake of terrorist attacks outside the EU. Reports are distributed to members of the PSC and the EUMC. The SITCEN has a small staff who receive information from a variety of sources including the EU's Satellite Imaging Centre at Torrejon, Spain. Apart from collecting information, there is also an outflow of information from the SITCEN to the member states.

SPECIAL AND PERSONAL REPRESENTATIVES

Solana is assisted by a number of special and personal representatives (EUSR) who are responsible for a geographical area such as the southern Caucasus or a thematic issue such as human rights. In mid-2006 the EU had seven special representatives in different regions of the world. These representatives were established under Article 18 of the Amsterdam Treaty, and they are supposed to represent and promote the interests and the policies of the EU. Three of the current EUSRs are resident in their country/region of activity, while the four others operate on a travelling basis. An EUSR is appointed by the Council through the legal act of a Joint Action. All EUSRs carry out their duties under the authority and operational direction of Mr Solana and are financed through the CFSP budget. These special representatives have varied in their ability to ensure added value to the CFSP. They have certainly not been tasked with ensuring the vital inter-pillar coherence so sought after, although a start was made in November 2005 with the double-hatted appointment of Erwan Fouéré to be both head of the Commission Delegation and simultaneously EU special representative in Macedonia. The experience with special representatives has generally been positive, but success depends considerably on the personality and political weight of the individual and his or her ability to gain the respect of diplomatic peers and the parties in the crisis area.

Box 3.4: EU special representatives

Erwan Fouéré (Ireland) was appointed EUSR in the Former Yugoslav Republic of Macedonia (FYROM) in October 2005. His mandate is 'to contribute to the consolidation of the peaceful political process and the full implementation of the Ohrid Framework Agreement, thereby facilitating further progress towards European integration through the Stabilisation and Association Process'. Interestingly this appointment was a first ever shared appointment as Mr Fouéré is simultaneously head of the Commission delegation in Skopje.

Pierre Mirel (France) was appointed EUSR for Central Asia in October 2006. His mandate is 'to contribute to the implementation of the EU's policy objectives in the region, which include promoting good and close relations between the countries of Central Asia and the EU, contributing to strengthening of democracy, rule of law, good governance and respect for human rights and fundamental freedoms in Central Asia as well as enhancing EU's effectiveness in the region, including closer co-ordination with other relevant partners and international organisations, such as the OSCE'.

Pekka Haavisto (Finland) was appointed EUSR for Sudan in July 2005. His mandate is 'to work towards a political settlement of the conflict in Darfur, to facilitate the implementation of the Comprehensive Peace Agreement (CPA) and to promote South–South dialogue, with due regard to the regional ramifications of these issues and to the principle of African ownership. He will also contribute to ensuring maximum effectiveness of the EU's contribution to the African Union mission in Sudan (AMIS).'

Adriaan Jacobovits de Szeged (Netherlands) was appointed EUSR for Moldova in March 2005. His mandate is 'to strengthen the EU contribution to the resolution of the Transnistria conflict in accordance with agreed EU policy objectives and in close co-ordination with the OSCE'.

Marc Otte (Belgium) was appointed EUSR for the Middle East peace process in July 2003. His mandate is based on the EU's policy objectives regarding the Middle East peace process, which include a two-state solution with Israel and a democratic, viable, peaceful and sovereign Palestinian state living side-by-side within secure and recognised borders enjoying normal relations with their neighbours.

Peter Semneby (Sweden) was appointed EUSR for the South Caucasus in February 2006 replacing Heikki Talvitie. His mandate is 'to contribute to the implementation of the EU's policy objectives, which include assisting the countries of the South Caucasus in carrying out political and economic reforms, preventing and assisting in the resolution of conflicts, promoting the return of refugees and internally displaced persons, engaging constructively with key national actors neighbouring the region, supporting intra-regional co-operation and ensuring co-ordination, consistency and effectiveness of the EU's action in the South Caucasus'.

Francesco Vendrell (Spain) was appointed EUSR in Afghanistan on 25 June 2002. His mandate is 'to contribute to achieving the implementation of the Union's policy in Afghanistan'.

Christoph Schwarz-Schilling (Germany) replaced Lord Ashdown as EUSR in Bosnia and Herzegovina in January 2006. He had a broad mandate, but his main focus was supporting the fight against organised crime in a more proactive way and implementation of police reform, working closely with other EU actors and local law enforcement agencies.

Aldo Ajello (Italy) was appointed EUSR for the African Great Lakes Region in March 1996. His mandate is 'to work closely with the UN and AU [African Union] and demonstrate the EU's desire to contribute to solving the crises in the region'.

Personal representatives

Mr Solana has also appointed a number of personal representatives to deal with sensitive issues. These include Annalisa Giannella (Italy), appointed in October 2003 to deal with proliferation of WMD; Michael Matthiessen (Denmark), appointed in January 2005 to deal with human rights in the area of the CFSP; Stefan Lehne (Austria), appointed in November 2005 to deal with the Kosovo future status process.

THE EU MILITARY COMMITTEE (EUMC)

The Nice Treaty provided for the establishment of an EU military committee (EUMC) and military staff within the Council. The EUMC is composed of representatives of the defence ministry of each member state. It provides military advice and makes recommendations to the PSC; and exercises direction of all military activities within the EU framework. The committee can provide advice either at its own initiative or on the basis of a request from the PSC. It is supposed to help develop guidelines for the overall concept of crisis management in its military aspects; provide risk assessment of potential crises, and management of military operations. Under Council authority it is also charged with planning, implementing and ending EU military operations. The EUMC is presided over for four years by an elected chairman, normally a four-star general, preferably a former defence chief. The chairman in 2006 was an Italian, General Mosca Moschini, who participates in the PSC and attends Council meetings when decisions with military consequences are made.

THE EU MILITARY STAFF (EUMS)

The EUMS, established in January 2001, has over 130 military personnel. Its function is to give the Council strategic options, which are, in turn, evaluated by the EUMC. It is in practice, therefore, the EUMC's support body, although formally it is a department of the Council Secretariat directly attached to the SG/HR. Like the EUMC, it is far from being an incipient EU military headquarters. The military staff has three main operational functions: early warning, situation assessment and strategic planning. It is the source of the EU's military expertise and it assures the link between the EUMC on the one hand, and the military resources available to the EU on the other. It has the responsibility to monitor, assess and make recommendations regarding the forces and capabilities made available to the EU by the member states, on training, exercises and inter-operability. It also liaises with military intelligence in the member states and inputs into the Situation Centre with military information. It also contributes to the development and preparation (including training and exercises) of national and multinational forces made available by the member states to the EU.

THE EU MONITORING MISSION (EUMM)

The EU Monitoring Mission (EUMM) is tasked with monitoring political and security developments (particularly border monitoring, inter-ethnic issues and refugee return). It provides the Council with information but can also help build confidence in unstable situations. Though it currently operates only in the Balkans, the EUMM model might be exportable to other peace-building situations to contribute to stabilisation while giving the EU an independent source of information. The monitors – slightly over 100 at present – are unarmed and wear white civilian clothing. The EUMM's chief is appointed by the Council and reports to it through the SG/HR. The problem with the EUMM is its lack of co-ordination with other CFSP elements, and many consider that it should be fully integrated into the EU security apparatus in order to fulfil its potential.

THE COMMISSION

The Commission plays a very important role in EU external relations, albeit a more limited role in the CFSP and the ESDP. In some areas, such as trade, it has exclusive competence. In other areas, such as development policy, it has shared competence with the member states. In the CFSP it remains 'fully associated' but has key strengths to bring to the table. These include its management of the EU budget, its network of delegations and its permanent presence in the troika. It has a lesser profile in the ESDP but nevertheless remains essential for complementary measures to support (and often finance) ESDP actions. The President of the Commission also has responsibilities in the external field and he is always present when there are summit meetings with third countries such as the US, China, Russia, India, etc. Within the Commission there are a number of major departments that deal with external relations, but nearly all directorate generals have some impact on foreign policy whether it is agriculture, energy, transport or fisheries.

During the EPC years the Commission had only a small staff dealing with foreign policy located in the Secretariat General. After Maastricht the Commission established a new directorate general (DG1A) to handle the CFSP. It was headed by the former Dutch foreign minister Hans van den Broek. This new DG soon found itself in competition with the more established DG1, responsible for trade policy, and headed by former British Conservative cabinet minister Leon Brittan. The frequently public disputes between van den Broek and Brittan were hardly conducive to efficient delivery of policy, and the reticence of the Commission throughout the 1990s to use its hard-won right of initiative in the CFSP, for fear of incurring member-state discomfort and opposition, compounded Commission weakness in the CFSP. The choice of the creation of DG1A, and the bureaucratic rivalry caused largely by the need to find Commissioners and Directors-General adequate portfolios, did much to keep the Commission from becoming the streamlined foreign service to which it might have aspired. The overall need to co-ordinate was counterbalanced by the perception that Commissioners' independence and their DGs' autonomy must be preserved. The relations between Brussels and the delegations are a case in point. There was no recognisable career development and training path for staff at headquarters or in the field, and as new delegations opened to cope with the changing emphases in world politics it was hard to ensure that staff abroad (including some 2,000 locally employed staff) were properly trained for the new functions they were to fulfil.

Under President Prodi a small grouping of Commissioners dealing with external affairs was set up with Chris Patten as chair. This reorganisation led to a slightly more coherent Commission approach to the CFSP. Patten's determination to improve the delivery of EU assistance was also appreciated by member states – and recipients. President Barroso has decided to continue and chair the Relex group himself. The current Commissioner for External Relations, Benita Ferrero-Waldner, is deputy chair of the Relex group. She is also responsible for the European Neigbourhood Policy (ENP) and the EuropeAid Co-operation Office. The other members of the Relex group include Peter Mandelson, responsible for trade; Louis Michel, responsible for humanitarian aid and development policy (he is also responsible for the European Commission Humanitarian Aid Office [ECHO]); and Olli Rehn, responsible for enlargement. From time to time other Commissioners whose portfolios touch on external relations, such as environment, economic and financial affairs, or justice and home affairs, may be invited to attend these meetings depending on the agenda. The Relex system has not really functioned as envisaged. Too often Commissioners plough their own furrow rather than seek to produce well-thought-out, comprehensive policy papers taking into account all the various aspects of external relations. The Commission sees its contribution to the CFSP/ESDP under the overall theme of conflict prevention, and its internal structures and procedures are being adapted to ensure that hitherto disparate policy areas form part of a coherent and co-ordinated whole. Though the Commission sensibly has not sought a role in the military dimension of the ESDP, it has argued that it has an important role in non-military dimensions such as defence-industrial co-operation, funding and training of police, customs officials and border guards, economic sanctions, de-mining operations, election monitoring, and restoring local administrations in societies emerging from conflicts.

The Commission was not created to be an actor in foreign and security policy. It neither recruited nor trained staff for these fields. Most officials working in the CFSP field have had to learn on the job. It is not surprising, therefore, that officials from the MFAs of member states do not always have a high opinion of the Commission's expertise in the CFSP. Commission expertise in other fields is, however, recognised. The directorate in DG Relex that interacts most closely with the Council is the CFSP directorate. Within the CFSP directorate falls the security unit, which is responsible for input to the Political Military (POLMIL) group, terrorism, arms control, small arms, non-proliferation, and the crisis unit. The other key policy unit comprises a team of some twenty officials covering conflict prevention, crisis management, the CFSP in Africa and the Commission contribution to the EU's rapid-reaction capacity, the financial mechanism known as the Rapid Reaction Mechanism. Two further units deal with the business of sound financial management and legal implications (the CFSP Counsellor) and operations under the COREU or

Cortesy network of inter-foreign-ministry communication and the preparation of briefings for Council meetings (the European Correspondent). In practical terms, the Commission has also built a secure 'crisis room' as a focus for the Commission's co-operation with the SITCEN and has insisted on parity with member states in reception of the information and documentation process in the SITCEN, while providing automatic transmission of information from its own heads of delegation to the Policy Unit.

The Commission also maintains a substantial network of delegations around the world, making it one of the larger diplomatic services. But few staff in the delegations or in DG Relex have a background in political or security issues, and they are often reluctant to speak on these matters at co-ordination meetings with member-state colleagues. Rather they prefer to stick to tried and tested areas of Commission competence such as trade and aid. The political reporting from delegations is understandably of variable quality as few have had the required training. This is unfortunate because, given the budget most delegations have to assist the local country, the senior staff have little problem getting access at the highest levels. Not all foreign ministers seem convinced of the need for the Commission delegations. Britain's former Foreign Secretary Jack Straw, speaking in the House of Commons on 25 May 2004, described the Commission's staff in delegations as 'all sorts of odd-bods from the EU running all sorts of odd offices around the world . . . it is not entirely clear what they are doing'. Patten was quick to respond, stating that the delegations:

> carry out detailed trade and other negotiations, to help support and coordinate the work of the Member States' own embassies, and to provide high quality political and economic reporting, frequently from countries where not all Member States are represented. Perhaps most importantly, they deliver over €5 billion of external and development assistance per year in support of the EU's agreed goals, and in support of the Union's policies.

Straw did not reply to Patten's letter. The Commissioner could have added some remarks about the exceedingly complicated structures and procedures he inherited concerning the delivery of assistance programmes. In 2001 the Service Commun Relex (SCR), the predecessor of Europe Aid (established in 2004), was managing over seventy budget lines on eighty different legal bases. It handled some 30,000 contracts with between 8,000 and 10,000 new ones a year. Total funds administered amounted to €418 million in 2001 involving 41,000 payments made. It was clear that the system needed an overhaul.

TURF WARS

There was much speculation when Solana and Patten were appointed that there would be constant turf wars. In fact, although there were occasional spats at official level, the two men worked reasonably well together. In a speech on 15 September 2002, Patten described the situation as follows:

> Javier Solana and I have different but complementary roles. We both develop external policies. Javier's role is to help the Council rally the Member States to our common policies and to represent those policies to the world. My role is to ensure that the EU can deliver on those policies, to come up with the necessary ideas and proposals, to implement them and to make sure that Europe's external action is consistent with its internal policies.

Yet, in a letter to member states' foreign ministers in November 2000 about the new crisis management arrangements, he underlined the Commission's concerns:

> My problem with Javier's proposal is that as soon as something is designated a 'crisis' he proposes it should at once become the object of a comprehensive Joint Action covering both Community and second pillar issues. Yet even in situations where possible military action creates an imperative for immediate decision-making, I would be unhappy about a Joint Action which strayed into the Community sphere.

Patten further warned about the submission of the Community method to the inter-governmentalism of the second pillar. In a communication of 7 June 2000, Patten himself argued that:

> the welcome creation of the CFSP High Representative has not helped. Indeed, it has given rise to some new institutional complications. It may also have increased the tendency for CFSP to usurp functions, which should be the responsibility of the Commission, e.g. the EC Monitoring Mission to the Balkans, which was dreamt up by CFSP and then left as an expensive baby on the Commission's doorstep.[1]

Patten further argued that 'ambiguity about the limits of the Commission's role is particularly acute in the security field' and he warned of the dangers of building parallel structures. Patten was also critical of the member states' approach in the CFSP. He accused them of making 'ringing political declarations which they were reluctant to underwrite in money and staff', and lamented the 'unresolved tension' between inter-governmental activities and community powers, so that the Commission gets left to wrestle with the contradictions and blamed for inadequate outcomes. Its role was 'that of the maid who is asked to prepare increasingly large and grand dinners in a poky kitchen with poor ingredients'.[2]

Solana described his function in an interview as 'to use the post of High Representative to create new momentum within the CFSP. We have to ensure that the EU provides a more coherent approach to the rest of the world. The Council has to guarantee that the Member States deliver on this' (*Financial Times*, 21 February 2000). In reality, though Solana may be regarded abroad as 'the EU's foreign policy chief', he is a chief with very few Indians and very little money. The Commissioner for External Relations, in contrast, has the money, the manpower, and ownership of most of the instruments, which are first- and third-pillar policies. The SG/HR is unable alone to order the use of specifically second-pillar foreign-policy instruments such as troop deployment or diplomatic *démarches*, while the Commissioner for External Relations has considerable autonomous control of the first-pillar instruments, which make up 90 per cent of the foreign-policy toolbox at the EU's disposal. The Commissioner has practical power. The SG/HR has political profile.

THE EUROPEAN PARLIAMENT

The European Parliament plays a very limited role in the CFSP but a slightly greater role in external relations overall. It is the budgetary power of the Union and can use this power to influence priorities. It also has to approve treaties with third countries. According to Article 21 of the TEU, the Presidency is required to consult the European Parliament on the main aspects and the basic choices of the CFSP and to ensure that the views of the Parliament are taken into account. Its committee on foreign affairs, human rights, common security and defence policy, chaired by Elmer Brok for many years, has two subcommittees, one on defence and another on human rights. One of the problems of the Parliament is that it has very limited research capacity compared to national parliaments or the US Congress. Another problem is that member states do not take it seriously, and there is a certain rivalry with the foreign and defence committees of national parliaments. Some MEPs would like to see more appearances by Mr Solana and Mrs Ferrero-Waldner at their debates.

CONCLUSION

The EU has developed a range of new institutions for the CFSP over recent years which, owing to the pillar system, are overcomplicated. Yet the system works and has some successes to its credit. More and more decisions are taken in Brussels, even though most will have been agreed in advance by the larger member states. Solana, Patten and Ferrero-Waldner have been bullish about the recent record, although many observers consider that there are still too many cooks in the kitchen. But most member states appear comfortable with present arrangements even though nearly all recognise the importance of changes in external representation in light of enlargement. These changes, if agreed, are likely to be incremental in nature. A review of the provisions regarding the CFSP and the ESDP in the constitutional treaty is offered below.

KEY QUESTIONS

Who makes EU foreign policy?
Explain the role and influence of the High Representative.
How could the EU improve its external representation?
Will there ever be an EU diplomatic service?

FURTHER READING

The institutional arrangements for CFSP are discussed in Regelsberger, de Schoutheete de Tervarent and Wessels (1997). Hill (1996) considers the actors in EU foreign policy. Eeckhout (2005) examines the legal foundations for EU foreign policy while Barbé and Herranz (2005) look at the role of the European Parliament. Patten's memoirs (2005) also provide some insights into his battles in Brussels.

4 Old and new member states

SUMMARY

The twenty-five member states of the EU all pursue their own national foreign policies with their own national foreign ministries and national diplomatic services. The idea of the CFSP is to create not a single EU foreign policy but rather a common policy in as many areas as possible. In foreign and security policy some member states are more important than others, and there is a trend towards informal structures such as the EU3 dealing with Iran. But the bottom line for most foreign ministers, including the large member states, is the fact that they are far more likely to achieve their national foreign policy goals by working through the EU than by working alone. The enlargement of the EU from fifteen to twenty-five member states in 2004 had a significant impact in some areas of EU foreign policy, particularly policy towards Russia and Ukraine. There was widespread concern in some older member states such as France and Germany that the new member states would be American 'Trojan horses', given their automatic support for the US in the Iraq war. There were also fears that it would become much more difficult to achieve a common foreign policy in a Union of twenty-seven or more members. It is true that the new member states have their own priorities, usually their immediate neighbourhood, and have been less interested in global issues, including development policy; but it would be unfair to blame them for lack of coherence on EU foreign policy.

INTRODUCTION

EU foreign policy is not made in Brussels. Decisions may formally be taken in Brussels, but it is the twenty-five member states of the EU (soon to be twenty-seven) who are the major stakeholders in the CFSP. The EU institutions are essentially the servants of the member states and can do very little without the agreement of capitals. With so many states of different size, history, tradition, interests and capabilities, it is not easy to forge a common policy. It is not always clear what are the common interests of Britain and Slovenia, Portugal and Estonia, Sweden and Malta. Inevitably the member states pay most attention to their immediate neighbourhood. Sweden, Finland and the Baltic states pay more attention to Russia than Spain or Ireland. France, Spain and Italy pay more attention to North Africa than Denmark or Poland. Greece and Cyprus keep a watchful eye on developments in Turkey. Then there are historical, often colonial, ties that impact on relations. For example, the UK is involved more than others in Hong Kong and Zimbabwe, the French more than others in Algeria and Chad, the Dutch more than others in Indonesia, Portugal more than others in Angola, Belgium more than others in the Congo, and so on. This historical experience can be very valuable if put at the service of the Union as a whole. The EU's involvement in East Timor would probably not have happened without the prodding of Portugal, which had close ties to the area. The decision to offer the western Balkans a roadmap towards EU accession in 2003 would not have happened without a push from Greece and Austria. At the same time, it is a common critique of the six-monthly rotating Presidency that these 'national' interests come to dominate the EU agenda and prevent any long-term strategic thinking or direction. The member states also have very different traditions and capabilities. Nineteen member states of the EU are members of NATO. Sweden, Finland, Austria, Ireland, Cyprus and Malta are all neutral or non-aligned states with no plans to join NATO. Yet the Nordics have a long tradition of strong support for UN peace-keeping operations, and this experience led the Swedes and the Finns to push for a stronger EU capability in this field. All member states are committed to ensuring the success of the Rapid Reaction Force (RRF), but there is considerable divergence in how much each member state spends on defence. The UK and France, for example, spend almost twice per head more than Germany on defence (see next chapter).

THE LARGER MEMBER STATES

Britain and France, both nuclear powers and permanent members of the UNSC, are the only two member states with some real power-projection capability, although nothing like that of the US. Both Britain and France have been involved in several military operations around the world since 1945. In recent times, the UK sent troops to fight in the South Atlantic, France in Africa, and both fought side by side in the first Gulf War and in the Balkans. Germany has a strong pacifist tradition as a result of its twentieth-century history but in the 1990s it began to play a more prominent role in international peace-keeping and is now playing a leading role in the Balkans and in Afghanistan. These three countries have significant diplomatic resources and also have foreign ministry buildings that remind one of the size and importance of the nation state. One only has to compare the magnificent pomp and splendour of the Quai d'Orsay with the functional Charlemagne (home to DG Relex) and Julius Lipsius (home to the Council Secretariat) buildings in Brussels to see how resources are divided between the member states and the EU. National diplomats also view their career development essentially within the framework of a national administration, although increasingly a secondment to Brussels is regarded as a useful career move. The EU3 have started to send top diplomats to the EU institutions to increase their influence in the CFSP system. The UK has provided Solana with his most senior official ever since his appointment in 1999; France Solana's deputy; and Germany the head of the Policy Unit.

Britain, France and Germany tend to see themselves on a different plane from other member states and often meet to discuss policy matters. This trend has become more apparent since the 2004 enlargement that tilted the balance heavily towards the smaller and medium-sized member states. Since 2004, Britain, France and Germany have been co-operating closely as the EU3 in negotiating with Iran, trying to persuade Tehran not to develop a nuclear weapons capacity. This diplomatic move caused some consternation at first, but it was soon recognised that the Big Three had rather more credibility than the normal rotating EU troika. How could one expect officials from Slovenia or Luxembourg to have had any experience in nuclear issues? There is a growing fear, however, that the Big Three may continue to operate in this manner, neglecting to consult the other member states, who on occasions may have useful opinions to give. It may be difficult for British or French diplomats to accept that officials in Riga or Tallinn know more about Russia than they do; or officials in Ljubljana know more about Croatia. Big Three co-operation was tested severely during the Iraq crisis, but soon thereafter the three powers agreed on a number of important steps, including the provisions in the draft constitutional treaty on the CFSP/ESDP and on new rules for EU–NATO co-operation. The Big Three try to co-ordinate their foreign policy as closely as possible, but there remain significant differences. The most often cited is the Anglo-American special relationship, but most member states (certainly France, Germany, Spain, Italy, Ireland, Poland) would all claim a special relationship with America. French, German and Italian leaders have also sought a special relationship with Vladimir Putin of Russia. The foreign ministers of the Big Three and their senior officials certainly prefer operating in a more restricted environment, whether it be the G8, various contact-group formations or just as a trio. As one of Joschka Fischer's aides told the author, trying to explain why his minister only came for the lunches at the GAERC, Germany's foreign minister did not wish to waste his time listening to his Cypriot colleague complaining at length about Turkey or his Estonian colleague about Russia.

Some other countries like Spain and Italy have substantial numbers of men in arms but little military-power-projection capability. These two countries often try to secure a seat when there are meetings of large member states. Italy was involved in the contact group dealing with the Balkans – and is a member of the G8. It has refused to support Germany's bid for a permanent seat on the UNSC on the grounds that there should be an EU seat. Spain, partly owing to its impressive record of economic growth in recent years, would like to be a member of the G8. Since joining the EU, Poland has also sought to portray itself as a large member state, an approach sometimes encouraged by the other larger member states. For example, French Interior Minister and presidential hopeful Nicolas Sarkozy has suggested that the EU should be run by an informal directoire comprising the six large countries – France, Germany, the UK, Spain, Italy and Poland. One can imagine the reaction of Sweden, Finland, the Netherlands and other member states to this proposal.

ENLARGEMENT AS A SECURITY POLICY

The impression that the new member states would be a hindrance to an effective and coherent CFSP/ESDP was raised long before the Iraq crisis. The candidates were united in rejecting this charge. As several of their delegates argued in the Convention on the Future of Europe in 2003, the problem of the efficiency of the CFSP had nothing to do with the enlargement of the EU. It is true that much of the concern about the CFSP after enlargement related to efficient decision-making in an enlarged Union in general, but the Iraq crisis was as much a split between old members as between old and new members. Overall the new member states brought greater diversity and limited capabilities to the table. Furthermore, enlargement led to an EU with a very different balance between big and small member states.

The enlargement of the EU has always been, and still is, a quintessential security policy. By extending the Union's norms, rules, opportunities and constraints to the eastern half of the continent – and later to South-East Europe – it has made instability and conflict in the wider region much less likely. It is also a security policy in its own right because the entrants have brought in interests and skills that broaden the scope of the common external policies. But the 2004 enlargement was unlike previous ones in size and scope and raised numerous questions. How would a twenty-five-member EU stretching from Estonia to Portugal, from Sweden to Cyprus, be able to define its strategic interests? To what extent would this affect the way in which the EU projects itself externally? How would enlargement affect the functioning of the CFSP/ESDP? What would be the attitude of third countries such as the US or Russia? Many considered that, in a Union of twenty-five, alliances and coalitions could easily shift according to the contingencies and the issues at stake. How would this affect EU coherence?

For almost half a century the countries of Central and Eastern Europe (CEECs) had no independent foreign policy. The ruling Soviet communist party made all decisions in Moscow. After the historic events of the late 1980s and early 1990s, the fall of the Berlin Wall, the collapse of communism, and the end of Soviet domination, one of the first decisions of the CEECs was to turn to the West for admission to the 'Euro-Atlantic' framework, in particular through membership of the EU and NATO. The EU was swift to offer financial assistance in 1989 through the Phare programme, and to sign 'association' agreements from 1991 onwards. Although these accords provided for co-operation in political, economic, cultural and other areas, they fell significantly short of the countries' aspiration for EU membership. The preamble of the agreements recognised membership as the wish of the associated states, without affirming it as the aim of the EU.

In terms of security, the CEECs perceived EU membership as a supplement to NATO membership because of the powerful 'bonding' effect of its institutions and policies; and it would also bring economic gains through full access to the EU's market and budgetary receipts from its policies. Hesitations on the EU side concerning eastern enlargement persisted in the early 1990s, with attention focused on other political priorities such as the creation of the single market, the negotiation of the Maastricht Treaty, and the preparation for the EFTA enlargement which brought Austria, Sweden and Finland into the EU in 1995. But in June 1993 a historic step was taken at the European Council in Copenhagen when the EU's leaders stated that 'the associated countries of central and eastern Europe that so desire shall become members of the Union. Accession will take place as soon as a country is able to assume the obligations of membership by satisfying the economic and social conditions.' This promise was accompanied by a statement of the conditions for membership. The 'Copenhagen criteria' stated that membership of the Union requires that a country:

> has achieved stability of institutions guaranteeing democracy, the rule of law, human rights and respect for and protection of minorities; the existence of a functioning market economy, as well as the capacity to cope with competitive pressure and market forces within the Union; the ability to take on the obligations of membership, including adherence to the aims of political, economic and monetary union.

Box 4.1: *Enlargement of the European Union*

Original members of the 'European Communities' of 1950s

Belgium, Germany, France, Italy, Luxembourg and the Netherlands

Joined by

1973
Denmark, Ireland and the United Kingdom

1981
Greece

---

continued

1986
Spain, Portugal

1995
Austria, Finland, Sweden

2004
Cyprus, the Czech Republic, Estonia, Hungary, Latvia, Lithuania, Malta, Poland, Slovenia and Slovakia

2007

Bulgaria and Romania

These three criteria, political, economic and administrative (the ability to take on the obligations of membership), were accompanied by a fourth criterion linking enlargement to the EU's internal reform, since 'the Union's capacity to absorb new members, while maintaining the momentum of European integration, is also an important consideration'. This fourth criterion was to come to the fore in 2005–6 after the failure of the French and Dutch referendums on the constitutional treaty. Between 1994 and 1996 all ten candidates presented their applications for membership. The EU divided the ten into two groups according to progress towards meeting the criteria but later brought them together so that they all joined the Union together on 1 May 2004.

The newcomers' foreign policies are mostly focused on their neighbours, not on the wider world. Like the smaller, older member states, they tend to interest themselves in just a few issues in foreign policy, rather than taking a global view. Some of the new members could become rather ambivalent about further enlargement of the EU. They have all publicly supported Bulgarian and Romanian ambitions to join, but they are more divided about Turkey, as are the present member states. The key issue for most is whether the integration of further countries will divert EU funds away from them and diminish their status. All of the new members have complex views about Russia and the EU's future relationship with it. Eight of the new members were under Soviet tutelage for almost half a century, and there is little desire for a close relationship with Putin's Russia. Stalin's attempts to wipe out central European political elites after the Second World War are not forgotten. Some countries suffered invasion, and the three Baltic states were annexed by the Soviet Union. Such experiences cause instinctive suspicions about Russia and raise concerns when some member states (notably Germany under Gerhard Schroeder) try to secure a privileged relationship with Moscow. The historical impact of Soviet policy is still present in the status of Kaliningrad and the question of the large Russian minorities in the Baltic states. For example, the EU made treatment of the

Russian-speaking minorities in Estonia and Latvia part of the accession criteria for those countries. It also negotiated transit arrangements and a visa regime with Russia for the people living in the Russian enclave of Kaliningrad, sandwiched between Poland, Lithuania and the Baltic Sea. Furthermore, Russia has still refused to ratify border treaties with Estonia and Latvia and is building a pipeline to Germany bypassing the Baltic states and Poland. These issues, and the human rights abuses in Chechnya and elsewhere, continue to cast a shadow on relations between many of the new member states and Russia. This more abrasive stance has also irritated some of the larger older member states, especially France and Germany. However, some politicians in the region are beginning to see the virtues of the EU developing a more substantive relationship with Russia, the southern Caucasus and other parts of the former Soviet Union. It is usually easier to deal with Russia, in economic and political matters, through the EU, assuming that the member states are united and speak with one voice. The new members have a full role in negotiating the EU's relationship with Russia, and it gives them a better position *vis-à-vis* Moscow than if they were negotiating bilaterally. As smaller members of the EU, they gain more standing in international negotiations by being part of the EU. Poland, however, annoyed many member states by blocking the start of the PCA negotiations with Russia in November 2006 because of a Russian ban on Polish meat exports.

INTERESTS OF NEW MEMBER STATES

Outside the Euro-Atlantic area the new member states have few special interests. Occasionally some offer their services as a bridge between the EU and its new neighbours, but such offers have not been pursued. For example, in the south, Malta and Cyprus as Mediterranean participants in the Barcelona Process suggested that they could play a special role with the countries of North Africa and the Middle East. For Cyprus, a solution to the division of the island is a top priority. Cyprus is also affected by any changes in the Greek–Turkish relationship, and it is clear that both Athens and Nicosia will monitor closely Turkey's progress towards EU accession. Malta has been particularly affected by illegal migrants seeking to enter the EU from North Africa and has been pressing the EU to take more responsibility in this area. Both island states have neutrality enshrined in their constitution and would have difficulty participating in any major EU military operation. For its part, Turkey has often blocked closer EU–NATO co-operation because of Cypriot involvement. The new member states accept the priority given to the Middle East and the Mediterranean, although some may harbour concern at the possible diversion of resources to the region to support the Barcelona Process. Countries from the south also fear that the EU's attention will remain concentrated on the east for the foreseeable future. Global governance has not been a major issue for the new member states, but they have gone along with the EU mainstream in wishing to strengthen the multilateral institutions. The newcomers have often sought a non-permanent seat in the UNSC and the chairmanship of the OSCE as both have been considered prestigious positions. The new member states have not been able to devote much attention to the problems of the developing world as they have been too busy concentrating on making a success of EU membership.

All the new members, however, have a strong interest in the formulation of those external policies of the enlarged Union that might affect their immediate vicinity. After all, most of them are on the new external frontier of the EU. The permeability and safety of the eastern borders and all common 'direct neighbourhood' policies will become vital interests and shape their behaviour on the CFSP and other issues. The condition of national minorities, cross-border trade and visa regulations, energy and environmental issues, Balkan stability, relations with Belarus, Ukraine, Moldova and, of course, Russia are all priority issues. This does not mean that there is a CEEC 'bloc' on, say, relations with Russia (or Belarus). Like all member states, they tend to adopt positions that promote their national interests. On most international issues, the new members are increasingly 'European' in their preferences. They support the EU on issues like non-proliferation, the Kyoto Protocol, the death penalty and the ICC, despite strong US pressure. Even before accession, they usually voted with the EU in the UN and aligned themselves with the EU's common positions on the CFSP. Their voting patterns were motivated not by a wish to curry favour with the EU but by their changing views on international affairs. As they moved closer to membership, the CEECs became increasingly 'socialised' in the EU's ways of doing business. Their political classes have grown to think like the EU's current members, including on international issues. In some old member states there was another widely held view that the new members would not only be pro-American but would also seek to turn the EU into no more than a free trade area as the British are suspected of doing. But these countries did not make enormous efforts to join the Union in order to turn it into a free trade area. They already had most of the economic benefits prior to accession: free trade in industrial products, foreign direct investment and a large amount of aid. What they want from membership is full partici-pation in the political decisions being made in Europe, including foreign policy, security and defence.

BULGARIA AND ROMANIA

As regards the two countries that joined in 2007 – Bulgaria and Romania – it is quite natural to expect them to become more proactive with regard to their neighbours upon membership. The same was true of the 2004 enlargement countries – especially Poland, which has been the most vocal and active of the accession states in other foreign policy areas. Its involvement in Iraq, its preoccupation with Ukraine and its participation as an equal in the Franco-German–Polish 'Weimar Triangle' are examples. Romania and Bulgaria, as well as Hungary and Slovenia, are strong supporters of increased attention to the western Balkans, but compared to Poland's proactive approach to the eastern dimension of the EU they keep a rather low profile in expressing views on the further development and timing of the roadmap. Romania is more proactive with regard to Moldova and has advocated Moldova's inclusion in the Stabilisation and Association Process, i.e. in the group of 'potential candidates' for EU membership. The accession of Romania and Bulgaria may also see a revival of EU interest in the Black Sea Economic Co-operation (BSEC) organisation. Launched in June 1992 as a regional economic initiative, the BSEC has eleven members (Albania, Armenia, Azerbaijan, Bulgaria, Georgia, Greece, Moldova, Romania, Russia, Turkey and Ukraine). The BSEC was launched almost simultaneously with two other frameworks of regional co-operation – the Baltic Sea Co-operation and the Barents Euro-Arctic Co-operation. Interestingly, the EU showed much more involvement in the two northern co-operation initiatives where the European Commission is a member of the Council of the Baltic Sea States and is regarded as one of the founding partners of the Barents Euro-Arctic Council, even if its status is different from that of the member states. Attempts to get the EU involved in BSEC in the same way have so far been unsuccessful.

ATTITUDES TOWARDS THE US

When most central and eastern European countries (CEECs) announced their support for the US invasion of Iraq they seemed to vindicate Donald Rumsfeld, the US Defense Secretary, who announced in January 2003 that the EU's new members would be Washington's loyal allies, part of 'new Europe' as opposed to the 'old Europe' of Germany and France. The test of loyalty over Iraq came at a difficult time as the US Senate was about to ratify the second enlargement of NATO. The Iraq war was a special case, however, and the US cannot count on automatic CEEC support for further military adventures. Clearly the new member states have much to thank the US for, notably as regards NATO enlargement and providing considerable support after the end of the Cold War. Most have vocal minorities in the US; and several, led by Poland and the Baltic states, consider that they have a special relationship with the US. But the limits on this relationship were also evident when the US refused to lift its visa requirements for Poles despite Poland's involvement in the Iraq war and despite special pleading from the Polish president. No country wants to be placed in the dilemma of choosing between the EU and the US. The new member states all seek good relations with the US while recognising that their destiny is with the EU. For the foreseeable future, however, there will remain serious scepticism about the hard security capabilities of the EU. NATO will remain the preferred body for military action, and some new member states, e.g. Bulgaria, have been invited to host US military bases relocating out of Germany.

ENLARGEMENT AND THE CFSP/ESDP

Given the problems of twelve or fifteen member states reaching agreement on foreign policy, many feared it would be impossible with twenty-five. The results have been better than many feared. During the years prior to accession the ten candidate countries were 'shadowing' the CFSP for a number of years and there were no problems uncovered in the accession negotiations concerning the CFSP chapter. In the period of shadowing the CFSP the accession states normally gave unqualified and disinterested support to the Union. This was largely because their priorities were the accession negotiations and the adoption of the *acquis*. Furthermore, what they were invited to do by the Union was hardly onerous: aligning themselves with EU declarations and *démarches*; joining EU joint actions and common positions. In practice, the CFSP meant for the candidate countries mainly rhetoric rather than action. Some candidates had more problems with bureaucratic changes. As regards the positions 'Political Director' and 'European Correspondent' required for participation in different CFSP meetings and working groups, many candidate countries were slow to make the necessary changes and appointments in their MFAs. In establishing new positions to deal with CFSP structures, the candidates were experiencing similar problems to the turf wars of previous years in the MFAs of old member states. Many also had difficulty finding sufficient qualified personnel for the many positions needed under the CFSP system. They also had to find and train people to cover parts of the world they knew little or nothing about. One Baltic-state diplomat told the author that they had no one in the foreign ministry with any real knowledge of Africa or Latin America when they joined the EU in 2004.

In the first two years after enlargement, the views of the new member states diverged very little from those of the old member states. Clearly the new member states have brought considerable experience of their eastern neighbours to the EU table, and this has had an impact. The enlargement from fifteen to twenty-five member states has also led to renewed debate about the EU's role and position in all international organisations. Although nuances still persist (due also to their different historical experience, geopolitical position, sheer size, and available resources), some discernible common features also seem to emerge. The CEECs have all been strong supporters of NATO and suspicious of the ESDP. The decision, adopted by the Alliance at its Prague summit in November 2002, to invite the seven central and eastern European countries still outside it to join NATO by May 2004 reinforced their 'NATO-first' approach, at least in the short term. Once they became members, the CEECs' attitude changed towards a more balanced assessment of priorities and goals. Some residual ambivalence over the implications of the ESDP remains and may resurface in the presence of unexpected developments in the region and/or in transatlantic relations. Potential differences between new and old member states on the respective roles of the EU and NATO were raised in the Convention on the Future of Europe. The Dehaene Working Group Report noted that:

in certain cases the understanding of the Western interest will differ between the US and the EU and this may put CEECs into an uncomfortable position. Moreover, if America shifts its strategic priorities towards East Asia and the Middle East, the CEECs will of necessity become more reliant on the EU for security, making it difficult for them to pick and choose between NATO and the EU.

In spite of their relatively short record of freedom of action (and, for some, sheer independence) on the international scene, all the CEECs have, over the past few years, been increasingly engaged in peace-support operations – mostly, but not exclusively, in the western Balkans. As a rule, they have done so as modular components of bigger multinational units and under foreign command. Much as the contributions have been limited in absolute numbers and restricted in their functions, they have proved the willingness and ability of the applicants to participate and perform in peace-support operations. In most CEECs, participation in NATO-led or EU-led missions is seen as a driving factor towards some sort of role specialisation. Such specialisation is about making a virtue out of necessity: financial, technical and human resources are scarce and have to be channelled and focused on viable objectives. This is all the more important since all the new member states are engaged in overhauling and modernising their military forces. Moreover, the way in which, notably, the Czechs have focused on developing chemical-weapon decontamination units, or the Romanians mountain light infantry, represents important success stories. In other words, functional role specialisation (military as well as civilian) is a path that could soon prove unavoidable, even for current EU members. The almost generalised creation of multinational units on a sub-regional basis seems to have become more substantial and less symbolic than before, along with the joint leasing or 'pooling' of certain capabilities (aircraft and logistics).

Similar constraints, and opportunities, apply to the new member states' defence procurement policy proper. While most countries are still substituting or upgrading old equipment from the Soviet era, the need to become more interoperable with NATO allies is putting additional pressure on public budgets and decision-makers. Procurement policy, however, remains largely driven by political considerations, taking increasingly into account the added value of domestic job creation in high-tech sectors that may prove crucial in the future. Much will depend on how the EU responds to increased US pressure, especially on the new member states, to 'buy American' and follow Washington's lead also on operational matters. Polish participation in the postwar military administration of Iraq raised eyebrows in several EU capitals. Applicant countries were invited to contribute to the achievement of the EU Headline Goals and all attended successive capabilities-commitment conferences and relevant defence ministers' meetings. In 2003 the candidates were all invited to participate in the first two ESDP operations: the EU Police Mission (EUPM) in Bosnia and Herzegovina, and the peace-stabilisation operation 'Concordia' in Macedonia.

THE CONVENTION ON THE FUTURE OF EUROPE

The foreign and security policy views of old and new member states were presented clearly at the Convention on the Future of Europe. The Convention established two working groups on foreign and security policy, under former Belgian Prime Minister Jean-Luc Dehaene, and defence policy, under French Commissioner Michel Barnier. The Dehaene report was rather modest in its recommendations, a reflection of the substantial divisions within the working group. Amongst the conclusions were proposals for:

- a 'double hatted' EU foreign minister, with enhanced authority and a foot in the Council and in the Commission
- more qualified majority voting (QMV) in the CFSP
- moves to strengthen the EU voice in international bodies
- the establishment of an EU diplomatic service.

The Barnier working group also revealed significant divisions between the members but it came up with rather more ambitious proposals than the Dehaene report. Specifically it proposed:

- the creation of an EU Armaments and Research Agency
- a solidarity clause to combat terrorism
- enhanced co-operation for those wishing to move faster on the armaments front and on defence policy.

The views of old member states largely reflected traditional positions. The neutral and non-aligned countries (Sweden, Finland, Austria and Ireland – Denmark also attached itself to this bloc) were very cautious about any mention of common defence and armaments policy. The UK, Spain and Portugal were willing to move ahead but on a largely inter-governmental basis. France, Germany, Greece and Belgium were prepared to go even further and accept some Community measures such as qualified majority voting (QMV) on the CFSP. Prior to the Iraq war, the UK had been considering accepting an extension of QMV, but its opposition stiffened as a result of the war. The UK also opposed the name 'minister' for the new EU foreign minister and had reservations about the proposal for an EU diplomatic service – or 'external action service' as it was named.

With a few exceptions, the accession countries adopted a low profile in these debates. Their twin preoccupations were a possible weakening of ties with the US and a premature creation of the ESDP at the expense of NATO. There were also concerns at the possible dangers of a two-speed Europe developing in the defence field. Estonia was the only country to propose that enhanced co-operation should be developed outside the framework of the EU institutions. Their representative, Henrik Hololei, argued that member states were certainly free to make their security policy choices:

but closer cooperation in the military field should not take place within the Union but, rather, outside it. Otherwise our half-hearted attempts will make divisions within Europe plain to see. This will, on the contrary, diminish the influence of the Union in the world instead of improving it.

Most candidates accepted in principle the rationale behind enhanced co-operation and the progressive framing of a common defence policy. There was little enthusiasm for a mutual defence clause, although none of the candidates objected to the proposed solidarity clause on terrorism and civil disasters. Both the Poles and the Czechs proposed that the EU should establish appropriate forms of co-operation with NATO. Overall the candidates took a supportive position on the CFSP and a more cautious position on the ESDP. Their views, therefore, were not too dissimilar from those of old member states. They supported the establishment of a European Defence Agency, and most of them supported 'flexibility arrangements' even if under certain conditions. Their concerns were related to preserving the transatlantic link, not duplicating structures and capabilities, not creating rivalry with NATO and not being excluded from co-operation. The accession states already in NATO seemed to be more self-confident and less defensive on the still-divisive issue of 'flexibility' in security and defence issues.

With regard to institutional and decision-making issues in the CFSP/ESDP the new member states do not have the potential and the power to become the motor for further integration but they cannot be considered as a brake. What has been perceived as a struggle between small and big member states on the institutional issues is maybe better described in terms of a struggle between supporters of the Community method and supporters of the inter-governmental method. Most of the big member states would prefer to see the CFSP develop on an inter-governmental basis and under the leadership of some kind of 'directorate'. Virtually all new member states – all of them except Poland rather small and medium-size countries – support a more coherent CFSP but lean towards the Community method. Perhaps the key issue for the CEECs in the debate on the CFSP and on institutional reform has been 'equality'. Despite Poland's flirting with big powers, its Minister of Foreign Affairs, Cimoszewicz, could have spoken for all the accession states when he commented on 12 March 2003: 'The CFSP is built on dialogue of partner states. No state can impose its opinion on other states. Some recent statements could be interpreted as expressions of an underlying belief that "all states are equal, but some are more equal than others". This is certainly far from helpful.'

CONCLUSION

Member states remain the masters of the CFSP. Differences between member states will persist, although the areas of disagreement continue to narrow. The new member states have adopted a low profile in the CFSP, apart from policy towards Russia and Ukraine (support for the Orange Revolution), but there remain concerns about the implications of some proposals on the ESDP side. These concerns centre on possible duplication with NATO and ensuring that the US is not marginalised by any changes. The Iraq war exposed fault lines within the present member states and caused a rift between 'old Europe' and 'new Europe'. It is unlikely that the unfortunate letter-diplomacy escapade will be repeated. Lessons have been learned. The new member states have brought limited military and diplomatic resources to the EU table. Apart from Poland and Romania, few have sizeable military establishments and nearly all face problems of restructuring of their armed forces. Many are facing problems in adapting to NATO requirements, and hence their capabilities in the medium term are unlikely to improve significantly. Some do, however, have niche capabilities, e.g. in chemical weapons. Their diplomatic services vary considerably in size and experience. Some have tiny services that did not even exist fifteen years ago. Some have larger networks with experienced diplomats and a range of diplomatic missions. In short the variations mirror the position in the present member states. But enlargement opens up a number of important issues including the establishment of an EU diplomatic service, complementary to national services. It will also increase pressure to reduce the number of European seats around the table at international meetings. On the military side, financial pressures will lead to more sharing, and some states may be faced with difficult questions, e.g. over the continuing purpose of their air forces. But the new member states are unlikely to be a brake on further development of the CFSP/ESDP.

KEY QUESTIONS

Can there be an EU foreign policy on top of twenty-five national foreign policies?

Explain why the EU3 like operating together.

How have the new member states influenced EU foreign policy?

Are the new members likely to remain more pro-American than old member states?

What defence capabilities do the new member states bring to the EU?

FURTHER READING

Hocking and Spence (2002) look at the changing role of national foreign ministries operating within the EU. Manners and Whitman (2000) also look at the role of member states, while Regelsberger (2003) considers the impact of the enlarged EU on the institutions. A 2006 EU–Institute for Security Studies Occasional Paper (*The Baltics: From Nation states to Member States*), no. 62, by Kestutis Paulauskas, argues that the Baltic states have been too pro-American in their foreign policy and now need to align themselves more with the EU mainstream.

5　The defence dimension

SUMMARY

It is most unlikely that the EU will ever have its own army, but it is building up substantial military capabilities, largely for peace-keeping purposes, and has gained valuable experience in several small but important missions in different parts of the world. The EU's failure in the Balkans during the 1990s was the catalyst that propelled the Union to agree the Helsinki Headline Goals (HHGs) in 1999. There is strong public support for the EU to play a greater role in security policy but less support for spending more on defence. Given the limited resources, it is important that the EU meets its military targets and secures better value for its expenditure on defence. The creation of the European Defence Agency (EDA) is a step in the right direction. In the aftermath of the Iraq crisis, Solana produced a security strategy paper that outlined potential threats to the Union and how the EU might best respond. This was a welcome first step for the EU in moving towards a common security doctrine. The EU has also made limited progress in defining a new relationship with NATO.

INTRODUCTION

The founding fathers of the EU always envisaged an eventual security role for the Union. Indeed, after the establishment of the ECSC in 1952, defence was the next item on the integration agenda. But it proved too sensitive an area, and after the failure to set up a European Defence Community (EDC) in 1954 security and especially defence policy was not considered as part of the remit of the EU for a further four decades. Defence functions were considered to fall firmly within the domain of the Atlantic alliance and/or national governments. The Maastricht Treaty established the CFSP, which in principle included 'the eventual framing of a common defence policy', which could 'in time lead to a common defence'. In order to 'elaborate and implement decisions and actions with defence implications', however, the Union was to request another organisation, the Western European Union (WEU), to act. The WEU was created in 1954 out of the 1947 Brussels Treaty and included those EU members that were also NATO allies. The WEU was thus seen as 'an integral part' of the development of the Union, but its limited role only lasted until the end of the 1990s. With the advent of the ESDP most of the functions of the WEU were incorporated into the Union (Deighton, 1997).

ST-MALO

In June 1992, shortly after the signature of the Maastricht Treaty, the EU agreed a new set of missions, distinct from traditional territorial defence, that became known as the 'Petersberg tasks' (after the hotel near Bonn where ministers met). These tasks were described as 'humanitarian and rescue tasks, peacekeeping tasks, and tasks of combat forces in crisis management, including peace-making'. The acceptance of the Petersberg tasks was recognition of the EU's willingness to engage militarily when necessary, but fulfilment of these tasks was handicapped by the outdated structures and poor capabilities of the defence forces in most member states. What changed the attitudes of at least some member states was the dismal military performance of Europe in the Kosovo crisis. American planes flew 90 per cent of the bombing missions that were designed to force the Serbs out of Kosovo. As a result, the EU's two most important military powers, Britain and France, issued a historic declaration, at St-Malo, in December 1998, that for the first time called on the EU to develop 'the capacity for autonomous action, backed up by credible military forces, the means to decide to use them, and a readiness to do so, in order to respond to international crises'. According to the declaration, such a commitment would not put into question either NATO or other national defence arrangements because the Union would take military action 'where the Alliance as a whole is not engaged' and 'without unnecessary duplication'. The St-Malo agreement was highly significant as it brought together the two main European defence camps led by France and the UK; the former saw the potential for a European defence policy to strengthen European autonomy and break free of their dependence on the US through NATO, whilst the UK led the camp in which NATO remained the key pillar for defence and security policy. It was the election of a new pro-European Labour government in May 1997 that led to a change in the UK position.[1]

THE HELSINKI HEADLINE GOALS

In June 1999, at the Cologne European Council immediately after the Kosovo war, the Union as a whole embraced the St-Malo declaration. Six months later, the Helsinki European Council agreed to establish a Rapid Reaction Force (RRF) and also agreed on the establishment of new EU structures to manage the ESDP. It was remarkable that all member states signed up for the ESDP, including the traditionally neutral and non-aligned countries (Sweden, Finland, Ireland, Austria). Indeed, Sweden and Finland were the twin driving forces behind this initiative as a result of their long-standing support for UN peace-keeping operations. Since 1999 the ESDP has developed steadily. The Helsinki Headline Goals called for the member states to be able, by 2003, to deploy within sixty days and sustain for at least one year military forces of up to 60,000 persons capable of the full range of Petersberg tasks.[2] The Nice European Council in December 2000 then agreed the permanent structures of the Political and Security Committee, Military Committee and EU Military Staff. The Laeken European Council in December 2001 approved the European Capability Action Plan (ECAP), which called on member states to 'mobilise voluntarily all efforts, investments, developments and coordination measures, both nationally and multinationally, in order to improve existing resources and progressively develop the capabilities needed for the Union's crisis-manage-ment actions'. The Seville European Council in June 2002 reached agreement on financing military crisis-management operations. The ESDP was given a further boost in Solana's security strategy, which stressed that the Union needs 'to develop a strategic culture that fosters early, rapid and, when necessary, robust intervention'. The paper also drew attention to the inadequate capability the EU member states obtained from their considerable defence spending. Member states must make better use of the €160 billion devoted annually to defence (the US spends around €420 billion). The document emphasised that this required the transformation and modernisation of European armed forces to reduce duplication, share tasks and create more multinational capacity. The ESS was an important push to the member states to try to remedy their key civilian and military capability weaknesses.

Two reports by the EUMS, reviewing all European military capabilities and member states' commitments, revealed significant shortfalls in forty-two areas. At the second commitments conference in November 2001, a third catalogue was produced, under which the shortfalls were documented and monitored for improvement. By May 2003 the HHGs were considered as met by the Union, even though considerable shortfalls still remained in a number of critical areas: strategic and tactical lift; sustainability and logistics (including air-to-air refuelling); effective engagement (including precision weapons); survivability of force and infrastructure (including rescue helicopters); command and control functions (including communications, satellites and surveillance). Predating this EU initiative, NATO had launched the defence capabilities initiative (DCI) at its Washington Summit in March 1999, which had already identified fifty-eight key shortfalls. Like the EU, NATO found it difficult to get member states to improve their capabilities. Even worse, the two organisations were focusing on almost identical capability shortfalls but could not co-ordinate sufficiently to have joint meetings, even after agreeing security arrangements, known as 'Berlin Plus', for inter-institutional exchanges. US Secretary of Defense Donald Rumsfeld has been particularly scathing of European failure to boost its defence spending. At the 2006 Munich security conference he condemned the nineteen NATO nations that were spending less than 2 per cent of their budget on defence (the US spends 3.7 per cent).[3]

In June 2004 the EU agreed new targets for civilian and military readiness. It recognised that existing shortfalls still needed to be addressed as the initial Helsinki commitments had led to a surplus of capabilities in some areas such as soldiers (over 100,000), combat aircraft (over 400) and ships (100), and an absence of capabilities in other areas such as strategic airlift and tactical transport (including helicopters). The new 2010 Headline Goal was described as follows:

> Building on the Helsinki Headline and capability goals and recognising that existing shortfalls still need to be addressed, Member States have decided to commit themselves to be able by 2010 to respond with rapid and decisive action applying a fully coherent approach to the whole spectrum of crisis management operations covered by the Treaty on the European Union. This includes humanitarian and rescue tasks, peace-keeping tasks, tasks of combat forces in crisis management, including peacemaking. As indicated by the ESS this might also include joint disarmament operations, the support for third countries in combating terrorism and security sector reform. The EU must be able to act before a crisis occurs and ensure preventive engagement to avoid that a situation deteriorates. The EU must retain the ability to conduct concurrent operations, thus sustaining several operations simultaneously at different levels of engagement.

This ambitious statement was not very helpful in clarifying what type of forces the EU should seek to build up, nor how many operations the EU could undertake at the same time. Further ambiguity was added with reference to 'joint disarmament operations', which could include anything from providing personal security to UN inspectors to full-scale invasion as in Iraq. Perhaps in anticipation of such criticisms the new Headline Goal 2010 outlined a process for achieving these objectives with some specific milestones: to establish a civil–military cell within the EUMS; to establish the European Defence Agency (EDA); to complete by 2007 the establishment of the Battle Groups; to acquire the availability of an aircraft carrier with its associated air wing and escort by 2008; and to create a European Airlift Command by 2010. Every six months a progress report is submitted to the Council, and ministers meet to review progress in developing capabilities. These are ambitious but not unrealistic targets. For example, the EU is well advanced in meeting its target for Battle Groups. These consist of highly trained, battalion-size formations (1,500 soldiers each) available at fifteen days' notice and sustainable for at least thirty days (extendable to 120 days by rotation). They should be flexible enough to undertake operations in distant crisis areas, under, but not exclusively, a UN mandate, and to conduct combat missions in an extremely hostile environment (mountains, desert, jungle, etc.). As such, they should prepare the ground for larger, more traditional peace-keeping forces, ideally provided by the UN or member states. They should also be compatible with the NATO response force.

CONSTITUTIONAL TREATY PROVISIONS

The articles covering defence in the constitutional treaty provided recognition that in this area, more than in others, some member states are more equal than others. There remained the commitment to 'the progressive framing of a common defence policy', and this could lead to a common defence 'when the European Council, acting unanimously, so decides'. The most important change, however, was in the acceptance of a new form of 'permanent structured cooperation' within the Union that would allow those member states whose military capabilities fulfil higher criteria and which have made more binding commitments to one another in this area to carry out missions on behalf of the EU. In blunt terms this acknowledges that Britain and France bring rather more military assets to the table than Malta or Cyprus. The constitutional treaty stated that permanent structured co-operation would be open to any member state that demonstrated its willingness to develop its defence capabilities and participate in the main European equipment programmes, and in the EDA; that had the capacity to supply by 2007 at the latest targeted combat units for the missions planned with support elements including transport and logistics.

The treaty went on to state that to achieve these objectives those states participating in permanent structured co-operation should co-operate to achieve approved objectives concerning the level of expenditure on defence equipment, and regularly review these objectives in the light of the security environment and the Union's international responsibilities; bring their defence apparatus into line with each other as far as possible, particularly by harmonising the identification of their military needs, by pooling and, where appropriate, specialising their defence means and capabilities, and by encouraging co-operation in the fields of training and logistics; take concrete measures to enhance the availability, inter-operability, flexibility and deployability of their forces. There were complicated proposals for the use of QMV in taking decisions under permanent structured co-operation, but experience suggests that member states would be very reluctant to break from the traditional principle of unanimity in defence matters.

Another change was the mutual solidarity clause, which, while acknowledging the commitments of NATO members, stated 'if a Member State is the victim of armed aggression on its territory, the other Member States shall have towards it an obligation of aid and assistance by all means in their power'. This was more a political gesture than an attempt to create an EU defence alliance but it served to underline the basic solidarity between member states. The treaty also proposed extending the scope of the original 'Petersberg tasks' to encompass 'joint disarmament operations, military and advice assistance tasks, conflict prevention and post-conflict stabilization'. This consensus gave grounds for hope that even in the absence of a new treaty the member states would be ready, willing and able to work along the lines outlined in the treaty.

FUNDING THE ESDP

Although there is general support for the ESDP among the member states, there is still cause for concern over the financing of the ESDP and the amount Europeans spend on defence. Speaking to the Senate Foreign Relations Committee on 8 February 2006, General James Jones, SACEUR, expressed concern about the low level of commitment to NATO of a number of European allies. Of the twenty-six members, only seven were meeting their pledge to earmark 2 per cent of their gross national product for defence spending. Beyond that, some countries were paying 70–5 per cent of their defence budget for salaries. Jones said, 'a country that spends more than 50 percent for that purpose cannot be a significant contributor to the alliance'.[4] European defence spending began to stabilise around the mid-1990s after a period of decline in the immediate aftermath of the Cold War, and present levels are likely to remain stable for the foreseeable future. EU member states are under strong pressure not to expand public expenditure, owing both to the EU's self-imposed financial discipline and to low rates of growth. This will have an impact upon defence budgets as well as on other areas of public spending. Nevertheless, the US has been putting enormous pressure on Europe, especially since 9/11, to increase defence spending and address the so-called 'capabilities gap'. Partly owing to massive new funding after 9/11, the US is now not just in a class of its own but is approaching the point where it will spend as much as the rest of the world put together. In Europe, however, there is little enthusiasm for increased spending on defence, nor would an increase in spending necessarily provide more military capability, unless accompanied by reform of inefficient procurement processes, ministerial bureaucracies and relevant industrial sectors.

Furthermore, some defence expenditure is aimed at deterring neighbours, as the case of Greece and Turkey, rivals in the Aegean Sea, clearly proves. Apart from these two states, only Britain and France can claim to spend large sums per capita in the defence field. In addition the amount of money spent on pure defence is not an adequate measure of the contribution that is made to promoting security in the broadest sense. There is a need to take into account expenditure on other policy areas including development, crisis management capabilities, enlargement policy and even climate change. In this broader context EU contributions to international security are on a par with American expenditure. For instance, European countries contribute three times as much as the US to development aid and pay almost twice as much into the UN budget. Together, the EU bears the main military burden of peace-keeping operations in the Balkans and largely finances peace-building in the region. It is also responsible for the lion's share of civilian aid in the Middle East as well as of post-conflict reconstruction in Afghanistan.

There is, however, no room for complacency. The EU has a defence budget problem, starting with the strong imbalance between personnel and equipment expenditure that affects almost all members, and ending with the small amount (a quarter of the US total) that they spend on R&D. The main problem lies with the quality of European defence spending, i.e. with the way in which EU member states allocate their limited resources. Defence procurement is fragmented and nationally focused, thus dispersing financial means that could be better used for the common good without duplicating assets. The existing co-operative programmes, such as Eurofighter, Meteor or A400M, are all ad hoc and purely inter-governmental, creating extra costs and delays. The overall level of investment is largely insufficient if measured against the shortfalls that the member states have agreed to address together. Uneven spending across EU countries, even among the main spenders, further creates a potential 'burden sharing' problem inside the Union. Neither do the member states use comparable budgetary or procurement systems, which further complicates policy co-ordination and convergence. Even if it was possible and accepted, simply spending more would not necessarily generate the required capabilities, since 'pork barrel' politics is well established in the defence field. Even if spending better were to take precedence, however, spending more would become all the more necessary: savings are certainly possible in the short term, but reconfiguring expenditure will in itself require an investment of time and money (in terms of early-retirement schemes for redundant personnel, base closures, etc.); while increasing capabilities will mean buying or leasing new equipment off the shelf.

A further problem is that member states still do not all share the same views on the scope of the 'Petersberg tasks'. There is certainly a broad consensus over their so-called 'low end', for which most of the necessary resources, including those related to non-military crisis management, are already available both across the Union (member states) and in Brussels: the Commission's rapid reaction mechanism; the EC humanitarian office (ECHO); Europe Aid, plus the Council Secretariat. By contrast, 'high end' missions are more controversial among the member states. Differences do not necessarily lie in the amount of military force involved on the ground, although air power varies significantly, but rather in the description and mandate of the envisaged mission, including the desirability of NATO (read US) involvement. Such differences represent an important part of the reality of EU crisis management, whereby the member states' forces cannot be considered a single unit, unlike the American ones.

ESTABLISHING A DEFENCE-INDUSTRIAL BASE

Compared to the US, the EU does not get enough 'bang for its buck' (or euro) in defence procurement. After many years of hesitation, the member states, the European Commission and the defence industry are collectively pushing for a breakthrough at the EU level on armaments policy. The argument is that, if defence spending is not to increase, one obvious way of bridging capability gaps is through increased armaments co-operation. Joint procurement of the necessary equipment would offer savings through economies of scale and reduced duplication. However, this might not be such an easy option to achieve: despite much rhetoric about the need for greater armaments co-operation within the EU, actual results are so far disappointing. European defence-industrial consolidation is still patchy, and defence procurement remains oriented towards national needs. Two dominant features are evident in the defence-industrial scene: a growing monopolisation in the aerospace and defence-electronics sectors; and a lack of consolidation of mostly subsidised, and protected, national capacities in the other sectors. Given US preponderance in the military technology field there is concern that Europe will be marginalised in fighting capacities of the future. There is also a concern that the US will completely dominate the arms market unless Europe can combine forces. The political concern is a longstanding one, and as yet the US has shown no signs of wanting completely to create force postures and technologies that will make co-operation with key European partners impossible (and perhaps even less so after Iraq). The balance is needed both for the US in restraining its tendencies to seek technological solutions to international security threats and for Europeans to invest in key enabling and inter-operability capabilities to enable them to project their forces in a timely manner, if necessary with partners to meet their security objectives. Neither the US nor Europeans seem ready, nor can afford, fundamentally to undermine their shared desire to achieve this balance, but the pressure is mounting in both the EU and NATO to move beyond policy frameworks to creating usable and larger numbers of deployable armed forces.

The defence-industrial concern is equally complex because, whilst some sectors of industry consider that a European market would offer them a firm basis on which to compete internationally, others do not and worry that such a European market would end their privileged relationships with national governments that ensure their existence. It is further complicated by the internationalised nature of some larger defence companies and US reluctance to allow European firms to compete for American defence procurement contracts. Within the EU there is a danger that strategic goals and defence-industrial policy are not in synergy. There is also a need to ensure that the limited budget spent on research and development results in efficient outputs. It will be a major challenge to achieve both better co-ordination and coherence. The EU needs to ask the right questions about its future capability needs in order to influence the current procurement process. Engaging in a broader debate about the role and future of the EU as a strategic actor and what it needs from an ESDP will complement present bottom-up approaches. In adapting to the demands of being a global strategic actor with a common defence policy, the EU now needs to take its general statements under the new Headline Goal 2010 and make progress on its key benchmarks, not least developing scenarios that test member states' commitments to providing sufficient troops and capabilities to meet the need for concurrent, sustainable and projectable forces. This is a critical aspect for the new debate in understanding how credibly the EU is planning to take up its international responsibilities mapped out in the ESS. This is the only way force planners can move forward and provide credible analysis on the types of capabilities available for different crises.

THE EUROPEAN DEFENCE AGENCY (EDA)

There have been many efforts over the years to inject more efficiency into defence procurement in Europe. These efforts have often failed owing to the lack of political will and with employment considerations trumping economic efficiency. But in an era of shrinking defence budgets, and with the cost of new weaponry rising, there has been a new willingness to promote closer co-operation. This led to the establishment of the European Defence Agency under a June 2004 Joint Action of the EU following a proposal in the European Convention and endorsed in the constitutional treaty. The EDA has four main roles:

- developing defence capabilities in the field of crisis management
- promoting and enhancing European armaments co-operation
- strengthening the European industrial and technological base
- creating a competitive European defence equipment market as well as promoting research aimed at leadership in strategic technologies for future defence and security capabilities.

Although all member states may join the EDA, only a small number (France, the UK, Germany, Italy, Sweden and Spain) have significant defence-industrial sectors. This means that most member states are consumers rather than producers of defence equipment. The importance of the EDA is that it brings all defence development issues under one roof and under the responsibility of the SG/HR and defence ministers. The eighty-strong staff (with a €25 million annual budget) should provide some much needed fresh impetus and top-down orientation as opposed to the current bottom-up approach. There is also an important role for the Commission in promoting procurement, security research and cross-pillar co-operation. In recent years the Commission has been deeply involved in examining different aspects of the state of play of the defence market and defence-industrial policy. In a communication dated 11 March 2003 and entitled 'Towards an EU Defence Equipment Policy', the Commission identified seven priority areas: action standardisation, monitoring of defence-related industries, intra-community transfers, competition, procurement rules, export control of dual-use goods, and research. The Commission also financed a report by experts in 2004 entitled 'Research for a Secure Europe'. Its key conclusion was that security research is an essential pillar of future European security and as such should require substantial appropriate resources to the tune of €1 billion (reaching up to €1.8 billion) per year. Whilst meeting EU security needs, it would also help the EU to meet the Lisbon economic criteria and the agreed target of 3 per cent spending on R&D of all Community research spending. The Commission has also sought to mitigate the protectionist clause (Article 296 in the TEU) that states 'any Member State may take such measures as it considers necessary for the protection of the essential interests of its security which are connected with the production of or trade in arms, munitions and war material'.[5]

THE ESDP IN ACTION

Despite all these obstacles and limits, the ESDP has evolved considerably in a short time. Since January 2003 it has been engaged in several missions including in Bosnia-Herzegovina, the Former Yugoslav Republic of Macedonia (FYROM), the Democratic Republic of Congo, Georgia and Aceh. These missions have performed a variety of tasks, from law enforcement and cease-fire monitoring to security and humanitarian crisis management. On the whole, over 8,000 police and military personnel have been involved in these missions. These operations have been important test cases for the Union's ability to apply some of the security policy instruments it envisaged under the Helsinki and Feira headline goals. Although limited in scope and time, these ESDP engagements have given the EU added confidence and are the first hands-on manifestation of the EU's security and defence dimension, which may lead to more ambitious interventions in the future.

Box 5.1: ESDP missions

Since January 2003: police mission (EUPM) in Bosnia and Herzegovina to assist local police in rebuilding the police force and in the fight against organised crime and corruption. The mission has been extended until the end of 2007. This was the EU's first ever civilian crisis-management operation under ESDP and involved over 500 police officers, about 80 per cent from EU member states and 20 per cent from third states, performing monitoring, mentoring and inspection activities.

March to December 2003: military operation Concordia to stabilise the situation in Macedonia. EU forces, a modest 350 lightly armed military personnel from thirteen member states, monitored the implementation of the August 2001 Ohrid framework agreement, which settled the ethnic conflict between Macedonian Slavs and Albanians. The EU force was able to draw on NATO assets and capabilities under the 'Berlin Plus' agreement of December 2002.

December 2003 to December 2005: police mission to build a professional police force in the Former Yugoslav Republic of Macedonia (EUPOL PROXIMA).

June to September 2003: military operation Artemis in the Democratic Republic of Congo under French leadership to stabilise the security situation and improve the humanitarian situation in the Ituri district. The force had about 1,800 soldiers, mostly French. Artemis was the EU's first military operation outside Europe and the first that did not rely on NATO assistance.

December 2004: the EU took over the formerly NATO-led SFOR operation in Bosnia and Herzegovina, codename EUFOR Althea – this is the largest EU crisis-management operation to date (approx. 7,000 soldiers) and is intended to stabilise the security situation and allow political and economic reforms to proceed.

July 2004 to July 2005: EUJUST Themis civil mission in Georgia to reinforce the rule of law.

Since April 2005: European police experts have been advising police forces in the Democratic Republic of Congo as part of Operation EUPOL Kinshasa.

Since May 2005: also in the Democratic Republic of Congo, European experts have been supporting the security-sector reform process (Operation EUSEC Congo).

Since July 2005: civil operation EUJUST Lex: training of senior Iraqi judicial officials at training sites outside Iraq in the establishment of modern criminal justice based on the rule of law.

July 2005: to assist the African Union's Operation AMIS II peacekeeping mission in Darfur Province in Sudan, the EU decided to launch an operation to provide the African Union with practical support both in the military and policing fields (e.g. by transporting African peace-keeping troops to the area of operations).

September 2005: launch of the EU observer mission in Aceh. At the request of both parties to the conflict, the EU (with the participation of a number of ASEAN states) has been monitoring the implementation of the peace agreement between the Indonesian government and separatists in Aceh Province in northern Sumatra, and more particularly the hand-over and destruction of weapons by the fighters of the Free Aceh Movement (GAM), the release of imprisoned GAM activists, the reintegration of GAM fighters into civil society, the withdrawal of

continued

Indonesian troops and police units from the region, and the observation of the human rights situation.

15 November 2005: Israel and the Palestinian Authority conclude an agreement on opening the Rafah international border crossing from Gaza to Egypt. Implementation of the agreement is intended to bring a significant improvement in the political climate in the region. Under this agreement, approximately seventy EU observers in the course of a year will supervise access and traffic at the border.

Since 1 December 2005: the EU has been performing an observer mission at the Ukrainian–Moldovan border (border assistance mission/BAM). Unannounced inspections by initially fifty EU observers for a period of eighteen months are designed to bring an improvement in Ukrainian–Moldovan co-operation on border controls. It is hoped that the mission will also help create the conditions for solving the conflict in Transnistria.

1 January 2006: launch of a police mission in the Palestinian Territories (EUPOL COPPS). A sustainable, efficient police force complying with recognised international standards is to be established under Palestinian responsibility during a mission of at least three years' duration. Thirty EU experts will advise Palestinian police officers.

When the EUPOL PROXIMA mission ends, the EU Police Advisory Team (EUPAT) in Macedonia will assist the EU Special Representative's office for a transition period until May 2006. The European Commission will then continue the support work with projects of its own.

These ESDP operations highlight the willingness of the EU to take concrete action in crisis-management tasks and to adopt a flexible approach towards command of such operations. This flexibility reflects the reality that certain member states have the necessary structures to take the lead in multinational operations and that in a Union of twenty-five it will not always be possible to include everyone in an operation, as was attempted with 'Concordia'. The numerous ESDP operations launched in 2003–6 represent an important confidence boost for the Union. The missions show that the EU is capable of reacting to ongoing or emerging humanitarian/security crises and able to contribute to peace enforcement, reconstruction and stabilisation. Of course this will be all the easier to achieve whenever and wherever there is no major disagreement with the Americans over the respective roles of NATO, the EU and other possible formats and/or coalitions. The current blossoming of the ESDP, therefore, should help put the EU's dismal performance over Iraq in perspective, allowing the demanding European public to be slightly more optimistic about the scope of shared interests and policies under the ESDP. At the same time, it is important to recall that EU missions thus far remain very limited in scope and still depend heavily on the leadership, commitment and interest of major EU member states. Certain member states in particular may not always be keen on engaging their national assets and capabilities within an EU framework: e.g. in the Ivory Coast or Sierra Leone, where France and Britain, respectively, preferred to act autonomously, applying the subsidiarity principle to peace support. Other (especially new) member states may prefer to act militarily only or primarily within NATO and/or with the Americans. The fact is that the EU has no military capabilities at its own disposal. Moreover, significant command and control capability shortfalls among member states mean that any complex high-end operation would have to depend on NATO support. True, 'Concordia' implemented the Berlin Plus agreement, yet the long-term relationship between the Union and NATO remains to be fully defined. Besides, EU operations thus far, while important symbolically, are not complex operationally. None of the current operations, with the exception of 'Althea' involving more than 6,000 troops, pushes EU military capabilities and political will to the limit, but a new Balkan mission would be a problem. In this respect, the EU remains untested across the full spectrum of peace-support missions.

Much remains to be improved, tested, learned and fine-tuned, yet EU progress in crisis management in a short period has been quite remarkable. The geographical and strategic scope of its action is still subject to significant evolution. For the time being, it encompasses the immediate proximity of the EU (the western Balkans, Moldova) and, potentially, the wider cultural/historical/economic proximity represented by some post-colonial states in Africa (Congo) as well as further afield (East Timor). It is not by accident that these areas are also the main recipients of EU direct aid and assistance schemes, and that they are on the receiving end of preferential trade arrangements, although the Union is still far from linking up effectively all the policy tools at its disposal. The functional scope of EU security policy is likely to be varied, mixed in both space and time, and encompassing economic, civilian and also military components. One problem area, however, is financing the ESDP. The ESDP budget climbed from €47.5 million in 2003 to €102 million in 2006. But this still resulted in an empty kitty by mid-2006, and if the EU were to undertake a mission in Kosovo it would need a 50 per cent increase in the ESDP budget.

EU–NATO

For two major organisations situated just a few miles apart in Brussels, relations have been very poor. Until the mid-1990s there was almost no contact between the EU and NATO. For most people, one did economics and the other defence. This began to change slowly with the end of the Cold War; but some member states, notably France, were always wary of expanding NATO's role. Paris always had a vision of an independent European defence, a vision that was not shared by many other member states. The US was always keen to assert the primacy of NATO in security matters and for many years was suspicious of the EU's plans for the ESDP, fearing that it would undermine NATO. These fears were crystallised in 1998 when US Secretary of State Madeleine Albright warned the EU that the ESDP should only proceed if it took account of the 'three Ds': (1) no decoupling from NATO. ESDP must complement NATO and not threaten the indivisibility of transatlantic relations; (2) no duplication of NATO command structures; and (3) no discrimination against European NATO countries that were not members of the EU. The US also insisted that there should be no EU caucus in NATO. This was a strange point to make, for two reasons. First, there were no plans for an EU caucus within NATO. Second, it seemed to contradict long-standing US demands that the EU should speak with one voice. Washington was also concerned at the limitations it encountered in fighting the Kosovo war with nineteen members around the table. For some time after 9/11 the US seemed to prefer operating with 'coalitions of the willing', with Afghanistan and Iraq as examples. But the major problems encountered in both countries brought the US back to seek NATO support to help achieve US objectives.

NATO Secretary General Jaap de Hoop Scheffer has lamented the lack of EU– NATO co-operation. In a speech on 14 April 2005 he said: 'We also need to strengthen the relationship, and the dialogue, with the EU. And let me be frank there is plenty of room for improvement.' The Secretary General was speaking shortly after two separate EU and NATO missions to Darfur – the two organisations could not agree on a joint humanitarian mission. NATO's problems stem from the lack of consensus on what NATO should be doing. It was set up in 1949 to confront the Soviet threat. When that threat disappeared in 1991 there was confusion about its role. Was it to remain a strictly defence alliance? Should it go global? Should it be used to tackle terrorism and, if so, how? How far should it expand? The US preference for coalitions of the willing and its refusal to use NATO, despite its offer under Article V, after 9/11 was a shock to many members. Gradually the US began to recognise that it needed NATO and pushed the alliance into a difficult role in Afghanistan. In November 2005, Jaap de Hoop Scheffer concluded that NATO had to face the challenges 'when and where they emerge, or they will end up on our doorsteps'. At the same time he said that NATO could not become the world's policeman, given its limited resources. In January 2005, German Chancellor Gerhard Schroeder sparked a debate about the most suitable forum in which to conduct a trans-atlantic strategic dialogue. Neither the EU nor NATO, he argued, was really adequate. This debate continued into 2006, with many influential Americans arguing that NATO should develop a global role while some Europeans warned of NATO over-reaching itself.[6]

Like the EU, NATO is also developing a 20,000-strong rapid reaction force for high-intensity operations and seeking to improve its capability. Although NATO has a longer tradition of dealing with the capability-generation and defence-transformation process, it is still struggling, like the EU, to meet commitments. There is, of course, much overlap between EU and NATO forces, yet there has been little work on a common-capability agenda. For several years a key obstacle for developing EU–NATO relations at a working level was the difficulties in achieving security arrangements to support an inter-institutional relationship, which became known as 'Berlin Plus'. Its origins refer to the 1996 NATO ministerial in Berlin where foreign ministers agreed to make NATO assets available to WEU-led operations in a bid to boost European defence within NATO. Between 1999 and December 2002, the EU and NATO were prevented from formalising this agreement because of blocking manoeuvres by, alternatively, Greece and Turkey. Eventually agreement was reached in December 2002 which led to a further series of agreements covering a NATO–EU security agreement; assured access to NATO assets and planning capabilities for EU-led crisis management operations; terms of reference for different command options; and arrangements for coherent and mutually reinforcing capability requirements. Berlin Plus is thus a series of institutional arrangements between the EU and NATO that enable them to exchange information securely and to establish the manner in which NATO makes available its assets. As a result, the EU can now work on the assumption that it has access to the NATO capabilities it requires, even when the formal decision to do so will be taken on a case-by-case basis. The two organisations now engage in more regular contacts, but there is still some underlying tension concerning roles and command functions. For instance, the need for the EU to have its own advanced planning capability, such as NATO has at SHAPE, was thought to be redundant now that the Union has recourse to such assets under Berlin Plus. However, the Union's interest in places such as central Africa highlighted a very interesting question: Who at NATO would have the plans for such an operation?

CONCLUSION

There are some positive signs that at last the member states of the EU, prodded by the institutions, may be getting serious about defence. There is a broad recognition that too much money is being wasted on conscript armies and out-of-date equipment. There is also recognition of the benefits to be gained from sharing costs in security research and procurement. But the pursuit of effective security policy supported by appropriate defence policy and capabilities has been a difficult process at the national level, and it would be unfair to expect instant results from the EU. However, the national level has developed a sophisticated approach of discussing military capability needs based not only on defence-industrial policy but also increasingly on a discussion about strategic interests and security requirements. The EU must not ignore this in its bid to develop mechanisms and processes which appear disconnected at a time of changing institutional and legal competences. Any new framework for assessing capabilities and armaments policy must be based upon strategic objectives and military needs, and respond to a changing security environment. How can the EU combine immediate security pressures, owing to concerns over terrorism and the proliferation of WMD, and the need to develop a strategic framework that provides for the generation of defence capabilities as well as satisfying a hungry defence industry? This question may provide the impetus for a profound step-change in the level and intensity of debate at the EU level that has hitherto been absent.

Defence transformation will be a key element. The figures are well known. The member states of the Union have over 1.2 million men and women in uniform but struggle to put more than 150,000 into the field at any one time. There is a clear need to improve deployability and mobility. Proposals have been made for a European defence White Paper and an EU defence strategy. Both make eminent sense. With the new constitutional treaty and the ESS, the ground has been prepared for a change in approach. Public opinion also expects the members of the EU to act together in tackling the new security threats. But, although expectations are rising, and even if the European Council has adopted a security strategy and launched a number of ESDP operations, member states and the EU institutions still have a long way to go in refining the institutional architecture, integrating the different policy instruments and providing clarity on concepts left unclear in the ESS. Failure to achieve synergies in European defence and security capabilities will represent a significant missed opportunity to facilitate the development of the ESDP in the future and for Europe to take up its stated international responsibilities and strategic role.

Finally, too many of Europe's elite have failed to rethink the utility of force in the modern world. Most European defence establishments are still configured on the basis of fighting an industrial war, as happened against Germany in 1939–45. But the conflicts of the past two or three decades have not been about a possible attack on Europe or, indeed, for the most part, inter-state conflicts, but rather intra-state conflicts such as Sudan, Yugoslavia, Liberia, etc. The institutions set up during the Cold War have been slow to adapt and even slower to interact in any meaningful way. Both the EU and NATO will be around for some time to come, but the cards are increasingly stacked in the EU's favour as the most comprehensive security organisation. It simply has a much larger 'toolbox' than NATO to tackle the new security threats.

KEY QUESTIONS

Should the EU have its own army?
How would Europe cope if US forces went home?
What should be the EU's security priorities?
Is there a danger of duplication between the EU and NATO?
Why does the EU fail to reap the benefits from joint procurement?

FURTHER READING

Smith, R. (2005) discusses the limitations of military power. Sloan (2002), Schimmelfennig (2004), and Howarth and Keeler (2003) assess the security roles of the EU and NATO. Deighton (1997) examines the WEU in some detail. There are many good articles on defence published by the EU Institute for Security Studies. See also the websites of the Council (www.ue.eu.int), NATO (www.nato.org) and the European Defence Agency (www. eda. eu.int).

6   Transatlantic relations

SUMMARY

The US is the most important partner of the EU, but the relationship has been under increasing strain for some time, partly but not only because of differences over the Iraq war. The EU and the US often share a similar analysis of threats but then take different views on how to counter such threats. This has led some people to ask whether the EU and the US are actually friends or rivals. EU–US relations are also complicated because many member states consider they enjoy a special relationship with the US. Many Americans have their roots in Europe, but their forefathers often left to escape famine or persecution. Isolationism has been an important feature of American history despite the global engagement since 1945. Public perceptions are also evolving, with very high numbers of Europeans expressing distrust of the Bush administration. There are different perceptions of the EU in the US. Some view the EU as irrelevant while others consider it a potential rival. The second Bush administration has sought to improve relations with the EU, but there remain important divergences especially with regard to international law. The EU–US economic and trade relationship is the most important in the world and a stabilising factor in transatlantic relations.

INTRODUCTION

The US is by far the most important partner of the EU, and the EU–US relationship is arguably the most important geopolitical relationship in the world. The two blocs dominate world trade and provide by far the lion's share of economic, development and technical assistance. They account for over 70 per cent of global expenditure on defence. (The US, however, spends three times more than the EU.) The two sides co-operate in numerous areas around the world, ranging from Iran and Ukraine to the Balkans and Sudan. A flood of American officials are regular visitors to the EU institutions in Brussels. EU officials are also keen to engage with their US counterparts. As Jim Cloos, the former Director for the US in the Council, explained to a group of visiting journalists in March 2006:

We need the Americans in many areas. If you go around the world, and look at what the problems are, you rarely, if ever, encounter cases where it would be better to work without or against the Americans. But the reverse is also true, even though this took a little more time to be registered in some quarters in Washington. The second Bush administration has clearly come to the conclusion that EU–US relations matter and has acted on that.

Yet transatlantic relations remain strained, largely as a result of the war in Iraq and the unilateral approach of the first George W. Bush administration. Despite the many areas of co-operation, there are many areas of disagreement covering political and strategic issues as well as economic and social issues. Part of the problem is that there has never been a high-level EU–US discussion on the nature of the new security threats and how to deal with them. Instead there have been countless communiqués and statements pledging both sides to combat terrorism and tackle the problems of WMD. Many Europeans have been very critical of the US approach to fighting the 'war on terror', and the images from Guantanamo and Abu Ghraib prisons have severely damaged the US in European eyes. Another major divide is over global governance and the role to be accorded to the UN and other multilateral institutions. Americans claim that, while both sides stand for 'effective multilateralism', the US puts the emphasis on 'effective' while the EU places its faith in 'multilateralism'. There is some evidence that the growing number and seriousness of these disputes, including over Iraq, the Israel–Palestine conflict, dealing with 'rogue states' and terrorism, global warming and arms control, may already be undermining the trust necessary to tackle global problems together. Furthermore, transatlantic disputes are having a major impact on European foreign and security policy, and even on the process of European integration. Despite the fine words of President Bush when he visited Brussels in February 2005, there are doubts whether the US is still committed to a strong, united Europe speaking with one voice. The US continues to harbour suspicions about European defence plans.

The twin geopolitical earthquakes of the collapse of communism in 1989–90 and the US response to the 9/11 terrorist attacks have had an inevitable impact on transatlantic relations. As the EU has grown in size and stature (single currency, enlargement), so it has taken on more responsibility for security in its neighbourhood. Its post-Cold War agenda was dominated by efforts to unite the continent for the first time in history by peaceful means. By and large the US has been supportive of this process, while reducing its strategic interest in Europe as a result of challenges elsewhere. The US has also been at pains to stress the continued importance of NATO while emphasising that it will accept no military challenge from any quarter. According to the 2002 National Security Strategy, 'America has, and intends to keep, military strengths beyond challenge'. US priorities have been homeland security, the war on terrorism, and promoting change in the wider Middle East. These different agendas have led to a growing divergence between America's perception of its moral leadership and European perceptions of a military-minded America obsessed with rogue states and weapons of mass destruction.

It is worth noting that the 1990s were not exactly a decade of transatlantic bliss. Indeed, many of the current disputes have their origins in the 1990s when, for most of the decade, the Clinton administration faced a hostile Congress, largely uninterested in foreign policy, and European governments were deeply concerned at the 'hands off' approach of both the Bush senior administration and the new Clinton administration towards the Balkan conflict. While Bush senior won plaudits in Europe for his statesmanlike handling of the collapse of communism, he was unwilling to engage the US in the Balkans. As Secretary of State James Baker remarked, 'We do not have a dog in that fight.' Clinton continued this non-engagement; and the 1992–4 period was a time of major crisis, with the Europeans and the Americans pursuing different policies in the Balkans. The British and the French had significant numbers of troops on the ground under UN auspices. The Americans had no troops on the ground and preferred to arm some of the belligerents. Eventually the US intervened militarily to secure the Dayton agreement and later again intervened to resolve the Kosovo crisis (Bildt, 1998; Holbrooke, 1998). The lesson was finally learned that the EU and the US co-operating rather than competing brought peace to the Balkans. Despite these difficulties, the Clinton administration was overall pro-European. It had many people in its senior ranks with direct experience of the EU, and Clinton himself was temperamentally inclined to European ideas and solutions. But there were disputes in several areas, including tackling 'rogue states', global warming, the ICC, the failure to ratify the Comprehensive Test Ban Treaty (CTBT) and the treaty banning land-mines. It is therefore wrong to believe that EU problems with the US started when George W. Bush took over the White House in January 2001 (Cameron, 2005).

THE NEW TRANSATLANTIC AGENDA (NTA)

Both Bush senior and Clinton recognised the growing potential of the EU as a partner for the US and were keen to provide some structure to EU–US relations. But the structures established in 1990 and 1995 were never given the necessary unstinting political support on either side of the Atlantic to ensure success. The 1990 Transatlantic Declaration committed the US and the EU to regular political consultations at all levels (biannual summits, ministerial and senior-official as well as working-group meetings). The flowery declaration committed the EU and the US:

> to further strengthen their partnership in order to: support democracy, the rule of law and respect for human rights and individual liberty, safeguard peace and promote international security, by cooperating with other nations against aggression and coercion, by contributing to the settlement of conflicts in the world and by reinforcing the role of the United Nations.

In 1995 the US and the EU moved a stage further with the signing of the New Transatlantic Agenda (NTA) proposing joint action in four major fields:

- promoting peace and stability, democracy and development around the world
- responding to global challenges
- contributing to the expansion of world trade and closer economic relations
- building bridges across the Atlantic.

The NTA confidently affirmed that:

> the ties which bind our people are as strong today as they have been for the past half century. For over fifty years, the transatlantic partnership has been the leading force for peace and prosperity for ourselves and for the world. Together, we helped transform adversaries into allies and dictatorships into democracies. Together, we built institutions and patterns of cooperation that ensured our security and economic strength. These are epic achievements.

In connection with the adoption of the NTA, a joint EU–US Action Plan was drawn up committing the EU and the US to a large number of measures within the overall areas of co-operation. As an extension of the NTA efforts, agreement was reached at the 1998 London summit to intensify co-operation in the area of trade, which resulted in the Transatlantic Economic Partnership (TEP). The TEP covers both bilateral and multilateral trade. Bilaterally, the TEP addresses various types of obstacle to trade and strives to establish agreements on mutual recognition in the areas of goods and services. Furthermore, there is co-operation in the areas of public procurement and intellectual property law. Multilaterally, focus is on further liberalisation of trade within the World Trade Organisation (WTO) in order to strengthen world trade. In connection with each summit, time is sometimes set aside for meetings with representatives of one or more of these dialogues. The most advanced dialogue is the Transatlantic Business Dialogue (TABD). Other dialogues include the Transatlantic Legislators Dialogue (TALD), the Transatlantic Consumer Dialogue (TACD) and the Transatlantic Environmental Dialogue (TAED). The TALD has struggled to secure appropriate recognition with the Congress, while the other dialogues have had little impact owing to a mix of apathy, lack of funding and lack of interest. In addition to direct bilateral EU–US relations based on the Transatlantic Declaration and the NTA, a great deal of economic interplay between the two takes place in the international multilateral economic forums: the G7/8, the WTO, the International Monetary Fund (IMF) and the World Bank.

Central to the NTA structures is the Task Force (TF) and the Senior Level Group (SLG). The TF is a group of officials from the US, the EU Presidency, Council and Commission that plays a key role within the NTA in identifying and dealing with all aspects of transatlantic co-operation. It also decides which issues should be passed on for attention at the SLG, which is responsible for preparing the summit meetings. The SLG is supposed to monitor the work of the TF and report back to it on progress at summits. But these senior officials are usually overworked and have less and less time to travel for short meetings. Hence there has been a new willingness to carry out pre-summit discussions by video conferencing. There is little doubt that the bureaucratic structures underpinning the NTA have been useful in discussing EU–US disputes and even helping to resolve some issues, mainly in the trade field. But overall the NTA has had a mixed record. The various attempts to involve business, consumers, environmentalists and others in structured 'people to people' dialogues have had little sustained success. There has also been no real substantive discussion at the highest political level – for example, on threat perceptions – partly because of the inability on the EU side to speak with one voice on sensitive political, security and economic issues. The rotating six-monthly EU Presidency has not been conducive to promoting such a dialogue, and many member states, not just the UK, prefer operating on bilateral channels. Indeed, member-state ambassadors are often judged at home by the length of audience they secure for their president or prime minister with the president of the US (visits to Camp David and the Bush ranch at Crawford count as bonus points!). On the US side, successive administrations have not viewed the EU as their prime or even principal interlocutor on foreign and security policy issues.

BUSH AND UNILATERALISM

There was considerable sneering in Europe at George W. Bush the candidate. He was widely portrayed in the European media as an unsophisticated cowboy, keen on the death penalty and unsympathetic to the environment ('the toxic Texan'). On taking office, these prejudices were confirmed as the new administration seemed to go out of its way to denounce the Kyoto Protocol, sabotage the ICC, refuse to sign or ratify arms-control agreements, and proceed with national missile defence. European concerns were further heightened by the new administration downgrading the importance of the Middle East peace process and North Korea (both Clinton priorities). Global institutions were scorned. The best spin on working through international institutions came from Richard Haass, then Head of Planning in the State Department, who talked of *à la carte* multilateralism. As far as Europe was concerned, there were very few in the senior ranks of the administration with any direct experience of the EU (Bob Zoellick being a notable exception). The experience of Condoleezza Rice, Donald Rumsfeld, Colin Powell, Dick Cheney, Paul Wolfowitz, etc., was of Europe during the Cold War when NATO and bilateral relations played the dominant role. The new administration showed little desire to interact with the EU, a body that seemed to many to cause problems (e.g. stopping the Honeywell–General Electric merger, defeating the US in the WTO and preventing the import of genetically modified foodstuffs). It was no surprise when in 2002 the Bush administration unilaterally decided to reduce the number of summits with the EU to one per year. Congress also showed little interest in maintaining close relations with the increasingly powerful and multilingual European Parliament.

9/11 – THE DAY THAT CHANGED AMERICA

The terrorist attacks of 9/11 changed the US in a fundamental manner – but inevitably they did not have a similar impact on Europe. There was of course an immediate and genuine outpouring of shared grief and outrage epitomised by the famous headline in *Le Monde*, 'We are all Americans now', and the willingness to invoke Article V of NATO. There was also support for the measured US response in defeating the Taliban regime in Afghanistan. For its part, the EU responded swiftly by agreeing on the introduction of a European arrest warrant, the adoption of a common definition of terrorism, agreeing new international legal instruments, combating the funding of terrorism and strengthening air security. But few Europeans really understood the mix of angst, desire for revenge and uncertainty pervading American society. Few Europeans grasped just how much 9/11 affected US thinking, especially on security policy. For the first time since Pearl Harbor, Americans had a sense of their own vulnerability. Bush declared a 'war on terror', and overnight national security became top of the agenda, domestic and foreign. European hopes that 9/11 would temper US hostility to multilateralism were soon dashed. By early 2002, EU–US divergences became clearer, with most European governments distancing themselves from the President's 'axis of evil' speech and the new, openly proclaimed pre-emptive-strike doctrine. Many Europeans doubted whether military might alone could defeat terrorism or tackle the roots of terrorism. The US talked of a 'war on terrorism'; Europeans talked of 'a fight against terrorism'. Americans retorted that Europeans did not take defence seriously and pointed to the huge transatlantic gap in military capabilities. A related dispute concerned 'rogue states', with few Europeans even prepared to use the term and preferring a policy of conditional engagement rather than a policy of isolation and sanctions. Such disputes, especially over US legislation on Cuba and Iran, had soured EU–US relations for several years.

WHAT COMMON VALUES AND INTERESTS?

During the Cold War common interests and shared values were widely assumed between Europe and the US. Both shared the same commitment to democratic institutions, liberal values, human rights and regional stability. Both had a common interest in an open international trading system, access to world energy supplies and preventing the spread of weapons of mass destruction. But there are many who question whether the EU and the US still share the same values, pointing to sharp differences on the death penalty, gun culture, violence, healthcare, social and economic models. Many of these differences were exposed in films such as *Bowling for Columbine* and *Fahrenheit 9/11* by Michael Moore. The growing influence of religion has also been highlighted as a major cultural difference impinging on politics. Robert Kagan has described two worlds: that of a Europe which is 'entering a post-historical paradise of peace and relative prosperity, the realization of Kant's Perpetual Peace'; and that of the US, which 'remains mired in history, exercising power in the anarchic Hobbesian world where international laws and rules are unreliable and where true security and the defence and promotion of a liberal order still depend on the possession and use of military might'. He suggests that these differences are likely to endure (Kagan, 2003). Francis Fukuyama, another close observer of transatlantic relations, wrote *The End of History* in 1992, declaring 'the triumph of common Euro-American values'. By 2003 he was writing about the 'deep differences' within the Atlantic Alliance and arguing that the current split in transatlantic relations was not a transitory problem as the US was at a different point in its history with regard to international institutionalism and international law (*National Interest*, May 2003).

On the European side, Chris Patten, the former Commissioner for External Affairs, was a sharp critic of the US, and pleaded for the US to return to supporting the international 'rule book' that it helped establish after 1945 to promote democracy, the rule of law and the opening of international markets. It had been a 'pretty successful formula', and one that people on both sides of the Atlantic have found it easy to identify with. So why, he asked, did some people now want to abandon it? The real future challenge for the US and the EU was to try to understand each other's interests and concerns better; and to make the global rule book more successful (Patten, 2005). In an interview with the *Financial Times* on 8 January 2003, Javier Solana attributed the widening gulf between the EU and the US to a confrontation between the religious vision of world affairs in the White House and the secular vision of the Europeans. According to Solana, 'it is a sort of binary model, it is all or nothing. For us Europeans, it is difficult to deal with because we are secular. We do not see the world in such black and white terms.' Certainly, since 9/11, Bush has divided the world into 'good-versus-evil' and asked countries if they are 'with us or against us'. Religious exhortations abound in his speeches. For example, in his State of the Union address of February 2003 he stated 'the liberty we prize is not America's gift to the world, it is God's gift to humanity'. It is highly doubtful that any European politician would ever use such rhetoric. In his 2004 State of the Union address, he devoted several paragraphs to the benefits of sexual abstinence and not a word about the Middle East peace process. In terms of their respective worldviews, therefore, there is a different approach to several important issues between the EU and the US.

US ATTITUDES TO EUROPE

The Iraq war had a significant impact on how Americans view Europe. A 2002 poll conducted by the Council on Foreign Relations and the German Marshall Fund showed that Europeans and Americans shared a similar worldview in many respects. Americans preferred working through multilateral channels as much as Europeans. A clear majority of Americans would have preferred the US to have UN support for fighting in Iraq. But with the wrangles in the UNSC over Iraq, and prompted by administration criticism of France and Germany, public attitudes also changed. Britain was perceived as a far more reliable ally than France or Germany. After Iraq, there was a change in attitudes, with a majority of Americans wanting to see a strong EU as a partner for the US in tackling global security threats. But this had little impact on the Congress, which rarely thinks of the EU as an entity. In addition to the well-known aversion to foreign travel, only a handful of Congressmen have regular contact with their European counterparts. Europe-bashing is popular and brings some media attention. Rumsfeld has been particularly critical of old Europe (critical of US policy on Iraq) compared to new Europe (those supportive of US policy). He seemed to relish the disarray in the Union caused by the Iraq war. Leaving Iraq aside, there is no single US reaction to the EU. There are still those who broadly support the twin goals of widening and deepening; others would prefer just widening, with Turkey included. Some are sceptical as to whether the EU can really move forward as a cohesive foreign policy actor. But there is a growing number who doubt whether such a move would be in US interests. They point to the problems the US has faced when the EU has managed to speak with one voice (ICC, Kyoto, trade) and suggest that the US should rather intensify its policy of divide and rule. What this implies is that the EU should do more to convince the US that the idea of uniting Europe is not at the expense of the US. At the same time this will require a certain psychological adjustment on the part of the American foreign and security policy elite to recognise the EU as the principal partner of the US.

EUROPEAN ATTITUDES TOWARDS THE US

European attitudes towards the US have changed dramatically owing to the Iraq crisis. In 2002 there were clear majorities supporting US foreign policy. But in 2003, with the approach of war, there were massive anti-war demonstrations throughout Europe. These demonstrations were an indication of a genuine European public opinion on a major issue. Interestingly, the largest anti-war demonstrations occurred in the UK, Spain and Italy, the three countries that gave Bush the strongest support over Iraq. Post-Iraq, there was an alarming slump in European public support for US foreign policy. On average only 25 per cent favoured US foreign policy (see Pew Institute and GMF polling data). There have been bouts of anti-Americanism in Europe ever since the 1950s. General de Gaulle proclaimed in 1965 that the 'United States is the greatest danger in the world today to peace', and left the NATO military structure in 1966. Opposition to the Vietnam war, deployment of cruise missiles in Europe, and Reagan's talk of the Soviet Union as an 'evil empire' caused condemnation of the US. But opposition to the policies of the first George W. Bush administration reached unprecedented heights.

European governments were sharply divided in their response to Iraq and other issues affecting EU–US relations. The UK has traditionally tried to maintain its 'special relationship' with Washington at the same time as acting as a bridge between the US and Europe. Germany, a traditional uncritical ally of the US during the Cold War, caused consternation in America when its chancellor successfully fought an election campaign on opposition to war in Iraq. France, usually the pack leader in opposition to US global hegemony, also angered Washington with its threat to use its veto in the UNSC to prevent UN approval of the US-led attack on Iraq. Apart from Iraq, member states have not always demonstrated solidarity or coherence on other issues. There have been divisions within the EU on how to respond to US plans for missile defence, to US attempts to sign bilateral treaties with accession states exempting them from the ICC and on trade sanctions.

A SOLID ECONOMIC AND TRADE RELATIONSHIP

On the plus side, the US and Europe enjoy a very healthy and solid economic and trade relationship based on a combined GDP at around 60 per cent of the world total. The transatlantic relationship defines the shape of the global economy as either the EU or the US is the largest trade and investment partner for almost all other countries. Every day the two sides turn over more than €3 million in goods and services. Transatlantic trade comprises approximately 20 per cent of each side's overall foreign trade. European exports to the US totalled €260 billion in 2005, while imports from the US amounted to €195 billion. Mutual investments have contributed even more than actual trade to integration: more than 60 per cent of foreign investments in the US come from the EU and over 50 per cent of US foreign investments go to the EU. By year-end 2004, the total stock of two-way direct investment reached $1.45 trillion (composed of $871 billion in EU investment in the US and $628 billion in US investment in the EU), making US and European companies the largest investors in each other's market. This huge investment relationship is in marked contrast to the EU and US relationships with Asia that are largely trade-focused. Few people know that France is the largest single investor in Texas. Likewise the US invests more in the Netherlands than it does in Japan. Of the ten largest private-sector employers in the United States, five are European firms. Despite the very significant trade levels across the Atlantic, the most important element of the EU–US economic relationship is the investment engagement of both parties in their counterpart's economy. The relationship directly supports 12 million jobs.

In 2003 there was much talk of a boycott of French and German goods in the US because of their opposition to the Iraq war. Congress changed the name of 'French fries' to 'Freedom fries' in the Capitol Hill restaurants, while insulting remarks were made about 'cheese-eating surrender monkeys'. But even in these troubled times US investment in France and Germany – and vice versa – actually increased. Despite transatlantic tensions over Iraq, corporate America invested nearly $87 billion in Europe in 2003. US investment flows to France in 2003 rose by more than 10 per cent to $2.3 billion, and US affiliates more than doubled their profits in France to $4.3 billion. French firms were also among the largest European investors and largest foreign sources of jobs in the US – corporate France invested $4.2 billion in the US in 2003. US foreign affiliate income from Europe surged to a record $77.1 billion in 2003, a 30 per cent jump from 2002; and 2003 was also a record year for profits of European affiliates operating in the US. Despite the strong euro, European affiliate earnings of $46.4 billion easily surpassed earnings of 2002 ($32 billion) and 2001 ($17.4 billion), and the previous peak in earnings of $38.8 billion in 2000. As regards European boycotts of American products, there was a temporary slump in sales of Coca-Cola, Marlboro cigarettes and McDonald's in 2003 but little else (Hamilton and Quinlan, 2004).

The EU and the US are also each other's main foreign assets locations. Corporate America's foreign assets totalled over $7.8 trillion in 2004. The bulk of these assets – roughly 60 per cent – were located in Europe. Most of the top destinations for US investment in the world in 2002 were European: the UK (1), the Netherlands (3), Switzerland (4), Germany (6), Belgium/ Luxembourg (8) and France (10). The UK is the most important market in the world for corporate America. Indeed, US assets in the UK are more than 50 per cent larger than the entire US asset base in Asia and almost equivalent to the combined overseas affiliate asset base of Asia, Latin America, Africa and the Middle East. Affiliate sales also represent the primary means by which European firms deliver goods and services to US consumers. In 2001, European affiliate sales in the US ($1.4 billion) were over four times larger than European exports to the US. Contrary to most assessments of transatlantic drift since the end of the Cold War, Europe's investment stake in the US has deepened dramatically since the fall of the Berlin Wall: income of European affiliates in the US rose more than tenfold between 1990 and 2003 – from $4.4 billion to $46 billion.

Very similar levels of integration are also visible when it comes to the labour markets. The bulk of corporate America's overseas workforce is employed in Europe, not in low-wage countries like Mexico, China or India. Of the nearly 10 million workers employed by US foreign affiliates in 2001, roughly 43 per cent work in Europe. The US also 'insources' more jobs from Europe than it 'outsources' across the Atlantic. In 2001, European affiliates of US firms directly employed roughly 3.2 million workers, while US affiliates of European firms directly employed just over 4.2 million US workers. Employment-related trade is substantial in many US states and European regions. In total, and adding indirect employment, it is estimated that the overall transatlantic workforce numbers some 12–14 million workers. The importance of deepening the transatlantic economic relationship was stressed by the European Commission in May 2005 when it adopted a communication with the snappy title 'A Stronger EU–US Partnership and a More Open Market for the 21st Century' (Com [2005] 96). Both sides then adopted a declaration at the June 2005 summit entitled 'A US–EU Initiative to Enhance Economic Integration and Growth' which spelled out the next steps to be taken in the close economic partnership. The list included regulatory co-operation, capital markets, innovation and technology, trade, travel and security, energy, intellectual property rights, investment, competition, procurement and services. The importance of further reducing trade barriers was stressed in a 2003 OECD study which showed that deepening liberalisation could result in an increase of over 3 per cent in per capita GDP on both sides of the Atlantic.

The rise of the euro is often accused by the detractors of the common currency of undermining the eurozone's competitiveness at the global level. The rise of the euro, starting in the first semester of 2002, has been driven, to a large extent, by a growing US trade deficit. However, the loss of competitiveness for EU exports, caused by the appreciation of the euro, has not exerted any significant downward pressure on EU exports to the US and consequently on the US trade deficit. There has not been any trend reversal in the exchange rate so far, whereas the growth differential between both zones, the US and Europe, has not changed markedly since 2002. This tends to confirm the idea that European competitors at the global level have managed to face up to the euro's rise, containing their production costs to compensate for the inflationary pressure induced by the euro's appreciation. Surprisingly to many, this major economic relationship has continued relatively immune from problems in the political relationship and also with relatively little government interference. There were some American concerns following the two 'no' results in the referendums in France and the Netherlands, but these fears about possible negative effects on the EU swiftly subsided. There is thus a considerable stabilising influence as a result of the economic relationship. But now there is a more difficult agenda that needs to be tackled, which partly touches on moral issues, e.g. stem cell research, GMOs, and partly on sensitive areas, e.g. new regulatory frameworks. An additional problem is the American insistence on tightening controls of goods and people travelling to the US in an effort to combat terrorism.

THE MAIN EU–US TRADE DISPUTES

While trade conflicts regularly hit the headlines, they really only affect a very small percentage of the total trade flow (approximately 2 per cent of the overall flow). Given the size of the trade relationship, it is important to recognise that there will always be some disputes. The trick is to identify possible new disputes in good time and try to seek common ground. This applies particularly to 'new disputes' such as genetically modified foodstuffs, competition policy, drugs, standards, banking and insurance. The EU and the US have also rowed over issues such as the EU's desire to lift its arms embargo on China and the question of public subsidies to Airbus and Boeing. In a number of trade issues it is clear that the EU and the US are rivals, but the depth of the economic relationship is a strong anchor for the overall relationship. With the possible exception of agriculture, the disputes have been handled without excessive political animosity. Over the past several years, however, trade relations have been strained by the nature and significance of the disputes. Part of the problem may be that the US and the EU are of roughly equal economic strength and neither side has the ability to impose concessions on the other. Another factor may be that many bilateral disputes now involve clashes in domestic values, policy priorities, and regulatory systems where the international rules are inadequate to provide a sound basis for effective and timely dispute resolution.

Foreign Sales Corporation Tax

A long-lasting disagreement between the EU and the US was focused on the American Foreign Sales Corporation Act. This corporate taxation legislation was providing American companies with huge tax subsidies, illegal under the WTO. In October 2004 the scheme was finally abolished by the US after this system of export rebates was banned by the WTO, resulting in retaliatory sanctions from Brussels. There remain some question marks, however, as to whether the changes are sufficient to satisfy the EU.

The Helms–Burton Act

The Helms–Burton Act (the Cuban Liberty and Democratic Solidarity Act) was passed by the US legislature on 12 March 1996. This bill is aimed against Fidel Castro's regime. Its primary concern is property confiscated from current American citizens during the 1959 Cuban revolution. First of all, it denies visas to anyone who has done business with property that was confiscated during the revolution. Moreover, it gives American citizens the right to file in domestic courts for financial compensation for the property they lost. This right, though, is followed by the stipulation that the President has the right to waive this rule every six months if the courts are becoming inundated with lawsuits. As the bill contains provisions that seek to punish non-US companies or individuals for engaging in trade with Cuba, provisions that run counter to the spirit of international law and sovereignty, the European authorities attacked it with a complaint with the WTO. In retaliation the US authorities repeatedly suspended title III of the Act, which permits legal action to be brought against non-US firms.

The Iran–Libya Sanctions Act (ILSA)

The Iran–Libya Sanctions Act of 1996, renewed in 2001, is to stay in force at least until 2006. ILSA imposes sanctions on foreign companies that make an investment of more than $20 million in one year in Iran's energy sector, or $40 million in one year in Libya's energy sector. Prior to the suspension of UN sanctions against Libya, which was triggered by Libya's handover of the two Pan Am 103 suspects in April 1999, foreign firms were also subject to the sanctions if they exported to Libya technology that could be used to develop its energy sector, to develop weapons of mass destruction (WMD), to enhance its conventional military, or to maintain its aviation capabilities. In April 2004 the US lifted virtually all restrictions on trade and investment in Libya, and removed the country from the Iran–Libya Sanctions Act, after the country reached a final agreement on the Lockerbie 1988 terrorist attack, agreed to destroy its chemical munitions, missiles and components for a nuclear weapons programme, and to join international efforts to halt weapons proliferation. Traditionally sceptical of economic sanctions as a policy tool, the EU states took exception to ILSA as an extraterritorial application of US law. Some EU states criticised ILSA as a 'double standard' in US foreign policy, in which the United States worked against the Arab League boycott of Israel while at the same time promoting a worldwide boycott of Iran. As with the Helms–Burton Act, the EU has adopted a blocking statute that makes it illegal for any EU company to comply with ILSA. Moreover, in April 1997 the European Council decided that the EU would request the re-establishment of a WTO panel against the US should any action be taken against EU companies or individuals under ILSA or the Helms–Burton Act.

Boeing–Airbus subsidies dispute

The US and EU companies Boeing and Airbus are the world-dominating large civil aircraft producers. Being the two main world producers, both companies profit from government support. Despite the very complicated nature of the subsidies schemes, the WTO could find both the US and EU guilty of giving illegal subsidies to their manufacturers. Boeing, in particular, has since outsourced more of its components to countries such as Japan, and it is an aim of the new round of negotiations to bring such outside suppliers into the scope of a new US–EU subsidy code. For Washington, the main cause for going to the WTO is the direct launch aid that four of the European governments provide to Airbus for the launching of the A380 'superjumbo' plane, as well as the planned long-range, mid-sized A350. The heart of the negotiations will be over what should constitute an allowable subsidy.

EU customs

One of the newest attacks of the US officials against the EU concerns the European customs rules. The Office of the US Trade Representative (USTR) has reportedly asked the WTO to form a dispute-settlement panel in the case against the EU's customs regulation system. At the heart of the dispute are the differences among the EU members in their national customs authorities' operations. The USTR asserts that the lack of a single EU customs administration hinders US exports, particularly for small to mid-size businesses. Washington contends that the twenty-five-member EU is in violation of WTO rules that require its 148-member nations to administer their customs laws 'in a uniform, impartial and reasonable manner' and that they 'provide tribunals for prompt review and correction of administrative action relating to customs matters'.

Competition

The European Commission has intervened controversially in a number of high-profile cases involving US companies such as the Boeing–McDonnell Douglas merger in 1997, the Honeywell–General Electric merger in 2001 and the Microsoft anti-trust probe, which included a record €497 million fine in March 2004.

Although political differences in the past have not affected the economic relationship, this may not always be the case as there are deep differences of view regarding the Middle East, China and the whole concept of balance-of-power politics. Moreover the multilateral trading system needs to be strengthened, and a common approach to foreign policy sanctions that have a trade impact needs to be found. Last but not least, the EU and the US have to commit themselves not only to supporting the multilateral system, but also to working together to ensure a fairer international system, including strengthening regional groupings as cornerstones of the multilateral system.

A NEW PARTNERSHIP

There are signs now that both sides are willing to accept that they have different views on major issues but also a desire to work together where possible. Dan Fried, Assistant Secretary of State for European Affairs, said in a statement to Congress on 8 March 2006 that he had seen over the past year 'a shift in emphasis among Europeans from a focus on past differences to a commitment to work together on global challenges'. Tony Blair said after the Iraq war that, 'if we are going to have a strategic partnership between Europe and America, we have to work out the basis of that and how we make progress on issues that are difficult between us'. Javier Solana, in his European security strategy paper of June 2003, also emphasised the importance of a solid transatlantic relationship to tackle the shared threats of terrorism and WMD. It was also encouraging that the first overseas visit by Bush in his second term was to Europe. Largely as a result of the Iraq experience, there has been a rethink in Washington on the importance of the EU, and both Rice and Bush have made supportive statements of closer European integration. President Bush also praised the EU as a solid partner of the US when he visited Vienna for the annual EU–US summit on 21 June 2006. But there remain doubts as to whether the US will always see the EU as partner of first choice, or the individual member states. The temptation to divide and rule will always be there unless the Europeans show a united front.

Some have suggested that it might be useful to have a transatlantic treaty arguing that the EU has strategic partnerships with Russia, Canada, China, India and Japan – but not with the US. Most observers, however, think such an idea to be premature. It will take time to heal the wounds over Iraq and it will take time for the EU to resolve its external representation. Perhaps in a few years it will be opportune to revisit the question of a new transatlantic relationship. Then the EU will be faced with important questions including its willingness and ability to take care of its own security and the future role of NATO. Increasingly, many Americans (and Europeans) ask why the US should continue to defend Europe, through NATO and with some 100,000 troops on the ground, when Europe is as rich as the US, has more people in uniform than the US, and there is no longer any communist threat. The American attachment to NATO is somewhat ambivalent. The Pentagon had reservations about fighting war by committee after the experience in Kosovo. Following 9/11 the US rejected the offer of NATO assistance. Bush and Rumsfeld made clear their preference for coalitions of the willing. The metaphor was of a sheriff riding out leading a posse of allies to tackle the bad guys. This attitude did considerable damage to NATO, as did the concept of using NATO as a toolbox. On the other hand, the US was also concerned at the Europeans building up their own command and control centre for military operations (see Chapter 5).

CONCLUSION

The EU and the US are the two most important global actors and increasingly need each other to tackle many world problems successfully. They need to learn to work together where possible; differ when necessary; but try to narrow the areas of divergence. The annual summits need more focus, and arguably they should be increased to two a year. These summits must spend time discussing major strategic issues such as the future of China and Russia, and failed states. Both sides must continue the good work in areas of co-operation (the Balkans, the Middle East, Afghanistan, HIV/AIDS in Africa), plus the economic agenda – regulatory co-operation, financial services, civil aviation, digital economy, competition policy and more. The US should also reiterate its unambiguous support for a strong, united Europe, while the EU needs to improve its foreign policy co-ordination and implementation. The Congress and the European Parliament need to upgrade their relations, and there should be more exchanges and more use of video links. One of the problems of the renewed attempt to forge a strong transatlantic partnership is the feeling that both sides are doing it out of necessity rather than from conviction. There is also a high degree of anti-Americanism (or rather opposition to Bush-administration policies) in Europe, and continued resentment at Europe (or rather France and Germany) in the US. Furthermore, the EU has no real concept of how to deal with the world's only superpower and cannot engage it on areas it considers a priority such as Iraq, Afghanistan and North Korea. Too often there is a preference for bilateral as opposed to EU channels. But the current EU–US structures do not enable a serious discussion of many of these differences to take place. Neither is NATO an adequate structure for a transatlantic strategic dialogue.

For many years the US has encouraged the EU to speak with one voice on external affairs. Yet when the EU does manage to speak with one voice it often delivers a message that the US does not wish to hear. There have always been EU–US disputes (from chicken wars to gas pipelines) but they were never allowed to escalate out of hand during the Cold War. Without the Cold War glue, the number of disputes, covering political, economic, social and trade issues, has steadily increased. They range from divergent views on the Middle East and climate change to the imposition of steel tariffs and the death penalty. It will require some considerable political skill, therefore, to ensure that the partnership elements prevail over the dispute elements in the next decade. Much will depend on whether the US accepts EU insistence on working through and strengthening international institutions. The transatlantic relationship has survived the Iraq crisis, and few doubt that the partnership remains indispensable, especially in dealing with the array of new global threats. The new enlarged EU is inevitably preoccupied with internal problems, but enlargement has also brought in a group of countries who instinctively see the US as a force for good in world affairs. This will not be uncritical support because the accession states, like current EU member states, are firmly committed to multilateral institutions. If the US demonstrates a renewal of faith in multilateral solutions, then a new partnership should be possible. A precondition will be a stronger and more coherent EU as a foreign policy actor – something more difficult with the failure to ratify the constitutional treaty. At the same time the US also needs to make a psychological adjustment to accept the EU as a global partner, a partner of choice in tackling international problems. Certainly it will not be an easy adjustment on either side. For the foreseeable future, therefore, the EU and the US are likely to remain both friends and rivals.

KEY QUESTIONS

Is the US the EU's most important partner?
What are the main problems in transatlantic relations?

Are there differences in how the US and the EU see the future of NATO? Can trade relations be isolated from political issues?

FURTHER READING

US foreign policy is analysed in Cameron (2005), Kupchan (2002), and Christiansen and Tonra (2004). For the impact of the Iraq war on transatlantic relations, see Gordon and Shapiro (2004). For the Mars v Venus thesis, see Kagan (2003). Philippart and Winand (2001), and Peterson and Pollack (2003) provide good overviews of transatlantic relations, while Hamilton and Quinlan (2004) concentrate on the economic side.

7   The neighbourhood

SUMMARY

The EU pays considerable attention and devotes considerable resources to the states in its immediate neighbourhood. It has established various types of contractual relations (European Economic Area [EEA], Association Agreements, Partnership and Co-operation Agreements, Stabilisation Agreements, etc.) with its neighbours, and since 2004 the European Neighbourhood Policy (ENP). The ENP is now the flagship policy of the EU towards its neighbours, with individual Action Plans a central element. But the ENP does not offer the enticement of EU membership, and it is consequently much more difficult to promote change in these countries. The ENP embraces the countries to the south of the EU, most of which are also involved in the Barcelona Process, and to the east and south-east, excluding Russia and the Balkans. Russia and the EU have a so-called strategic partnership, but there is little content to the relationship. The western Balkans have their own roadmap towards EU accession. The EEA is the most advanced EU relationship, but the model is not relevant to the majority of the EU's neighbours.

WIDER EUROPE

The launch of the Wider Europe initiative in 2003, precursor to the ENP, was designed to offer those countries that had zero or very distant prospects of joining the EU closer association in EU policies. Former Commission President Romano Prodi described it as 'everything but the institutions'. There were two distinct groups of countries targeted for this new policy. The southern group were the countries of the North African littoral and the Middle East which, because of their geographical location, are excluded from the prospect of EU membership. The eastern group, comprising Russia, Ukraine, Belarus, Moldova, Georgia, Armenia and Azerbaijan, were not excluded geographically from the EU but were viewed as states far from meeting the EU accession criteria. The Wider Europe initiative was not received with much enthusiasm, partly because there were so many uncertainties. It was not clear which countries would be involved. It was not clear what would happen to existing contractual arrangements; or whether there would be extra money to support the initiative; or what programmes and policy areas would be open to the various countries; or who would draw up the proposed Action Plans and establish benchmarks for progress. The EU had been remarkably successful in imposing regime change in the candidate countries of central and eastern Europe. But there had been a massive carrot on offer. How would the new scheme work if there were no such carrot of EU membership on the table? In countries still on the enlargement track, such as Bulgaria and Romania, the Wider Europe concept was viewed as an unnecessary distraction (even though it was never designed to apply to them). In countries that hoped soon to be on the enlargement track – Turkey, Croatia, Macedonia – it was viewed with downright suspicion as a plot to put their candidature on the back burner. Even for those with distant prospects of joining the EU, such as Ukraine, there was a dislike of being lumped together to suit the whims of Brussels bureaucrats. And for another group of countries in the Caucasus – Armenia, Azerbaijan and Georgia – there were loud protests at their initial exclusion from the initiative.

The Wider Europe concept was designed to deal with the consequences of the 2004 enlargement of the Union from fifteen to twenty-five member states. Given the number of accession countries, it was inevitable that fundamental questions were asked about the nature of the Union and its limits. What were the final borders of the Union? It is impossible to give a definitive answer to this question, one that is posed increasingly by EU politicians and bewildered citizens. To the north the situation is clear. The only remaining countries outside the EU are Norway and Iceland. Both would have little difficulty fitting into the EU, given their membership of the European Economic Area (EEA). To the west Ireland and Portugal are the border states facing the Atlantic. To the south, the position is equally clear. Morocco once applied for membership but was politely told it was not European. North African states are thus slated to be good neighbours but can never join the family. The problems for the EU begin in the east and the south-east. The countries of the Balkans have been given an undertaking that they are all eligible for membership when they meet the Copenhagen criteria. But no one can state with any certainty when this might occur as it largely depends on progress in each country. Turning to the east, the EU has to deal with the rump of a superpower (Russia), a newly independent state as big as France but unsure of its identity (Ukraine), and five states with significant problems – Belarus, Moldova, Armenia, Azerbaijan and Georgia.

Russia is still suffering from the loss of its empire and the loss of its superpower status. President Putin has restored some order after the Klondike years under Yeltsin; but there are worrying indications that the Kremlin is steadily eroding the democratic gains of the 1990s. Moscow is also unsure how to deal with the EU, a strange and largely unknown animal in the eyes of most of the Russian elite. It expressed reservations about the consequences of the May 2004 enlargement that featured several ex-Soviet states, but was forced to accept the inevitable. In Ukraine the December 2004 Orange Revolution was welcomed in the West, while Putin's Russia was suspicious of the new president, Viktor Yushchenko. The EU had been exasperated at the failure of the former president, Leonid Kuchma, to introduce reforms and further exasperated at the constant Ukrainian demands to be given an association agreement and candidate status. While the EU was sympathetic to Yushchenko, there was much disappointment in Brussels at the failure to pursue real reforms during 2005–6. The EU is also in a dilemma over how to deal with Belarus, languishing under the authoritarian Lukashenko, and Moldova, home to thousands of unwanted Russian troops in the breakaway republic of Transnistria. As regards the Caucasus, a strong lobbying campaign ensured that they are part of the ENP, but the EU has shown little interest in the region beyond security of oil supplies. Given the myriad of unresolved political issues in the Caucasus, it is doubtful whether the intro-duction of 'agreed benchmarks' will make much difference to the situation.

THE EUROPEAN NEIGHBOURHOOD POLICY (ENP)

When it was launched in 2004 the ENP was seen to cover the immediate neighbours of the enlarged EU but not countries with an accession perspective (Bulgaria, Romania, Turkey, western Balkans). The ENP covers Israel, Jordan, Moldova, Morocco, the Palestinian Authority, Tunisia, Ukraine, Armenia, Azerbaijan, Egypt, Georgia, Lebanon and Algeria. There are no agreements yet with Syria, Libya and Belarus because ENP status requires a contractual agreement such as a partnership and co-operation agreement or an association agreement and none exists with these three countries. As Commissioner Benita Ferrero-Waldner explained:

> The aim of the ENP is to avoid new dividing lines on the continent and deepen relations between the EU and its neighbours. The ENP is not about enlargement but it is about mutual interest in supporting reforms and modernisation. Each country has its own agreed Action Plan that reflects its needs and priorities.

The ENP is supposed to be based on common values and interests including democracy, a market economy and responding to challenges such as crime, migration, health, the environment and terrorism. The ENP offers progressive integration into the EU's internal market and deepened political co-operation. The main drawback is the lack of additional money before 2007. The EU plans to use its experience gained in the transition process of central Europe to help the ENP countries. For example, it will boost the twinning schemes that enabled officials and experts to spend time in the ENP countries to train them in EU laws and standards.

The ENP Action Plans are similar in outline, but the content is specific to each country. They include: political dialogue; economic and social co-operation; trade-related issues, market and regulatory reform; co-operation in justice and home affairs; sectoral issues such as transport, energy, information society, environment, research and development; the human dimension, including people-to-people contacts, civil society, education and public health. The ENP builds on existing legal and institutional arrangements (Association Agreements, Partnership and Co-operation Agreements [PCAs], Barcelona Process) and established instruments (Association or Co-operation councils, committees and subcommittees) to implement and monitor the policy. From 2007, the ENP financial instrument (ENPI) will replace Phare, Tacis and MEDA and should allow for more flexibility in terms of funding priority programmes. The Commission proposed a budget of nearly €15 billion for ENPI, but this figure was reduced to just over €13 million as a result of the compromise over the budget at the December 2005 European Council. While the laudable aim of the ENP is to reward those states that help themselves, the ENP does not provide a framework for those states such as Belarus that show no signs of self-help. The lack of major new funding and the reluctance of the EU to open its markets fully also weaken the policy. Arguably the EU needs the co-operation of most of its neighbours to tackle problems of illegal migration, terrorism and cross-border crime as much as they need access to partial EU programmes. Without offering more than is currently on the table the EU may be facing a ring of states in distress rather than a ring of friends. The Commission did propose strengthening the ENP in a communication of 4 December 2006 (COM 726).

THE SOUTHERN NEIGHBOURS

The Mediterranean and the entire Middle East region (defined here as reaching from Morocco to the Gulf) are of crucial importance to the EU. Together with Russia, the region is the most important source of energy to the EU, and the EU is the main trading partner of all countries in the region. The Mediterranean countries send 50 per cent of their exports to the EU, and Europe is the largest foreign investor in its southern neighbours (55 per cent of total FDI). The EU is the largest provider of financial assistance and funding for most Mediterranean countries, with nearly €3 billion per year in loans and grants flowing to the region. In addition, the member states of the EU also provide substantial amounts of bilateral development assistance. The EU is also the main source of tourism. At the same time, it is the first destination for migrants, legal and illegal, who form sizeable diasporas (almost 10 million people altogether, mostly from the Maghreb) in countries like France, the Netherlands or Belgium.

The geopolitical situation of the Mediterranean and the Middle East has changed significantly since the Barcelona Process began in late 1995. The terrorist attacks of September 2001 and the war in Iraq have given the region a new centrality in global affairs. The EU is rightly concerned about the situation of its southern neighbours. European leaders worry that the south may not be able to cope with the challenges ahead (rising unemployment, social unrest, rapid urbanisation, globalisation, population growth, fundamentalism, water scarcity, etc.). Many Europeans fear that the flood of illegal immigrants into Europe will continue to swell and have a profound effect on the European labour market and its society. The region's precarious political, social and economic systems constitute a potential security threat. The southern shores of the Mediterranean thus pose huge challenges for the EU. The economies of the region are stagnating with their share of world trade declining. Unemployment is around 25 per cent with even higher rates for young people. Per capita income is around 10 per cent of the EU average, which leads to a continuing flow of legal and illegal migrants to Europe. The environment is under huge strain as a result of massive population increases and ill-considered development strategies. The leaders in the region also feel under threat, partly by US demands for more democracy and partly by EU attempts to impose conditionality. Many view the EU–Mediterranean relationship less as a partnership of equals, as stated in the Barcelona Process, than as a teacher–pupil relationship. The economic situation of the region has improved in recent years, thanks above all to substantially higher export revenues from oil and gas that remain the economic mainstay of the region, together with tourism. But politically nearly all Arab countries have been slipping further behind. The third Arab Human Development Report (2004) has rightly drawn attention to a long catalogue of deficiencies, including slow economic reforms and a lack of democracy. For these reasons, the EU has a major interest in the reform process among its southern neighbours. The first priority is political and economic reform – more democracy and respect for the rule of law, and more investment to tackle the massive problem of youth unemployment. The EU's 'governance facility', which provides support for capacity building, could be useful here. Another priority is improving the quality of education. Lastly, the region has to counter the rapid environmental deterioration of the region. The EU's influence, however, is much less compared to its relations with candidate countries on Central and Eastern Europe, as well as the Balkans. So far, the ENP's 'sticks and carrots' are insufficient to motivate national authorities to implement reforms that weaken their own power status.

THE BARCELONA PROCESS

At the Barcelona summit in November 2005, held to celebrate ten years of co-operation, very few Arab leaders actually showed up. Nevertheless, the summit was a useful occasion to take stock of achievements and shortcomings. The Barcelona Process was ambitious. Its goal was to convert the Mediterranean Sea into a zone of peace, stability and prosperity. To that end, the EU proposed: to establish a vast Euro-Mediterranean free trade area to be completed by 2010; to increase its development assistance substantially; to conclude Association Agreements with each of the neighbouring countries in the Mediterranean; to establish a political dialogue with all the countries around the Mediterranean including Israel.

Among the achievements of the first ten years of Barcelona were:

- All Mediterranean countries have negotiated Association Agreements providing for reciprocal free trade with the EU. Agreements are in force with Algeria, Morocco, Tunisia, Egypt, Jordan, Israel, the Palestinian Authority and Lebanon. An agreement has been negotiated but not yet signed with Syria. Libya is not formally part of the Barcelona Process and has therefore not entered into negotiations for an Association Agreement. But only Israel has lifted all obstacles to trade with the EU. The other neighbouring countries, with the exception of Syria and Libya, are in the process of completing free trade with the EU, but only Tunisia and Morocco will have abolished all tariff barriers on manufactured products and imports from the EU by the target date of 2010. The completion of the Euro-Mediterranean free trade area will therefore be delayed beyond 2015.
- Morocco, Tunisia, Egypt and Jordan signed a free trade agreement (Agadir Agreement) in 2004. It provides for free trade by 2006. This agreement has considerable potential in encouraging more intense trade relations between Mediterranean and EU countries, provided all parties apply the identical 'generous' rules of origin (the so-called pan-European rules of origin). Other Mediterranean countries are free to join the Agreement – Lebanon has already expressed its intention to do so, and other Arab countries in the Gulf might join in the future. Economic co-operation among the southern Mediterranean countries still remains in its infancy, owing to a lack of political will, low economic complementarity, inadequate transport links and high trade barriers. That may change in the future, as the level of development is bound to rise and trade obstacles will be progressively removed, including a more efficient handling of merchandise in ports.
- Both sides have proceeded with specific trade liberalisation measures on key agricultural products. Essentially, the EU grants tariff-free access for the main products coming from the south – potatoes, tomatoes, citrus products, olive oil, beans, etc. – during the winter season, but within rather modest tariff-free quotas. These arrangements are reviewed periodically. However, agricultural products amount to less than 10 per cent of bilateral trade between the EU and its Mediterranean neighbours. Its potential remains relatively modest whatever the protection applied by either side.
- There has been a timid expansion of regional arrangements including a Euro-Mediterranean parliamentary assembly, a cultural dialogue and a cultural foundation in Alexandria.
- The two sides have held a multitude of meetings, seminars and workshops. They meet every six months at foreign minister level and several times per year at the level of high officials to discuss such issues as terrorism, weapons of mass destruction, illegal immigration, liberalisation of

services, etc. Trade ministers have also met occasionally. This flurry of meetings and reciprocal visits certainly has had a useful socialisation effect, even if there have been only modest results. It has also been a useful opportunity for Arabs and Israelis to sit together.

Since 1995 the Barcelona parties have established numerous ministerial and official bodies to oversee the process but have failed to secure visibility and popular support. Not one person in a thousand in the EU, and even less on the other side of the Mediterranean, has any idea of what the Barcelona Process is about, though official documents remain widely optimistic. A Commission communication of April 2004 spoke of a 'strong partnership driven by a common political will to build together a space of dialogue, peace, security and shared prosperity'. Among the reasons why progress has been so slow are the political difficulties caused by continuing conflicts in the region (most notably the Arab–Israeli conflict), a reluctance to implement agreements, and the impact of the consensus principle. For pragmatic reasons, the EU has preferred to attempt to stimulate economic reforms – free trade, customs administration, protection of intellectual property rights, competition policies, macroeconomic stability – rather than to address politically sensitive issues relating to democracy or the rule of law. Progress has been greatest in such countries as Tunisia, Morocco and Jordan, which concluded Association Agreements almost ten years ago. The most regrettable shortcoming of the past ten years has been the slow pace of socio-economic development. Per capita income has gone up 1–2 per cent per year, compared to 4 per cent in Eastern Europe or even more in Asia. The Mediterranean region has thus fallen behind wider global developments. Their combined efforts towards reform have been insufficient in light of the huge challenges each country is confronted with, in particular rising unemployment and environmental hazards.

When the ENP was conceived it was primarily addressed to the countries of Central and Eastern Europe with distant prospects of membership. After some hesitation, it decided to offer the same type of structured relationship to its southern neighbours. This created some confusion, as the southern neighbours were contractually in a more advanced situation than the new eastern neighbours. Indeed, their Association Agreements were more substantial than the Partnership and Co-operation Agreements concluded with Ukraine, Moldova or the southern Caucasus countries. In accordance with this new approach, the EU agreed ENP Action Plans with Morocco, Tunisia, Jordan and the Palestinian Territories in 2004. These documents, valid for a three-to-five-year period, constitute a sort of 'checklist' of some 100 political, juridical and economic reform steps, which partner countries agree to, including appropriate timetables according to their political priorities. The EU and the partner country both have joint responsibility for the implementation of the Action Plans. But the EU has stated its readiness to reward the good performers. The Action Plans are innovative in relation to the past practice of bilateral co-operation: they provide an all-embracing blueprint for modernisation of legislation and executive practices, and their reach extends not only to the economic and financial spheres but right to the core of political issues, from election practices to freedom of assembly and the rule of law. Those governments that wish to proceed with reforms will find the Action Plans to be a useful tool, as they allow them to draw upon the extensive experience of EU countries, especially its newest members, in devising and implementing reforms from situations not entirely dissimilar to their own.

Compared to 1995, the overall setting in the Mediterranean has changed. Three of the former neighbours have 'changed sides' or are in the process of doing so: Malta, Cyprus and Turkey have become member states or are candidates for EU accession. Israel has distanced itself more and more from its Arab neighbours: it has turned into a high-tech country, not very different from an EU member state. Its political governance, technical rules and regulations have become similar to those applied by the EU, and it is more deeply integrated within the EU – through scientific and cultural changes, similarities of values and work/consumption patterns – than any other country in the region. It could become an ideal economic partner for its Arab neighbours if it were able to make peace with the Palestinians.

The nine Arab states (excluding Libya and including the Palestinian Territories) on the southern and eastern shores of the Mediterranean therefore constitute the primary 'target' of ENP in the south. It is there that the problems of governance, freedom, education, environment and, last but not least, demographic growth and employment will persist, with potential negative fallouts on the northern shores by way of illegal migration, drug-trafficking and even terrorism. A key priority is an EU–Mediterranean free trade area. The southern neighbours, most of them WTO members, will have to dismantle protective barriers among themselves and towards the EU in order to emerge with globally competitive manufacturing industries. The EU is trying to encourage its neighbours to improve the investment climate, abandon excessive 'red tape', accelerate privatisation and dramatically improve the quality of the judiciary, with special emphasis on commercial courts. As long as international business does not trust the effectiveness and independence of the judiciary, it will continue to shun the countries around the Mediterranean. The improvement of the business climate is, therefore, a key priority in the joint ENP Action Plans. Other priorities include educational reform, especially granting girls equal opportunities, and tackling the rapidly deteriorating environment. Cities are suffocating from toxic emissions and noise levels due to increasing traffic, scarcity of water, and pollution of riverbeds. In addition, industrial activity and maritime shipping have eroded the natural environment of the sea and rivers. Governments have seriously neglected this issue and have thereby exposed their growing populations to rising health hazards. The EU rightly insists on the need to clean up the Mediterranean Sea to protect it from oil and waste shipping spills.

Bringing democracy to the region

Both the EU and the US are committed to helping bring more democracy to the region. Although there were some encouraging signs of progress in 2005–6 (elections in Iraq, Palestine, Lebanon, etc.), the UN Arab Human Development Report paints a rather bleak picture of democracy's progress in the region. The report blames the 'freedom deficit' for a wide range of problems, including sluggish growth rates, poor performance in science and innovation, and widespread human rights abuses. Oppression is bad for governments, too, because it deprives them of legitimacy and provides outside powers with a pretext to intervene in Arab affairs. Indeed, many Arab regimes practise what the report terms a 'legitimacy of blackmail', sustaining their power by posing as the only protection against chaos or a takeover by Islamist extremists. Another common feature is what the authors call the 'black hole' state. Arab republics and monarchies alike grant their rulers such unchallengeable power as to 'convert the surrounding social environment into a setting in which nothing moves and from which nothing escapes'. The authors describe a life-long system that whittles away at personal freedoms, beginning with patriarchalism and clannishness in Arab family life, extending through to school systems that favour the parroting of fixed ideas rather than open inquiry, and on through to citizenship restricted by arbitrary laws and limits to free expression. Out of twenty-one Arab countries, seventeen prohibit the publication of journals without hard-to-get licences, seven ban the formation of political parties altogether, and three (Egypt, Sudan and Syria) have declared permanent states of emergency that date back decades.

Aside from piecemeal reforms in several Arab countries, the most significant trend noted is the growing acceptance, by governments as well as by the public, of the urgency of change. In recent years a broad consensus has emerged around the idea 'that the heart of the failing lies in the political sphere, specifically in the architecture of the Arab state'. Yet in no Arab country has pressure for change resulted in a fundamental shift of power away from long-ensconced elites. The ruling classes benefit too much from the status quo to accept reforms that may leave them worse off. The EU has never been totally serious about using conditionality to promote reform. There are clauses in the Association Agreements (Article 2) that provide for their suspension in light of violations of human rights and democratic principles, but they have never been invoked. Indeed, in 1992 the EU sat back and did nothing when the army intervened after the first round of voting in Algeria heralded the prospect of an Islamic party taking power. The EU also did nothing when the Israelis built a security wall on Palestinian territory.

One of the difficult questions for the EU is whether or not to co-operate visibly with the US in pursuit of its Broader Middle East and North Africa Initiative. Launched in 2003 with much fanfare, few resources and no consultation with the EU, the initiative is a major foreign policy priority of President Bush's second term and is a direct response to 9/11 and the 'war on terrorism'. Given the dismal public image of the US in the region, it is questionable whether the EU would gain anything from too open an association with the US. The EU has had a common position on the Middle East peace process for many years and enjoys a single seat (Solana) in the quartet (the US, Russia, the UN, the EU) that attempts to promote peace talks between the Israelis and the Palestinians. It also has a special representative (Marc Otte) who shuttles between Brussels and the region in an effort to encourage dialogue. The EU is also the principal funder of the Palestinian Authority. A related question is to what extent the EU and NATO should co-operate in the region. Although the EU is far more engaged than NATO, the Alliance does play a useful role in holding security dialogues with Mediterranean partners and promoting security-sector reform. There are some EU–NATO contacts but overall little overlap between the programmes of the two organisations.

THE GULF

The nine Gulf countries – from Iran to Yemen – are almost as important to the EU as the Arab countries around the Mediterranean. It is there that half of the world's oil reserves and a third of the known gas reserves are situated. Also, the prospects for economic growth for the coming twenty to thirty years appear much brighter than in the Mediterranean, thanks to further rising prices of fossil energy. The intensity of economic, cultural and political links with the Gulf countries is substantially lower than for the Mediterranean neighbours, owing to greater geographic, historic and cultural distance, but above all to the fact that the Gulf countries look beyond Europe for their economic and political ties. Asia is their future export outlet; and the USA is the provider of 'security' and higher education for them, with the notable exception of Iran. The EU has therefore made efforts to engage in a productive dialogue. Co-operation Agreements have been in force with the six Gulf Co-operation Council (GCC) countries for more than fifteen years and with Yemen for almost ten years. The EU has been trying to establish contractual links with Iran for more than fifteen years, without success so far. The EU and GCC foreign ministers meet once a year for a broad exchange of views. But the overall level of contacts is much lower than with any of the Mediterranean countries. Until 2004, the EU Commission had not a single full-fledged delegation anywhere in the region.

Given the importance of energy for Europe, the EU is seeking to intensify relations with the GCC and is considering plans for a more frequent energy dialogue and assistance for their WTO aspirations. Plans are also in hand for an EU–GCC free trade area. Some EU diplomats also believe that the EU should try to convince the three principal powers – the GCC, Iran and Iraq – of the need for a comprehensive security relationship among themselves. This would indeed be a difficult venture when Iran seems bent on acquiring nuclear power status, Iraq is busy restoring its sovereignty and the GCC shows signs of weakness. But the EU might be the only credible power to undertake such a task. What is clear is that the region will remain of critical importance to the EU for decades to come. The EU has no choice but to become deeply and permanently involved in the reform process, as a failure to reform could seriously affect the EU's security and future energy supplies.

RUSSIA

Russia signalled at an early stage that it did not see itself as part of the ENP. It held that its status required a special relationship with the EU. But despite soaring energy prices Russia remains a weak state with numerous political, social and economic problems. The authoritarian trends in Russia pose a problem for the EU, which is seeking to develop a values-based foreign policy. On the surface there is increasing co-operation between the EU and Russia on security affairs. Russia is a permanent member of the UNSC and the largest neighbour of the EU. In some areas, such as non-proliferation, there has been more in common between the EU and Russia than between the EU and the US. There has also been good co-operation on the Middle East, Iran, terrorism and the reform of the UN. But there are also differences in terms of how to deal with the neighbours. For example, the EU (critical) reacted very differently from Russia (uncritical) to the death of many demonstrators in Uzbekistan in 2005.

Moscow has also struggled to assert itself against rebellious provinces and regions such as Chechnya. It has an ageing population, an absence of a strong legal culture, and rising social problems, including an HIV/AIDS epidemic. Its leaders are also struggling to cope with a changed global system, a system that seemed very predictable until the collapse of communism in 1989–91. Many regret the loss of superpower status, and President Putin is on record as stating that the break-up of the Soviet Union was one of the worst calamities of the twentieth century. Russia has no desire to join the EU (or NATO) as it would be very uncomfortable with the constant interference and loss of sovereignty. It prefers to align its policies when convenient with the West and welcomes opportunities to play on the stage with G8 partners. Russia was the chair of the G8 in 2006. The terrorist attack on the Beslan school in 2004 was a traumatic affair for Russia as it displayed Russia's weakness. There were swift fears of an international conspiracy to undermine Russia and a consequent determination not to compromise with the separatists or terrorists. Russia also tends to view foreign policy in zero-sum terms, a throwback to the Cold War mentality. Given Russia's weakness, it tends to be very defensive in foreign and security policy. It has proved very difficult, for example, to secure any movement by Moscow in the frozen conflicts of the Caucasus.

Partnership and Co-operation Agreement (PCA)

The legal basis for EU relations with Russia is the Partnership and Co-operation Agreement (PCA) that came into force in December 1997 for an initial period of ten years. It establishes the institutional framework for bilateral relations, sets the principal common objectives, and calls for activities and dialogue in a number of policy areas. It covers:

*   trade and economic co-operation: liberalisation of trade based on most-favoured-nation (MFN) treatment and the elimination of quantitative restrictions; legislative harmonisation; and provision on the establishment and operation of companies, services, current payments and the movement of capital, competition and intellectual property
*   co-operation in science and technology, energy, environment, transport, space and a range of other civil sectors
*   political dialogue: on international issues, democracy and human rights
*   justice and home affairs: co-operation to prevent illegal activities, trafficking in drugs, money laundering and organised crime. An Action Plan on combating organised crime was signed in June 2000.

Bilateral institutional contacts are to a large extent determined by the PCA. They include two summits each year, a permanent partnership council (ministerial level) and a co-operation committee (senior official level). In addition, nine subcommittees (working level) deal with technical issues while there is also a regular ministerial and official dialogue on foreign and security policy issues. A parliamentary co-operation committee has also been established, where members of the European Parliament and the Russian Duma meet on a regular basis. The PCA is due to expire in 2007 but it can be prolonged on an annual basis pending negotiations on a new EU–Russia agreement. A protocol was signed by the EU and Russia in April 2004 to extend the PCA to the ten new member states. Russia has found it difficult to come to terms with the fact that eight former communist countries, including three former Soviet republics, have joined the EU. While Moscow has tended to ignore its former satellites in Central Europe, it has continued to press the Baltic states for alleged maltreatment of the ethnic Russians living there. For several years Russia has refused to sign and ratify the border agreements that were agreed with Estonia and Latvia, partly using the issue as a hammer to beat Baltic heads. One of the most difficult issues for the EU and Russia to resolve was transit to the Kaliningrad *oblast*. A relic of the Second World War, Kaliningrad suffered severe socio-economic problems as a result of the break-up of the Soviet Union. After lengthy negotiations a specific transit regime, based on facilitated travel documents, came into effect in July 2003. The EU has also offered substantial financial assistance to support the socio-economic development of Kaliningrad.

Russia was also the subject of a 1999 EU common strategy that was supposed to inject greater coherence between the EU and member states in their policies towards Russia. Most observers agree that it has been a failure. EU member states have been unwilling to align their bilateral agendas and programmes with those of the EU. Chirac, Schroeder, Blair and Berlusconi have all sought to establish close bilateral and personal ties to Putin's Russia, sometimes at the expense of agreed EU policy. For example, in 2004, the Italian prime minister, while holding the rotating EU Presidency, was not even willing to defend EU policy on Chechnya when hosting Mr Putin for the six-monthly EU–Russia summit. Germany and Russia also agreed on a new pipeline route that bypassed Poland and the Baltic states. The current tendency simply makes it easy for Moscow to play off one member state against another, and the result is a weakened EU approach to one of its most important neighbours.

EU–Russia trade has been increasing substantially and amounted to €150 billion in 2005. For Russia, the EU was by far the most important trading partner, accounting for 50 per cent of total Russian trade. For the EU, Russia was the fourth most important trading partner (after the US, China and Japan). Steel and textiles are the main industry sectors covered by bilateral trade agreements. The Energy Charter that would provide a legal framework for investment, construction and transit of energy supplies has been awaiting ratification by the Duma for several years. This is an important issue, as Russia desperately needs EU investment to exploit new energy sources, many of which are in very inhospitable climes. In 2004, Russia finally ratified the Kyoto Protocol. Many considered this was a quid pro quo for EU support in helping Russia join the WTO. In terms of financial and technical assistance, more than €2.6 billion have been allocated to Russia under the Tacis programme since it started in 1991, with a view to promoting the transition to a market economy and to reinforcing democracy and the rule of law. Partly owing to bureaucratic problems on both sides, however, Tacis has had a limited impact. The European Commission Humanitarian Aid Office (ECHO) has been the most important donor active in the northern Caucasus. In addition, the EU provides financial assistance for non-proliferation and disarmament projects.

Four common spaces

Partly in recognition of the limitations of the PCA, and in the context of the EU–Russia strategic partnership, both sides agreed at the St Petersburg summit of May 2003 to start working on four 'common spaces'. It was decided to create a common economic space; a common space of freedom, security and justice; a space of co-operation in the field of external security; as well as a space of research and education, including cultural aspects. As far as the common economic space is concerned, the priority issues were identified as the energy dialogue, transport, the environment, and steps to improve the investment climate and pursue regulatory convergence. Preparations for Russia to join the WTO were also emphasised. Regarding the common space of freedom, security and justice, the priorities were to be border management and migration issues. The EU was unable to agree to Russian demands for visa-free travel but did agree to set up a working party to examine the issues, including the better use of existing flexibilities under the Schengen Agreement that provides for a passport-free area. Both sides also stressed the importance of working together in crisis management, and welcomed practical co-operation in ESDP operations.

Chechnya

The most sensitive issue, however, remains the situation in Chechnya. The EU, while condemning terrorism in all its forms, has called for a peaceful and durable solution to the current conflict, based on the territorial integrity of Russia, the creation of representative institutions and respect for human rights. The assassination of Chechen President Kadyrov in a terrorist attack on 9 May 2004, bombings in Moscow, two planes blown up and the terrible school siege in Beslan have demonstrated the ongoing seriousness of the situation. Russia was stung by Dutch Foreign Minister Bot's suggestion after the tragedy in Beslan that the EU might be able to help if the full facts were known. Moscow's response was that this was an 'internal affair' despite the fact that it had loudly proclaimed that the attack was carried out by 'international terrorists'. The EU has called on Russia to co-operate with the UN, the Council of Europe and the OSCE to investigate all claims of human rights abuse and to prosecute those found responsible. The EU, as the largest donor of emergency aid, remains concerned about the humanitarian situation, at the low level of access to Chechnya for aid providers, at the treatment of internally displaced persons and at the modest pace of reconstruction in the region.

The future bilateral agenda will likely continue to be clouded by Chechnya and the authoritarian trends in Russia. At the same time, the EU is aware that Russia is a vital partner in terms of energy supply (mainly natural gas) and in resolving some sensitive international situations, ranging from the Middle East to Belarus and the southern Caucasus. On the practical front, the focus is likely to be on the establishment of the four common spaces. An improved dispute-settlement procedure for the PCA was adopted in April 2004. There are also ongoing negotiations on trade in nuclear materials, fisheries, satellite navigation (Galileo), veterinary co-operation and a readmission agreement. Russia has shown that it takes the EU seriously when it is confronted with a united voice. For example, it basically had to accept EU proposals for transit between the Russian mainland and Kaliningrad. The EU will need to remain firm and united in future if it is to develop its strategic partnership with Russia according to its own democratic principles and values.

Although some progress has been made in EU–Russia relations, there remains considerable mutual distrust, partly through ignorance of the other side's motives. What is needed is a frank dialogue covering all sensitive issues including values, multilateralism and minority rights. Moldova and Belarus should be on the agenda as well as the situation in the Caucasus. Russia is still driven by a great-power mentality that tends to view developments as a zero-sum game. It will be important to engage with the coming generation of Russian leaders to explain the importance of 'soft power' in international relations. The EU needs to do more to attract Russian students and facilitate travel for genuine business and tourist travellers. For its part, Moscow should accept the EU as a serious negotiating partner and not try to undermine it by seeking special deals with member states or bypassing PCA structures. Both sides are condemned to live with each other and will increasingly rub up against each other as a result of enlargement. But a genuine strategic partnership can only be developed if there is acceptance of common values. Russia will inevitably be confronted with its internal problems for many years. It has come to recognise the growing influence of the EU in certain areas but it does not see any need to make major concessions to achieve a rather nebulous 'strategic partnership' with the EU. The same holds true for Brussels. It knows that it is heavily dependent on Russian energy but it also recognises that the energy card is not a strong one – after all, Russia has to sell its oil and gas to live. Overall, therefore, there is no major underpinning of the relationship.

UKRAINE

The EU has found it difficult to establish a normal relationship with Ukraine, partly because of the lack of reform in that country and partly because it does not want to encourage Ukrainian ambitions of joining the EU. When President Kuchma was in power there was considerable EU reticence to go beyond the PCA that Ukraine enjoyed, like other ex-Soviet republics. In December 2004 there was a political earthquake in Ukraine following the 'Orange Revolution' when the pro-Western leader Viktor Yushchenko came to power, largely as a result of grassroots pressure for reform. The EU, in the guise of Solana plus the Presidents of Poland and Latvia, played an important mediation role in ensuring the peaceful outcome of the Orange Revolution. But the new government in Kiev also failed to make much headway with political and economic reforms, and this led to further EU doubts about Ukraine's ability to change as rapidly as it had planned. In March 2006, Yushchenko's party came third in national elections, forcing it into a coalition with the party led by Julia Timoshenko, his former prime minister whom he had dismissed in 2005. She in turn resigned after less than a year in office and was replaced by Viktor Yanukovych. Ukraine joined the ENP but continued to insist on a signal from the EU that it wanted to see Ukraine as an eventual member state.

THE SOUTHERN CAUCASUS

The EU's interest in the three countries in the Caucasus has been fragmentary. It hopes to play a constructive role in the 'frozen conflicts' in the region but is aware of its limitations. These conflicts include Nagorno-Karabakh, South

Ossetia and Abkhazia. In July 2003 the EU appointed a special representative to the southern Caucasus with a wide-ranging mandate to assist the process of reconciliation, the promotion of democracy and human rights, and regional co-operation. A final point was to enhance EU effectiveness and visibility in the region. Of the three countries in the region Azerbaijan is the EU's largest trading partner, although this primarily relates to cotton, oil and gas, and occupies a strategic location between the EU and Central Asia. A high-level dialogue on energy and transport in the Black Sea and Caspian Sea was launched at the Commission's initiative with the November 2004 Baku Ministerials, aimed at the development of a regional energy and transport market and its progressive integration with the EU market.

Box 7.1: The frozen conflicts

In 1992 the mainly Russian- and Ukrainian-speaking region of **Transnistria** sought to secede from Romanian-speaking Moldova. The Moldovan government in Chisinau was unable to enforce its sovereignty over the whole country as thousands of Russian troops remained in Transnistria. The OSCE, together with Russia and Ukraine, has been trying to broker a political settlement. In early 2006 the EU sent a border mission to help monitor and train customs officials on the Moldova–Ukraine shared border.

Abkhazia broke away from the Republic of Georgia when the Soviet Union disintegrated in 1991–2. The Georgian government in Tbilisi used force in an attempt to regain control over the region but was defeated in 1993 by Abkhaz forces, backed by Russian units. Subsequently, thousands of ethnic Georgians were expelled from the region. An uneasy truce has been in place since 1994, policed by Russian peace-keepers.

There was a similar situation in **South Ossetia**, which did not support Georgia's quest for independence in 1991. Attempts by the government in Tbilisi to regain control failed, and a fragile truce is maintained by Russian, Georgian and South Ossetian peace-keepers.

Conflicts between ethnic Armenians and Azerbaijanis broke out in the late 1980s, with the most extensive fighting taking place in **Nagorno-Karabakh**, a region that was part of Soviet Azerbaijan but whose population is largely Armenian. A 1994 ceasefire established de-facto Armenian control over the region. OSCE talks to resolve the problem have not met with success. Both Azerbaijan and Turkey keep their borders with Armenia closed.

THE EUROPEAN ECONOMIC AREA (EEA)

Many critics of the ENP have suggested that the EEA might be a more suitable alternative. But this would not be an option as the EEA agreement is tailored to the requirements of advanced industrial neighbours of the EU. The EEA has its origins in the European Free Trade Area (EFTA) that was created in 1960 by seven countries then less keen to go down the integrationist path pioneered by the original six founding members of the EU. Relations between the EU and EFTA were cordial, with the focus being on the gradual establishment of a free trade area for industrial products. Following the announcement that the EU intended to establish an Internal Market by 1992, Jacques Delors, then President of the European Commission, proposed a new and more structured form of partnership, which was to become the EEA Agreement. The EFTA states at that time – Austria, Finland, Iceland, Liechtenstein, Norway, Sweden and Switzerland – welcomed the idea, and formal negotiations with the EU (then the European Community) began in June 1990. The Agreement for a European Economic Area was signed on 2 May 1992 in Oporto and came into force on 1 January 1994. The objective of the EEA Agreement, as laid down in Article 1, is 'to promote a continuous and balanced strengthening of trade and economic relations between the Contracting Parties . . . with the view to creating a homogenous European Economic Area'.

Switzerland voted against EEA membership in December 1992, and has since maintained and developed its relationship with the EU through bilateral agreements. Following the accession of Finland, Austria and Sweden to the EU in 1995, the EEA was composed of just three countries – Norway, Iceland and Liechtenstein – that nevertheless wished to maintain the arrangements in order to participate in the Internal Market, while not assuming the full responsibilities of EU membership. All new Community legislation in areas covered by the EEA is integrated into the Agreement through an EEA Joint Committee decision and subsequently becomes part of the national legislation of the EEA states. The Agreement gives them the right to be consulted by the Commission during the formulation of Community legislation, but not the right to a voice in decision-making, which is reserved exclusively for member states. Through the double impact of the participation in the decision-shaping and the high level of integration of Community *acquis* into their national legislation, the EEA states are, of all the countries associated with the Union, technically the most closely linked to the EU. Politically, however, the fact that EU membership is not on the current agenda for any of the EEA countries distinguishes them from other close neighbours, including ENP partners, who have EU membership as a declared aim.

The EEA Agreement is concerned principally with the four fundamental freedoms of the Internal Market, i.e. freedom of movement of goods (excluding agriculture and fisheries, which are included in the Agreement only to a very limited extent), persons, services and capital. Horizontal provisions relevant to these four freedoms in the areas of social policy, consumer protection, environment, company law and statistics complete the areas that the EEA states take over Community legislation. As one of the primary obligations under the Agreement is to ensure equal conditions of competition, the substantive competition rules of the Agreement correspond to the Community *acquis* in this area. This covers the rules concerning cartels, abuse of dominant positions, merger control, state monopolies and state aid. In addition to the obligation to accept the Community *acquis* in the fields of the four freedoms, the Agreement contains provisions to allow co-operation between the Community and the EEA states in a range of Community activities: research and technological development, information services, the environment, education, social policy, consumer protection, small and medium-sized enterprises, tourism, the audio-visual sector and civil protection. Where the EEA states are admitted to participate in these programmes, they contribute to the budgets of the programmes in question and participate in the committees that manage them, but with no right to vote. The EEA states also make a financial contribution towards the reduction of economic and social disparities in the EU.

The EEA Agreement is made up of 129 articles as well as twenty-two annexes and forty-nine protocols. The annexes refer to the *acquis communautaire* applicable in the EEA. The protocols include provisions on specific areas such as rules on the origin of goods, transition periods for the EEA states in certain fields, and simplified customs procedures. The EEA Agreement does not cover the following EU policy areas: Common Agriculture and Fisheries Policies (although the Agreement contains provisions on various aspects of trade in agricultural and fish products); a Customs Union; a Common Trade Policy; a Common Foreign and Security Policy; Justice and Home Affairs (even though Iceland and Norway are part of the Schengen network) and the Monetary Union (EMU). The EEA states have not transferred any legislative competences to the EEA institutions, and all decisions on the EEA side are therefore taken by unanimity.

The EEA Agreement is implemented through a set of special institutional arrangements. The EEA Joint Committee is responsible for the ongoing management of the EEA Agreement. It is a forum in which views are exchanged and decisions are taken by consensus to incorporate Community legislation in the EEA Agreement. The Joint Committee is made up of ambassadors to the EU from the EEA states, representatives of the European Commission and EU member states. The Joint Committee may set up subcommittees, which prepare the decisions of the Joint Committee and where discussion of different aspects of the Joint Committee's work can take place. There are currently five such subcommittees. The EEA Council, composed of the foreign ministers of the EU and EEA states, provides political impetus for the development of the Agreement and guidelines for the Joint Committee. It meets twice a year, usually briefly and on the margins of an EU Foreign Affairs Council, and it is chaired for six months on a rotating basis. The EEA Joint Parliamentary Committee comprises members of the national parliaments of the EEA states and Members of the European Parliament (MEPs). The Committee is supposed to contribute, through dialogue and debate, to a better understanding between the Community and the EEA states of the fields covered by the Agreement.

The EEA is the most advanced arrangement that the EU has with any group of countries and reflects both their proximity to and long-standing ties with the EU, and also the high levels of their political and economic development. Globally, the EEA machinery runs smoothly after ten years of operation. The updating of the Agreement through the incorporation of new relevant Community legislation has become a day-to-day business, and some 4,000 EU legal acts are applicable across the EEA. The basic deal of the EEA is that the three states have access to the EU's Internal Market, pay substantial amounts for the privilege and yet have no real say in the legislation that they must accept in this area. It is true that EEA states can request consultations on matters of concern and they can also negotiate adaptations to Community legislation when this is called for by special circumstances and agreed on by both sides; but the reality is that the prevailing EU attitude is 'take it or leave it'. Compromises painfully negotiated among twenty-five EU member states are not going to be unravelled at the EEA stage. The EEA states, of course, do have the opportunity to influence the shaping of EEA-relevant legislation, i.e. proposals at the preparatory or pre-pipeline stage by the EU. This opportunity is enshrined in the EEA Agreement as a right for representatives of the EEA states to participate in expert groups of the European Commission, and to submit EEA comments on upcoming legislation. While the EEA states use these opportunities to shape legislation actively, they have little influence on the final decision on the legislation on the EU side. They can neither sit nor vote in the European Parliament or the European Council of Ministers (co-legislators on the EU side for most EEA-relevant legislation) and hence have to incorporate into the EEA Agreement what has ultimately been decided, if not necessarily shaped, by others.

CONCLUSION

The EU devotes more time, energy and resources to its immediate neighbourhood than to any other part of the world. Its various contractual arrangements with its neighbours reflect the level of political and economic development in each country. The more advanced the neighbour (e.g. Norway), the closer the arrangement. The EU has never gone out to solicit countries to join the EU but rather adopted criteria for membership. The carrot of membership has been very successful in promoting the reform process in those countries eligible for membership. Where membership is not on offer the Union has considerably less leverage. The ENP was launched to deal with the challenges resulting from enlargement. The eastern neighbours may be eligible for EU membership at some date in the future, but the southern neighbours do not have this option. It is an open question whether the neighbours will really make something of the Action Plans on offer. EU–Russia relations will remain difficult for some time to come. The roadmaps for the four common spaces are rather vague and contain neither deadlines nor plans for specific projects. But with more than 50 per cent of Russia's trade going to the EU and the number of Russians visiting the EU growing at 20 per cent a year the relationship is bound to become closer. Although the EU has little appetite for further enlargements, the EU will have little alternative but to become even more active with its neighbours in future. The ENP will be the main vehicle for these relationships.

KEY QUESTIONS

Why did the EU launch the ENP?

How would you assess the first ten years of the Barcelona Process?

What are the main EU interests in Russia? What does Russia want from the EU?

How have the new member states tried to influence EU policy towards Russia?

Could the EEA be a model for other countries in the EU's neighbourhood?

The ENP is doomed to failure, as it does not hold out the prospect of EU membership. Discuss.

Should the EU attempt to define the final borders of the Union? If so where should they be?

FURTHER READING

The wider Europe debate is covered in Dannreuther (2004) and the foreign policy aspects in Zielonka (2002). Given the newness of the ENP, there are more articles than books available. Some to consider are:

Aliboni, R. (2005) 'The geopolitical implications of the European neighbourhood', *European Foreign Affairs Review*, vol. 10, no. 1.

Balfour, R. et al. (2005) 'The challenges of the European Neighbourhood Policy', *The International Spectator*, vol. 40, no. 1.

Cameron, F. (2006) *The ENP as a Conflict Prevention Tool*, EPC issue paper no. 47.

Emerson, M. et al. (2005) *The Reluctant Debutante: The European Union as Promoter of Democracy in Its Neighbourhood*, Brussels: Centre for European Policy Studies.

Lynch, D. (2004) *The Russia–EU Partnership and the Shared Neighbourhood*, EU Institute for Security Studies, July. See http://www.isseu.org/new/analysis/analy090.html.

Tocci, N. (2005) 'The challenges of the European Neighbourhood Policy – Does the ENP respond to the EU's post-enlargement challenges?', *The International Spectator*, vol. 40, no. 1.

8   The Balkans and Turkey

SUMMARY

The next enlargement of the EU could well include the countries of the western Balkans and Turkey. Given the Union's internal problems and the prevalence of 'enlargement fatigue', no one can predict when the next enlargement will take place. The accession of Bulgaria and Romania in 2007 is likely to increase EU attention on the Balkans, which has been a very difficult policy area for the EU. In the early 1990s the EU failed to deal effectively with the break-up of the former Yugoslavia. It had to rely on the US intervening twice to stop Serbian aggression. The EU's early failures and the Kosovo war spurred the EU into a more coherent and strategic policy towards the Balkans. Gradually the EU developed a roadmap for membership agreed in Thessaloniki in 2003. The EU played an important role in the downfall of Milošević and brokered agreements in Bosnia, Kosovo and Macedonia. The Balkans remains important as instability there, whether political, economic or social, affects the stability of member states. Turkey is a major neighbour of the EU, and its accession would be of a very different order of magnitude from any Balkan country. It is also predominantly Muslim, and this causes hesitation in some European circles.

INTRODUCTION

The Balkans has been a major testing-ground of the EU's developing international role and in particular of the CFSP and the ESDP. Few could have imagined, when the CFSP was agreed in 1991, that it would have such a baptism of fire. In the summer of 1999, south-eastern Europe emerged from yet another violent conflict in the region. NATO forces had just ended a bombing campaign against the former Yugoslavia and had taken control of Kosovo. Yugoslavia was still under international sanctions, with detrimental effects on the whole region, especially from organised crime. Albania and Macedonia were recovering from the refugee influx due to the Kosovo crisis, which aggravated the situation in Macedonia to a degree that led to ethnic violence in the summer of 2001. While fighting had ceased in Bosnia and Croatia with the Dayton agreement in 1995, the situation resembled more an uneasy truce than good-neighbourly relations. Bulgaria and Romania, while on the path towards EU accession, suffered severely from the blocked trade routes through neighbouring Yugoslavia, especially along the river Danube.

By 2006 the situation in south-eastern Europe was very different. All the countries of the region have a clear European perspective. Bulgaria and Romania joined the European Union in 2007. Accession negotiations started with Turkey and Croatia in 2005. Macedonia's application for membership was given a mixed appreciation by the European Commission in October 2005. It made clear that Macedonia would have to undertake further significant reforms before accession negotiations could begin but proposed that Macedonia be granted candidate status. This position was then endorsed by the European Council in December that year. The other countries are progressing under the framework of Stabilisation and Association Agreements (SAAs). The catalyst for these positive developments has been the EU. The decision by President Barroso in 2004 to make the new European Commissioner for Enlargement, Olli Rehn, responsible for all the western Balkan countries in addition to Romania, Bulgaria and Turkey was not just a bureaucratic measure, but also a political message that the future of the region lies within the EU. Now the EU is widely recognised as the most important actor in the region. It has poured huge sums of money into reconstruction, engaged in conflict prevention and crisis management, promoted regime change throughout South-East Europe, and agreed a roadmap that should lead to eventual EU membership.

A TOUGH LEARNING EXPERIENCE

With the establishment of the CFSP in 1991 there were high hopes that 'the hour of Europe' had arrived. This was the unfortunate phrase used by Luxembourg's foreign minister, Jacques Poos, who was chairing the Presidency, in 1991. Sadly it took several more years of bitter experience, including the Kosovo conflict, before the EU began to develop the instruments and the political will to make an impact in the Balkans. The Balkans, however, will remain a key benchmark for assessing the EU's external performance. In the early 1990s the Europeans were sharply divided in their approach to the Yugoslav crisis, particularly on the issue of the recognition of the independence of Slovenia and Croatia. They lacked the cohesion, determination and instruments to bring the crisis under control. The US had been quite reluctant to become engaged as no important US security interests were at stake. Secretary of State James Baker famously remarked: 'We do not have a dog in this fight.' However, as the bloodshed worsened, and in the absence of a credible European effort, the US became more involved. In 1995 the US bombed Serbia into acceptance of a peace deal at Dayton, Ohio. During the following years the overall division of roles between Europe and the US did not change significantly. Europe still contributed the lion's share of soldiers, humanitarian assistance and international expertise, but its political influence was not commensurate. Four years later the EU again failed to play a determining role in the Kosovo conflict. The EU's cohesion had improved, but it lacked the military capabilities to end the conflict and had to watch as NATO (read America) bombed Serbia into submission. This second failure was to have a powerful catalytic effect in pushing Europe to develop its own military capabilities. After Kosovo, the EU's Balkans policy became more coherent and proactive, and the US–European relationship in the Balkans shifted to the point where the US has largely disengaged from the region and the EU has moved the Balkans from crisis management towards the enlargement process.

A number of factors were responsible for this development. First, the victory of democratic forces in Croatia and then in Serbia made it possible for the EU to move towards the development of a comprehensive policy towards the region. Second, all EU member states had learned lessons from the experiences of the early 1990s. In the course of the intense work on Balkan issues throughout the 1990s the EU had developed a common analysis and a shared interest in the stabilisation of the region. There was now sufficient agreement on the objectives to develop a more ambitious policy. Third, the CFSP had been greatly strengthened with the appointment of Javier Solana as the EU's High Representative in 1999. He and Chris Patten, the European Commissioner for External Relations, formed a good team and devoted considerable efforts to the region. The EU also began to develop its own military commitments enshrined in the Helsinki Headline Goals: a target of deploying 60,000 troops in the field for eighteen months for crisis-management purposes. Even as these forces were being developed, the EU played a leading role in managing the ethnic crisis in Macedonia and in mediating in the constitutional dispute between Serbia and Montenegro. Over a period of several years three of the EU's seven Special Representatives dealt with Balkan issues. The EU had also begun to develop a civilian and military operational capacity that in the first instance was deployed in the Balkans. In spring 2003 the EU took over the police operation in Bosnia from the UN. In the summer of the same year it took over from NATO in Macedonia, which in turn was followed by an EU police mission in December 2003. A year later, an EU force of some 7,000 replaced the NATO SFOR mission in Bosnia. While an outright military confrontation is almost inconceivable today, the challenges in the area of military security are issues of downsizing over-expanded armies without causing social disruption, converting the military-industry complex to civilian use, and building confidence between armies that in some cases fought each other only a few years ago. On the other hand, fighting organised crime still remains a formidable challenge to most of the countries, with direct implications for the rest of Europe as well. Finally, while generally much poorer and further handicapped by the recent conflicts, the Balkan states shared many features with their eastern and northern neighbours. Throughout the 1990s the EU had accumulated vast know-how in promoting the integration of the central and eastern European countries into European structures. It was logical that this experience would strongly influence its developing approach to the Balkans.

A NEW APPROACH

In 2000 the EU decided that the western Balkans needed a comprehensive new policy approach. It would continue to deploy their foreign-policy and crisis-management instruments in order to promote the stabilisation of the region, but it would also hold out the promise of association, of integrating the western Balkan countries gradually into European structures. The policy provided for the conclusion of comprehensive treaties with each of the countries, and it deployed important policy instruments, in particular in the areas of trade and assistance. Most important, the Stabilisation and Association Process (SAP) gave the countries the perspective of future membership of the EU. The SAA process was also linked to conditions including co-operation with the International Criminal Tribunal for Yugoslavia (ICTY), facilitating the return of refugees and promoting regional co-operation. At first this commitment was expressed rather tentatively, but it gained greater clarity in the course of the following years. A decisive meeting was the EU–Balkans Thessaloniki summit in June 2003, which clearly stated that the future of the Balkans would be in the EU and that progress in this direction would depend on the fulfilment of the same conditions and requirements that applied to other candidates. This was a reference to the 'Copenhagen criteria' setting down benchmarks for EU candidates relating to democracy, market economy and administrative capability. Moreover, Thessaloniki also decided to put several instruments of the enlargement process (partnerships, opening of Community programmes, administrative twinning, etc.) at the disposal of the western Balkan countries, thus further reducing the gap between the SAP and the pre-accession process. The perspective of EU membership linked to the step-by-step implementation of the SAP has become the major source of the EU's influence in the region. In its practical application the SAP involves a series of steps, ranging from the establishment of taskforces, feasibility studies on an SAA, the beginning, conclusion and finally the ratification of the Agreement. This in turn opens the way to application for membership, launching the candidate country on a similar process ultimately aimed at accession to the EU. At each of the steps of the SAP, progress is made dependent on the fulfilment of conditions formulated by the EU. The annual reports by the Commission introduced in 2002 are a further way regularly to assess performance. In 2004, European Partnerships were also concluded to commit the countries of the region to a set of reform priorities. The assistance offered within the framework of the Community Assistance for Reconstruction, Development and Stabilisation (CARDS) programme, much of which is now devoted to institution building, is also designed to support the same reform priorities.

While important foundations have been laid to improve the economic situation in the region, economic development is probably the biggest remaining concern. Growth rates in south-eastern Europe have risen substantially, but the rates and sustainability of economic growth are still disquieting. This is exacerbated by high unemployment and in parts severe lack of investment. Economic growth in the western Balkans rose above 5 per cent in 2004 for the fourth consecutive year, but all the countries continue to face significant structural challenges, in particular the decline of the old industries and underdeveloped agriculture. High unemployment and severe social problems continue to overshadow an essentially positive macro-economic picture. The EU has provided by far the lion's share of external finance, contributing some €6 billion to the region in the period 2000–5. With its threefold aim of stabilising the region, enhancing regional co-operation and supporting the region on its path towards European and Euro-Atlantic integration, the Stability Pact, established in 1999, has supported these positive developments in south-eastern Europe. With two prominent donor conferences in 2000 and 2002, significant support could be secured for the region, particularly for upgrading the necessary infrastructure. The focus has subsequently moved towards facilitating regional co-operation and promoting foreign direct investment (FDI). Attracting FDI is difficult on a purely national level, considering the size of the markets, but the current network of free trade agreements (FTAs), now being transformed into a regional FTA, establishes a market of 55 million consumers, clearly more attractive for investment (see www.stabilitypact.org).

The EU now has a stronger profile in the Balkans than ever before. Five years of the Stabilisation and Association Process have produced sufficient progress to validate the overall policy approach, but clearly not enough to allow complacency. During this time the western Balkans has undoubtedly become more stable, and the EU has also become an operational actor in the area of 'hard' security. Opening the perspective of EU membership to the countries of the region has had some important successes, notably in Croatia and Macedonia, but has not yet had its full mobilising impact in other parts of the region.

INSTITUTIONAL ARRANGEMENTS

In 1999 the EU proposed the Stabilisation and Association Process (SAP) for five countries of south-eastern Europe – Croatia, Macedonia, Albania, Bosnia and Herzegovina, and Serbia and Montenegro. In June 2000 the European Council stated that all the SAP countries were 'potential candidates' for EU membership. The SAP is a strategy explicitly linked to the prospect of EU accession. It is adjusted to the level of development of the individual country, allowing each to move at its own pace. In return for the prospect of accession and the assistance to achieve it, the countries of the region have to meet stringent political and economic requirements. The EU's assistance package consists of trade concessions (autonomous trade measures), economic and financial assistance (CARDS programme) and contractual relationships (Stabilisation and Association Agreements [SAAs]). The SAAs are the first comprehensive agreements between the EU and the Balkan countries. Similar to the Europe Agreements with previous candidate countries, the SAAs provide the contractual framework for relations between the EU and the countries of the western Balkans. At the Thessaloniki summit in June 2003 the European Council confirmed the European perspective for all Balkan countries. An array of new instruments was introduced to enrich the SAP, including salient aspects of the enlargement strategy.

CROATIA

On 29 October 2001, Croatia signed its SAA with the EU; it came into force on 1 February 2005. In June 2004 the European Council confirmed Croatia as a candidate country after the European Commission had issued a positive opinion on Croatia's application for EU membership. The opening of accession negotiations was scheduled for 17 March 2005, but was put off because of an assessment that Croatia was failing to co-operate fully with the ICTY. On 3 October 2005, following a statement of the ICTY chief prosecutor, Carla del Ponte, that Croatia was fully co-operating, the accession negotiations were opened. Shortly after the opening of the negotiations the Croatian general accused of war crimes, Ante Gotovina, was delivered to the ICTY in The Hague. Croatia hopes to join the EU by 2009, but observers see 2010 or 2011 as more realistic. Much will depend on overall political and economic developments in the EU.

FORMER YUGOSLAV REPUBLIC OF MACEDONIA (FYROM)

Macedonia signed its SAA with the EU on 9 April 2001; it came into force on 1 April 2004. Macedonia applied for EU membership on 22 March 2004. At its meeting in Brussels on 15–16 December 2005, the European Council granted candidate status to Macedonia after a positive report from the European Commission. However, it did not agree on a date for the opening of the negotiations. Speaking in Skopje in February 2006, President Barroso commended Macedonia's efforts in achieving stability and inter-ethnic reconciliation, but said that further reforms were necessary to meet the political and economic criteria for EU membership.

ALBANIA

On 31 January 2003 negotiations for an SAA between the EU and Albania were officially launched, but progress was very slow. The November 2005

Progress Report on Albania registered improvement in a number of areas, but called for better results in fighting organised crime and corruption, and in enhanced media freedom, further electoral reform and swifter property restitution. The Commission report noted that the Albanian economy was working according to the principles of a market economy 'only to a certain extent' and that extra efforts were required to align Albania with EU standards in several fields including free movement of capital, competition, agriculture and the environment. On 18 February 2006 the SAA with Albania was finally signed in Tirana by Commissioner Olli Rehn and Albanian Foreign Minister Besnik Mustafaj.

BOSNIA AND HERZEGOVINA

The European Commission approved on 18 November 2003 a Feasibility Study assessing the readiness of Bosnia and Herzegovina (BiH) to start negotiations for an SAA with the EU. The study concluded that negotiations should start once BiH had addressed sixteen key priorities. Following significant progress by BiH in addressing these priorities the Council authorised the start of SAA negotiations, which were formally opened in Sarajevo on 25 November 2005 during a visit by President Barroso. The Commission report of November 2005 was critical of the many obstacles impeding political and economic reform. The functioning of the central institutions was handicapped by complex structures, fragmented decision-making power and lack of resources. The country had to make serious efforts to improve its executive and legislative bodies. The report noted some progress in the economy but drew attention to the lack of market structures and the inability to transform the EU *acquis* into local laws in many key areas.

SERBIA AND MONTENEGRO

On 3 October 2005 the Council authorised the Commission to begin negotiations for an SAA with Serbia-Montenegro, and negotiations were formally opened on 10 October 2005. In line with the 'twin-track' approach, negotiations will be held with the State Union or the Republics in their respective fields of competence. In May 2006 a small majority voted in a referendum for an independent Montenegro. Both the EU and Serbia reluctantly accepted the result, and negotiations began to prepare Montenegro's secession from the union with Serbia. During his tour of the region in February 2006, Barroso reminded Belgrade of its duty to co-operate fully with the ICTY and deliver the suspected war criminals Radko Mladic and Radovan Karadzic to The Hague. The Commission report noted that there was still not full respect for the constitution in Serbia and insufficient democratic control of the armed forces. The Commission also stated that it expected Belgrade to adopt a constructive approach towards Kosovo. In its assessment of the economy, the Commission drew a mixed picture. It was more critical of the failure to achieve progress in visas (with Montenegro), asylum, migration and border controls.

OPEN QUESTIONS

There are also several open questions in south-eastern Europe that need to be addressed before the region can reasonably become a part of the EU. This applies not only to Kosovo but also to Montenegro. It is also impossible to envisage Bosnia joining the Union while still under the authority of an EU/UN High Representative. Of course, the question of when all of south-eastern Europe will be a part of the EU is still very unclear and will probably remain so for several years. The EU has come a long way in outlining a roadmap for the region, but the timeline is of course dependent on a multitude of factors including the ability of countries of the region to continue with their reforms and the willingness of the EU to continue with the enlargement process. The two no votes in France and the Netherlands were regarded as indications of enlargement fatigue among European citizens. A further complication is the heated discussion on Turkey's accession to the EU. With the accession of Romania and Bulgaria in 2007 the western Balkans have become an island within the European Union. The EU therefore has a clear interest in ensuring that these outstanding problems are addressed and that south-eastern Europe continues on its current path of stabilisation. In this respect, the clear perspective of European integration is likely to continue to be the key reform incentive in the region. Nevertheless, the necessary steps can only be taken by the governments in south-eastern Europe themselves. The timetable for accession is therefore largely in their own hands.

It is something of a paradox that, whereas the overall risk of conflict in the western Balkans has greatly diminished, the EU's involvement in hard security issues in the region is expanding rapidly. The paradox is, however, easily explained by the fact that the development of the ESDP really began only at the end of the Balkan wars, and EU military and police operations only became possible at the end of 2002. In view of the important European security interests at stake in the Balkans, it was the logical theatre in which to undertake the first ESDP operations. While the EU may be a latecomer as an operational actor in security policy in the Balkans, there remains much to do. The era of large-scale conflict might be over but, in parts of the region, the potential for inter-ethnic tensions and confrontation persists.

At the end of 2006 the situation in Bosnia can certainly be considered as essentially stable. In terms of consolidating the state structures and the return of refugees, progress over the past years has been remarkable. However, the reform efforts are not yet self-sustaining, and a significant security presence is still necessary to maintain the commitment to the Dayton agreement. In Kosovo, the tragic events of March 2004, which caused nineteen deaths, the destruction of 730 homes and twenty-nine religious buildings, as well as the displacement of over 4,000 people, illustrated clearly that this question remains the greatest challenge to security in the Balkans. Finding an agreement acceptable to both Pristina and Belgrade will be extremely difficult. The third post-conflict area where the EU remains strongly engaged, Macedonia, has developed encouragingly over the past years. There has been important progress in implementing the Ohrid framework agreement, which ended a brief period of ethnic conflict, and the ethnically mixed government appears committed to multi-ethnicity and to progress towards EU membership. The residual risks in Macedonia are mostly related to the danger of a spill-over of a renewed crisis in Kosovo. In December 2005, Macedonia was granted candidate status by the EU, although no date was fixed for the opening of accession negotiations. There was also no progress on the name issue – Greece refuses to recognise the name Macedonia because its northern province is also called Macedonia and it fears irredentist calls should it accept the name Macedonia for FYROM.

ORGANISED CRIME

While the EU remains deeply involved in seeking to resolve these open questions a new security threat has emerged in the region. As the risk of major conflict has receded, the focus has shifted from the military to the policing aspect. Organised crime, in particular trafficking in humans, drugs and weapons, is today the most pressing security issue, with a clear impact also on EU member states. Widespread poverty, weak state institutions and endemic corruption provide a fertile ground for criminal networks, which exploit the traditional transit role of the Balkans into western Europe. Combating organised crime and bringing war criminals to justice are therefore essential elements of the efforts to consolidate democracy in the western Balkans. The EU's approach to tackling these problems is multidimensional. It ranges from strict conditionality regarding co-operation with the ICTY in The Hague, to visa bans against individuals supporting war criminals and crime figures linked with extremist political groups, to police operations in Bosnia and Macedonia, to many CARDS programmes in the areas of rule of law and border security. This is complemented by activities of Europol and EU-sponsored activities within the Stability Pact. The multiplicity of projects and activities, which are complemented by bilateral measures by individual EU member states, cannot hide the fact that the overall record in this field is not altogether encouraging. Not only is there a distinct deficit in co-ordination among the various actors in this field, but also the resources and the manpower deployed are so far no match for the well-financed and smooth international and inter-ethnic co-operation of criminal networks.

UNEVEN PROGRESS

Overall progress in the Balkans is very uneven. By far the most advanced country is Croatia, with Albania lagging far behind. There are several explanations for the marked differences in progress. Historical factors, differences in capacity, constitutional issues and political commitment all play a role. The success of the accession process in Central Europe rested to a considerable degree on the fact that the political elite in candidate countries was largely united in its commitment to European integration. Whatever the political complexion of the government, the EU always found a partner willing to take the necessary tough decisions and to move forward on the accession agenda. This is not yet the situation in the western Balkans. The legacy of the wars and structural weaknesses make the political landscape even more volatile and unstable. While almost all political parties pay lip-service to the objective of EU membership, the European idea clearly does not as yet have the powerful uniting force that it did in Central Europe. All too often the political agenda is dominated by the nationalist past rather than by the European future, with the settling of old scores rather than the tackling of concrete challenges.

THE EU'S PROMISES

Despite the varying degrees of enthusiasm and willingness to take tough decisions, it is important that the EU should remain credible in keeping the promises set out at Thessaloniki. At the same time, the perspective of EU membership, although a powerful motor for reform, will not work without significant institutional and financial engagement. This may mean a change in the approach to funding for the region. The original idea of turning the status of 'Associate' (following the conclusion of an SAA) into an attractive longer-term option for the countries of the region has clearly not worked out as expected. Both Croatia and Macedonia submitted their applications for membership not long after their SAA came into force. The other countries of the region are likely to follow their example. An SAA is not seen as an objective in its own right, but merely as a stepping-stone towards pre-accession status. This view is perfectly understandable, since EU accession remains the ultimate objective and every country wishes to move towards the next stage as quickly as possible. But it is also reinforced by the EU's funding policy, which made pre-accession status more attractive financially than the CARDS assistance open to SAP countries. This led to an indefensible situation in which the most developed countries enjoyed the most generous EU assistance. The Commission has moved to change this, and from 2007 there will be no difference in funding between candidates and non-candidates in the region.

Case study 8.1: Kosovo

Until 1999, Kosovo was part of the former Yugoslavia. From 1974 to 1989, Kosovo enjoyed autonomy as a province of Serbia, a status that gave it almost the same rights as Yugoslavia's six republics. The majority of Kosovo's population is Albanian, but various other minorities live in the province, the largest of which are the Serbs. The conflict between Kosovo-Albanians and Kosovo-Serbs has a long history. The 1990s saw the break-up of Yugoslavia, formerly held together by communist rule, into its constituent republics. The Dayton Peace Agreement of 1995 marked the end of the war in Bosnia-Herzegovina, which had lasted from 1992 to 1995. The internationally negotiated agreement settled the relationship between the Republic of Bosnia and Herzegovina, the Republic of Croatia, and the Federal Republic of Yugoslavia (consisting of Serbia and Montenegro). Kosovo continued to be part of this rump state. The failure of the Dayton talks to address the already pressing tensions in Kosovo later turned out to be a crucial mistake.

When Milošević reached the top of the Serbian Communist Party, he substantially cut the autonomy rights of the province. He pursued an increasingly nationalist Serbian course and purged all state institutions of Kosovo-Albanians. In 1989 he lifted the autonomy status. This angered Kosovo-Albanians, who declared their separation from Serbia and established parallel institutions. They pursued their idea of an independent republic by peaceful means until the mid-1990s, when the Kosovo Liberation Army (KLA) began a guerrilla war against Serbian rule. Belgrade responded with repressive actions, also against the civilian population. The situation escalated in February and March 1998 when the conflict caused many Kosovo-Albanians to flee from the province.

The EU's efforts to put pressure on Belgrade yielded no result as it lacked the military means to back up its diplomacy. In early 1999 the Rambouillet peace conference, in which the US participated, ended in failure. On 24 March 1999 it was NATO that launched a bombing campaign to stop the attacks of Serbian forces in Kosovo. The air strikes lasted until June and finally forced Milošević to withdraw his troops. In June 1999, UNSC Resolution 1244 was adopted, turning Kosovo into a UN protectorate administered by the United Nations Interim Administration Mission in Kosovo (UNMIK). UNMIK comprises four pillars: Pillars I (Police and Justice) and II (Civil Administration) are led by the United Nations themselves, Pillar III (Democratisation and Institution Building) is administered by the Organisation for Security

continued

and Co-operation in Europe (OSCE), and Pillar IV (Reconstruction and Economic Development) is in the hands of the EU. The EU has made a substantial political, technical and economic contribution, especially through the European Agency for Reconstruction which implements Pillar IV of UNMIK, but not without some criticism.

In October 2005 the UN Special Envoy Kai Eide in his 'Comprehensive Review of the Situation in Kosovo' recommended the opening of negotiations to resolve the question of Kosovo's final status. The Security Council gave the go-ahead for them to begin, and the former Finnish President Martti Ahtisaari was nominated to lead the talks as the UN's Special Envoy. The EU also nominated the Austrian diplomat Stefan Lehne as the EU representative to the future-status process of Kosovo. The key question was whether Serbia would accept the independence of Kosovo.

In September 2004 the European Commission opened a Liaison Office in Pristina and the High Representative for CFSP appointed a Personal Representative to Kosovo in April 2004 (Torbjörn Sohlström since December 2005). In 2005 the EU announced that it could take over the rule-of-law functions from the UN by 2007. In terms of the SAA negotiations with Serbia-Montenegro, there is a special tracking mechanism for Kosovo (and for Montenegro).

TURKEY

Turkey is not just another enlargement. With a population of nearly 70 million in 2006 (and set to reach 100 million by 2035), Turkey would be the largest member state in the EU, with all the consequences for the institutions. It would also be the first predominantly Islamic state to be a member (assuming it joined before Albania or Bosnia) – an issue that frightens some people and enthuses others as it would disprove assertions that the EU was a 'Christian club'. Millions of people in the Middle East, North Africa and the Balkans are watching closely the progress of Turkey towards accession. More than forty years ago the EU agreed that Turkey was eligible for membership. Only in the last few years, with the determination of the Erdogan government to push through long-overdue reforms, has this become a realistic prospect. Regrettably, as Turkey has shown its determination to meet the Copenhagen criteria, there have been strident voices in the EU opposing Turkey's membership on the spurious grounds that Turkey does not share European values. This is code for saying that a predominantly Muslim country has no place in the EU. To put forward such arguments at a time when the West faces huge challenges in its relations with the Islamic world is incredibly short-sighted. A democratic, prosperous Turkey anchored in a predominantly Christian EU would be a tremendous asset for reformers throughout the Muslim world.

Turkey is an important regional power with interests in the Mediterranean, the Middle East, the Caucasus, Central Asia and the Balkans. All these areas are characterised by instability and pose potential security problems for the EU. Although there may be some differences, overall the EU and Turkey have similar interests in seeking to promote peace, prosperity and stability in these regions. Turkey has a number of outstanding problems with its neighbours, including Greece (the Aegean, Cyprus), Syria (the border, water) and Armenia (history). It has the largest armed forces (790,000) and spends proportionately more on defence (4.8 per cent of GDP) than any other European member of NATO. It thus has an important capacity to support ESDP operations, something that it is already doing as a candidate country. Turkey is regarded as a key ally of the US, but the run up to the US-led invasion of Iraq revealed that Turkey was willing to go against the wishes of Washington when its own interests were at stake. It has generally been supportive of the EU developing its own defence capability and structures while underlining the continuing importance of the Atlantic alliance. It hosted the 2004 NATO summit in Istanbul. The future of Turkish foreign policy will be influenced by a number of factors, both external and internal. The external factors include terrorism, developments in the Middle East, and the future of US and EU foreign policy. The internal factors include political stability, the willingness of the armed forces to remain under civilian control and resolution of the Kurdish issue.

Turkey is situated in a volatile region characterised by numerous conflicts. Turkey's accession would mean that the EU's new neighbours would include Iraq, Iran and Syria (plus Armenia, Azerbaijan and Georgia). The first Turkish priority is territorial integrity – hence Turkey's preoccupation with the Kurdish issue. There are some 13 million Kurds in Turkey plus a large diaspora throughout Europe. Turkey will be vigilant regarding future developments in Iraq given the large degree of autonomy enjoyed by the Kurds in northern Iraq. There are also significant Kurdish minorities in Iran (*c*. 6 million) and Syria (*c*. 1 million). Turkey should have a shared interest with the EU in helping to rebuild Iraq and ensure that it develops some political and economic stability. Like most member states, Turkey is suspicious of Iran's nuclear ambitions and of the political control of the clerics. But there are strong economic ties, especially in the energy sector. Turkish relations with Syria have improved in recent years as both sides have sought compromises on minority and water-management issues. There has been much speculation about Turkey's role as a model for other Muslim countries in the wider Middle East and Turkey's potential contribution to a resolution of the Arab–Israeli dispute. Turkey does not perceive itself as a role model and has shown no inclination to export its values, including secular democracy, to other countries. Similarly Turkey, which enjoys close relations with Israel, has been reluctant to be drawn into the Middle East peace process. If there were a settlement at some future date, and the EU was invited to play a role in economic assistance and/or peace-keeping, Turkey would most likely be willing to play a full role.

Turning to the southern Caucasus, Turkey has a troubled relationship with Armenia as a result of continuing disputes over the alleged genocide of 1915. There are no major problems with Georgia and Azerbaijan. Turkish economic influence has been growing in the Caucasus and in Central Asia, which could be useful for enhancing EU interests. There are also strong energy links, with a new pipeline bringing oil from the Caspian Sea to the Turkish coast. During the past decade, Turkey has played a constructive role in the Balkans, often working with the EU in peace-keeping missions and in promoting investment. The significant Muslim communities in the Balkans (Albania, Kosovo, Macedonia, Bosnia) would welcome a decision to open accession negotiations with Turkey. There may be a friendly race between Turkey and other Balkan countries to see who joins the EU first. Turkish–Russian relations have traditionally been cool, if not hostile, each fearing the ambitions of the other in the Caucasus and Central Asia. A strong increase in trade, however, has helped to improve relations between Moscow and Ankara. Both are members of the Black Sea Economic Co-operation (BSEC). Although it has few achievements to its name, the BSEC could receive a boost from Turkish membership of the EU (along with Romania and Bulgaria). Ukraine would likely increase its efforts to become a candidate country following a decision to open accession negotiations with Turkey.

The regular political consultations between the EU and Turkey over the past decade have revealed few differences. Turkey has played a prominent role alongside EU forces in peace-keeping operations in the Balkans and in Afghanistan. Ankara has ratified all major international agreements on arms control, proliferation and the UN conventions on terrorism. Its export-control policy is regarded as satisfactory. During the Convention on the Future of Europe, Turkey was broadly supportive of proposals to strengthen the CFSP/ESDP. It nevertheless favoured a reference to the NATO obligations of certain member states in the final text. Turkey has a good record in aligning itself with EU declarations, common positions and joint actions, although there have been some differences over human rights and Middle East issues. Turkish accession could provide a significant boost to economic and trade links between the EU and Turkey's neighbours. Transport links should be improved in the Balkans and to the Caucasus and Central Asia, thus facilitating trade and increasing Turkey's importance as a hub. Many of Turkey's neighbours have significant energy reserves, and Turkish accession could help secure access to these resources, possibly aided by the construction of new pipelines. Turkey will also play an important role in the EU's fight against terrorism and illegal immigration. At some stage it will likely seek to join Schengen. At the same time construction of new dams in south-east Turkey is causing problems for Syria and Iraq. If not properly managed, these could become EU problems as well.

Turkey's membership of the EU should not in itself pose any major new problems for the EU's external relations. But the Union will inevitably be drawn closer to several regions of continuing political and economic instability. Turkish membership could, however, be an asset for the EU in seeking to promote its interests in these regions. Whether the EU emerges as a global actor will depend more on the political will of all member states and the readiness to make maximum use of the new treaty provisions than on the addition of any one new state, even one as large and important as Turkey. Turkey is the seventeenth-largest economy in the world and has enjoyed high growth rates in the period 2000–5. If it were to continue with these growth rates, by 2014, the target date for accession, it would not be too far from the EU average in terms of GDP per head. But Turkey has a long road to travel and will have to maintain the pace of reforms introduced by the Erdogan government in 2003. It continues to infuriate even its best friends in Europe by regular lapses in human rights, such as the attempted prosecution of the leading author Panuk for writing about the massacre of Armenians by the Turks in 1915, still a taboo subject in Turkey. Another very sensitive subject is Cyprus. According to the Greeks, Turkey invaded Cyprus in 1974 and engaged in ethnic cleansing. According to the Turks, they moved forces to Cyprus to protect Turkish Cypriots who were in danger of being killed by Greek Cypriots after a military coup.

CYPRUS

The unresolved problem of Cyprus may be viewed as one of the biggest failures of EU policy over many years. In 1961, Cyprus became independent from the colonial power, the UK, which nevertheless insisted on maintaining two sovereign military bases on the island. The island had two principal ethnic communities, roughly 75 per cent Greek Cypriots and 25 per cent Turkish Cypriots. In 1974, after a period of internal unrest and fears of a plot to unite Cyprus with Greece, Turkey invaded the island in an effort to 'protect' Turkish Cypriots allegedly under threat from the Greek Cypriots. The international community condemned the Turkish move; and no state, apart from Turkey, recognised the self-proclaimed Turkish Republic of Northern Cyprus (TRNC). The government in Nicosia was regarded as the only legitimate authority, even though it was not in control of the northern part of the island. Cyprus remains divided today, despite innumerable attempts to find a solution.

In 1995, Cyprus applied to join the EU and was given a qualified green light by the European Commission. The EU considered that Cyprus should not be denied membership because of the intransigence of the TRNC leader, Mr Denktash. It was not thought that the Greek Cypriots would oppose any reasonable proposal to reunite the island. Cyprus was thus allowed to proceed through all stages of the accession negotiations without any commitment not to oppose a UN-brokered deal. In 2004, after months of difficult negotiations, and after the departure of Mr Denktash from the political scene, the UN Secretary General, Kofi Annan, put his proposals to both sides. Essentially he proposed a package deal whereby there would be a confederal political structure, an exchange of territory, a settlement of property issues, and Turkey would also withdraw its troops from the island. In April 2004, in separate referendums, the north voted 65 per cent in favour of the Annan plan, but it was rejected by 76 per cent of the Greek Cypriots. The EU had campaigned hard for a yes vote and was left looking helpless. EU Commissioner Verheugen said he felt betrayed by the negative vote in the south. But, despite the no vote, Cyprus acceded to the EU on 1 May 2004. There was no attempt to put Cypriot membership on hold until the island was reunited – the long-term goal of the Union. After May 2004 the EU promised the north improved trade and a financial package, but both measures were blocked by Nicosia. Eventually, in February 2006, the Council agreed a package of €139 million for northern Cyprus. The Cypriot attitude greatly annoyed several member states. The former British Foreign Secretary, Jack Straw, was perhaps the most outspoken when he declared in January 2006, after a disputed visit to the north of the island, that:

> had EU membership been proposed under the current circumstances, neither the British government nor most European governments would have touched the idea of allowing a divided Cyprus into the EU. We want to see a unified Cyprus, but the current approach of the government of Cyprus does not in any way represent movement toward a united Cyprus and objectively is likely to lead to the opposite result.

CONCLUSION

Throughout the 1990s the western Balkans were nearly always the top priority of EU foreign ministers. Today the Middle East, Iraq, Afghanistan, the struggle against terrorism and WMD proliferation sometimes have an equal or higher priority on the agenda. Competition for the attention of decision-makers, but also for the administrative and financial resources of the EU, has become fierce. Yet there can be no doubt that, because of its geographical proximity and the EU's massive involvement over the past decade, the western Balkans remain a central challenge for the EU's external relations. The stability of the region is intrinsically linked to that of the EU, and the EU's credibility as an international actor thus depends to a large extent on its success in the Balkans. Unlike in 1991, the EU today has the experience, the instruments and the appropriate strategic concept to help the western Balkan countries meet the challenges at hand. What is now required, first and foremost, is the determination and staying power to build on the progress achieved and to bring – in close co-operation with its partners in the region – the 'Europeanisation of the Balkans' to a successful conclusion.

The EU's performance in the Balkans during the 1990s left much to be desired. But the difficult learning experience led to progress in the defence field and a new resolve to offer the countries of the region a roadmap towards future

EU membership. But the region has a very negative image with European public opinion; and, given the undoubted enlargement fatigue in the Union, no one can predict when, if ever, the various countries will be ready for accession. By mid-2007 it may be clearer just how many countries are in the frame as it is expected that the status questions surrounding Kosovo and Montenegro will be resolved by then. The Balkans will be quite a mouthful to chew, but it is the question of Turkey's possible membership that is likely to give the EU indigestion. If Turkey continues with its current reforms, there should be no prima facie reason to exclude it. But the issue of Turkish membership has become highly sensitive in many member states; and France, for one, has promised a referendum if and when the negotiations are completed. At present it is difficult to see how the French people would endorse Turkish accession. Perhaps a settlement of the Cyprus dispute would go some way to calming fears about Turkey. But thirty years of failed negotiations offer little encouragement.

KEY QUESTIONS

How did the EU perform in the Balkans during the 1990s?
What are the main difficulties facing the western Balkans?
Is the EU ready, willing and able to accept the western Balkan countries as member states?
What are the prospects for regional co-operation?
What are the pros and cons of Turkish EU membership?
How would Turkish accession impact on EU foreign policy?
Cyprus was a major failure of EU foreign policy. Discuss.

FURTHER READING

Owen (1995), Holbrooke (1998) and Bildt (1998) offer differing accounts of the Balkan quagmire in the 1990s. Hannay (2004) provides a masterful summary of the fruitless efforts to find a solution in Cyprus, while Goulard (2004) offers a powerful polemic against Turkish membership of the EU.

9   The EU and Asia

SUMMARY

Asia, with more than half the world's population and with several major countries growing rapidly, is becoming increasingly a priority for the EU. Originally relations between the EU and Asia were focused on trade and economic development, but now it is seeking to develop political relationships involving its three 'strategic partners' – China, India and Japan. The EU is also supporting regional integration efforts such as the ASEAN and the SAARC. Europe–Asia region-to-region meetings are conducted through the ASEM process. The EU has struggled to secure acceptance in the region as an actor. It has perhaps secured most recognition from China, but this may be due to Beijing's interest in securing an ally in its dealings with the US. In 2006 more EU Commissioners visited China than went to any other country.

INTRODUCTION

In the second half of the twentieth century there was a fundamental realignment of European and American relations with Asia. For almost 200 years the Europeans were the main colonial powers in Asia. After the Second World War, the US became the main military power in Asia, and Europe faded in terms of security provision and interests. The US became the dominant external power in security affairs, politics and economics. Washington formed alliances with Japan, Korea and the Philippines; and provided a de facto guarantee to Taiwan. Many Asians studied in the US and many emigrated there. Asian affairs, thanks to strong ethnic lobbies, were thus given greater prominence in America than in Europe. As the EU consolidated there was much talk in the early 1990s of a new trilateral world based on the emerging EU, the US and Asia (mainly East Asia). It was recognised that the European relationship with Asia was much weaker than either the EU–US relationship or the US–Asia relationship. But elite opinion on all three continents considered that this triangular relationship was a key building block for the future of the world. There was much talk of the 'Pacific century'; and Americans mused, first, about the challenge from Japan and, later, about the challenge from China. The financial crisis of 1997–8 put paid to dreams of the 'Pacific century', and talk of a trilateral world faded. Now there is talk of resurrecting the idea.

As regards the EU, it has struggled to find a balanced relationship with Asia. Only in the past few years, with the launching of the Asia–Europe Meeting (ASEM) process in 1996, has the EU sought to deal with Asia as a region. Otherwise, it has laid more emphasis on bilateral relationships with Japan, China, India and Korea. The ASEAN has always been treated slightly differently by the EU, partly because of the hopes that it might develop closer political and economic integration along European lines. Today the emphasis remains on deepening bilateral relations. EU–China ties, for example, have enjoyed a major boom in the past few years. But there is also a recognition that the EU and Asia have to deepen their region-to-region dialogue, not least to balance the respective dialogues between the EU and the US and Asia and the US.

Asia is a crucial partner for the EU in many key areas. Asia has been the cradle of several of the world's major religions and has an unparalleled cultural richness. Asia accounts for over half the world's population, more than a quarter of world GDP and just under a quarter of international trade. Asia accounts for 21 per cent of EU exports and a steadily increasing share of FDI. Much more than Europe, Asia is tremendously diverse, economically and politically, socially and culturally, and also in terms of scale. The region includes the two most populous countries in the world (China and India) and some of the smallest (Brunei and Bhutan). It includes some of the richest countries in the world (Japan and Singapore) and some of the poorest (eight Asian countries are on the UN list of LDCs). India is the world's largest democracy, while there are several non-democratic countries in the region. East Timor, a subject of EU–Asian disputes in the past, is one of the world's newest sovereign countries. Europe also has a very diverse background, but a number of important differences stand out. There are only democratic states in the EU, and the spread of wealth between countries is much more even in Europe than in Asia. Despite the increase from fifteen to twenty-five members in 2004, the EU is more homogeneous than Asia. Perhaps the greatest difference is that the EU has achieved a far higher degree of political and economic integration than Asia and has further ambitions both to deepen integration and to become a more important global actor. Such Asian aspirations are in their infancy. The financial crisis of the late 1990s (to which the European response was largely passive) seems to have galvanised Asians into renewed efforts at regional co-operation on economic and trade issues and, more slowly, on political and security issues. The renewed efforts to promote the ASEAN are being mirrored in East Asia and South Asia. Europeans watch these developments with great interest, and stand ready to offer advice based on their own successful efforts at integration. However, Asian diversity and the differences in political cultures and political systems, as well as Asian reluctance to share sovereignty, will continue to hinder political integration in Asia. A key question is the future of

China. Although it has begun to exercise a new and more positive role in the region, there remain considerable uncertainties about its future internal development and its external goals. There are major concerns about the impact of its high growth rates on the environment and the world markets for energy and natural resources. There are also concerns about its future relations with the US, Japan, India and, above all, Taiwan.

THE EU AND ASIA – SHARED INTERESTS

There are many shared interests between the EU and Asia covering political, security, economic and social issues. Asia and Europe share the same security concerns with regard to terrorism, drugs and illegal immigration. Combating religious extremism is another growing shared interest. Asia is home to many troublespots (North Korea, Afghanistan, Taiwan, Kashmir) that impact on Europe as well as on the US. Given the unilateral tendency in US foreign policy, one can detect a growing willingness of some on the Asian side to discuss security issues with the EU. The EU's 'soft power', and its ability to promote peace and security through development aid, economic assistance and non-military security co-operation, is increasingly welcome in Asia. For example, in Afghanistan, the EU is the largest donor in terms of humanitarian aid and assistance for reconstruction, with over €1 billion pledged for 2002–6. The EU also provides the lion's share of peace-keepers in Afghanistan. The EU contributes over 60 per cent of the UN budget and 70 per cent of official development assistance.

On the economic side, Asia is the fastest-growing market for European goods, and there has been a boom in European FDI in the region. This, in turn, has led to increased use of the euro in financial markets and for trade. Together, the EU and East Asia account for nearly half the world's gross domestic product. Close co-ordination between the two continents on economic, trade (WTO/Doha) and financial matters is therefore a necessity. Asia's trade relations with the EU have increased tenfold since the early 1990s. The EU now imports over €230 billion from Asia and exports over €140 billion to the region annually. Asia is now the EU's third most important trading partner and its fourth most important investment destination. However, there are marked regional variations within this overall booming relationship. EU trade with South Asia lags far behind East Asia, although India's impressive economic growth rates are beginning to change the balance.

Concern for the environment is a further issue shared by Europe and Asia. Co-operation on Kyoto has been good, but there are many other problem areas that could be tackled together, such as sustainable natural resource management (e.g. forestry), the management of urban development, and energy security. European experience and technology is advanced in this area and could be of interest to Asian partners. However, many Asian countries – above all, China – still seem too concerned with economic growth to accept European advice on sustainable natural resource management. China has recently turned into a net importer of crude oil, and the country's ever-growing need to import oil and other raw materials gives rise to concern in Europe and Asia respectively. Only the US consumes more crude oil than China (China has recently overtaken Japan as the second-biggest consumer of crude oil), and China is only at the early stages of its economic development. Migration is an increasingly sensitive issue, and Asia is the source of potentially significant migratory flows to Europe. The EU and Asian countries have started a dialogue on this common challenge in the context of the ASEM and are beginning to develop common approaches. Despite considerable progress in recent years, the level of mutual awareness between Europe and Asia is still less than one would expect, given the existing level of contact. Clearly there is considerable scope to promote greater inter-regional exchanges in the fields of education, culture and tourism.

Many of the above points were noted in a communication from the Commission in 2001 that discussed the framework for a strategic partnership between the EU and Asia. This paper was significant as it proposed a region-to-region approach on several major issues. At the same time, the paper restated the EU's intention to maintain and deepen its relations with sub-regional bodies such as the ASEAN. The follow-up to the Commission proposals has varied owing to a mix of national interests, a lack of regional cohesion, and disputes over issues such as human rights.[1]

ASIA–EUROPE MEETING (ASEM)

As the name implies, the ASEM is an informal forum for European and Asian leaders to meet and discuss common challenges. Meetings are held at the level of heads of government, foreign ministers and senior officials. The first ASEM summit was held in Bangkok in 1996; the second in London in 1998; the third in Seoul in 2000; the fourth in Copenhagen in 2002; the fifth in Hanoi in 2004; and the sixth in Helsinki in 2006. Singapore was the driving force in the early days, with France perhaps the most enthusiastic on the European side. In the early years of the ASEM there was a feeling on both sides that Asia–Europe relations could be developed from trade and economic issues to cover political and security issues as well. The Copenhagen meeting, for example, issued a strong declaration on fighting terrorism. Some also thought the ASEM could be a useful counter to the US-dominated Asia-Pacific Economic Forum (APEC). Remarkably, the ASEM is the only major forum involving key countries where the US is absent. ASEM partners are all EU member states, the European Commission and the following Asian countries: Brunei Darussalam, China, Indonesia, Japan, Korea, Malaysia, Philippines, Singapore, Thailand, Vietnam and Burma/Myanmar.

Despite the initial fanfare, the ASEM also did not gain much priority in the EU. This may have been because the objectives were rather vague, such as 'addressing political, economic and cultural issues, with the objective of strengthening the relationship between Asia and Europe, in a spirit of mutual respect and equal partnership'. The ASEM thus remains an informal EU–Asia dialogue forum lacking instruments and capabilities to implement joint EU–Asia initiatives. Despite the ASEM's successes in bringing European and Asian politicians, academics and others together, some still refer to the forum as a 'talk shop' lacking the political will to move beyond an informal dialogue. The ASEM still has no real secretariat (not even its own website yet), and the information available on the ASEM's work is still very limited. It has established a number of taskforces (e.g. an EU–Asia economic taskforce), but both the EU and the Asian side seem yet reluctant to implement the taskforces' recommendations. The absence of European ministers at ASEM meetings has led to irritation on the Asian side and accusations that the ASEM is not receiving sufficient high-level attention from the Europeans.

Relations were also damaged by the long-running dispute over how to treat Burma/Myanmar. This dispute led to the cancellation of two ASEM ministerial meetings in July 2004 and threatened the holding of the fifth ASEM summit in Hanoi in October 2004. Asians argue that the EU should not endanger the entire relationship because of problems in one country and charge the EU with hypocrisy in singling out Burma. The EU says that it is not prepared to sit at the same table as a military dictatorship and wants to see the military regime replaced with a democratically elected government and an improvement of Burma's human rights record (including the release of Nobel Peace Prize winner Aung San Suu Kyi) before accepting Burma as part of the ASEAN and the ASEM. While ASEAN nations in 2003 strongly urged the military regime in Burma to live up to its promise to introduce democratic change, some ASEAN countries amended their viewpoint indicating that Burma would be engaged in the 'ASEAN way'. This was then interpreted in the EU as a retreat from previous commitments on human rights and a signal from the ASEAN not to interfere in their internal affairs. Despite the deepening of EU–ASEAN relations, the principle of non-interference in the internal affairs of member states formulated in the ASEAN charter has proved a stumbling-block to closer ties. The 'ASEAN way' of political decision-making is likely to continue to clash with EU-style policy-making of interference and willingness to share sovereignty. Given the importance of the global challenges facing Europe and Asia, and their common approach on many issues, it is vitally important that the two sides overcome their differences on Burma. The ASEM summit in Hanoi was rescued at the last minute by a face-saving formula acceptable to both sides. The majority view of members on both sides is that the ASEM process is too important to let the Burmese military dictatorship hijack it. Nevertheless, the Burma issue left a sour taste in the mouth, and it will be important to reflect on how to develop the ASEM most productively in the future.

GROWING ASIAN REGIONALISM

The ASEM is perhaps more important for the Asian side because there is no other forum that encompasses all Asian countries. Increasingly, South-East Asia and North-East Asia co-operate with each other through the ASEM or the ASEAN 'plus 3' (i.e. China, Japan, South Korea). India is also linked to the ASEAN via the ASEAN Regional Forum (ARF). The EU is a full member of the ARF and is actively contributing to peace and security in Asia through the forum. The ARF, however, is still confronted with the criticism of being a regional security 'talk shop' lacking the instruments to implement policies and security initiatives. Despite the ARF's shortcomings, however, Asian nations acknowledge that the EU as a 'distant power' with limited strategic interests in Asia can play a meaningful role in the region's security through a forum whose character is still mainly consultative and not designed to implement legally binding policies.

Given the lack of common institutions and the diversity of the continent, there is very little in terms of explicit common policy objectives agreed among all Asian countries. However, there are common types of challenge shared by all Asian countries. On trade and investment, all countries are linked with common challenges and opportunities in the context of globalisation and progressive trade liberalisation. Almost all countries in the region are members of the WTO or are in the process of acceding to it. Many Asian countries also face the task of adapting their regulatory environments, for example in order to improve corporate governance and the stability of financial systems. At the same time, Asian exporters face yet another common challenge – to adapt their products to meet changing EU regulatory requirements, notably in the areas of health and environmental protection.

EAST ASIA

East Asia is by far the most important region for the EU in terms of politics and economics. Japan and China are the EU's top trading partners in Asia, with Korea lagging some way behind. The EU is, however, committed to a peaceful solution to the nuclear crisis on the Korean peninsula. EU–China relations have increased dramatically in the past few years, with several EU heads of government and several EU Commissioners visiting Beijing and the Chinese prime minister visiting Europe. Relations are driven primarily by mutual economic interest but also by the desire of each side to play a bigger global role. Unlike the US, China does not view the EU as a threat to achieving its eventual goal of unification with Taiwan. Indeed, Beijing seems to view the EU as a possible counter-weight to the US. Significantly, China produced its first-ever strategy paper in October 2003 that focused on the EU. It coincided with a Commission communication that highlighted the 'shared interests and challenges in EU–China relations'. It stated that the EU and China had:

an ever-greater interest to work together as strategic partners to safeguard and promote sustainable development, peace and stability. Interests converge on many international governance issues, notably the importance both attach to the role of the UN in physical and environmental security and to that of the WTO, where both have much to gain from further trade liberalisation. Indeed, the growth in the bilateral trade relationship is striking: two-way trade exceeded €115 billion last year, making China Europe's third largest trading partner, albeit with a substantial surplus in China's favour. Moreover, EU firms remain important investors in China. Mutually beneficial co-operation in the JHA, scientific and technical fields has also been growing apace in recent years, with a number of new agreements in process, and the EC's assistance programme continues at significant levels. Europe thus has a major political and economic stake in supporting China's successful transition to a stable, prosperous and open country that fully embraces democracy, free market principles and the rule of law. The EU has much to offer here, stemming in part from its own experience in integrating accession countries from East and Central Europe.

The paper concluded that the EU aim was to assist China in its transition to a stable, prosperous and open country that fully embraces democracy, a market economy and the rule of law.[2]

The astonishing economic growth in China has led to a boom in trade and European FDI. Total trade in 2005 was estimated at €130 billion, making China the EU's second-biggest trading partner after the US. China has also become the economic engine for Asia, accounting for more than half of total regional trade compared to just 11 per cent in 1999. EU–China relations have also expanded to cover many other areas. The EU was supportive of China's bid to join the WTO, but problems remain in at least two sensitive areas. The EU continues to maintain an arms embargo against China following Beijing's use of military force to crush peaceful pro-democracy demonstrations in Tiananmen Square in June 1989. Despite strong pressure from China to lift the embargo, the EU has decided to keep the embargo in place until Beijing improves the human rights situation in China. The decision to keep the embargo in place, at least for the time being, was made despite French and German pressure urging the EU to open the Chinese market for European weapons manufacturers. The other contentious issue is the EU's refusal to grant China market-economy status, criticising the lack of transparency and accountability of Chinese enterprises. This issue will remain on the EU–China agenda until the Chinese achieve the recognition they desire.

Meanwhile co-operation has intensified on many other fronts. At the sixth EU–China summit, in Beijing in October 2004, the EU and China agreed to develop jointly the EU's Galileo radio satellite navigation system despite US concerns that China is mainly interested in the military use of the system. China also supported the EU candidate (France) over Japan as the site for the world's first large-scale nuclear fusion plant, a $12 billion project known as the International Thermal Nuclear Reactor. Apart from science and technology, other fruitful areas for co-operation include the fight against terrorism, proliferation, tackling failed states, and health (SARS). The September 2006 summit agreed to start negotiations for a new EU–China strategic partnership agreement.

The future direction of China will have important repercussions for Europe and Asia. Will the present moderate policies in external relations continue or will China be tempted to use its growing military power to achieve its goals? What will be the environmental impact of China's voracious appetite for natural resources? What will happen when the economic bubble bursts? How long can an authoritarian leadership maintain power faced with such rapid social and economic changes? The EU can be a moderating influence on China, but ultimately the Chinese will have to decide their own path. China could develop into a constructive and influential global actor with a reformed political system; or it could fail to meet its many domestic challenges, including high and rising inequality and unemployment, massively indebted and unreformed companies in key sectors, emergent social unrest and an unsettled leadership transition.

Relations between the EU and Japan are highly developed and generally trouble-free. For many years it was a trade-dominated relationship, reflecting the fact that Japan's economy is nearly 60 per cent of Asian GDP; but more recently, since the signing of the 2001 EU–Japan Action Plan, there has been an emphasis on political and security co-operation. The Action Plan calls for closer co-operation to promote global peace and security through the strengthening of the UN system, continued co-operation to achieve the elimination of WMD, joint efforts to promote concepts of human security including human rights, humanitarian assistance and development assistance to the most vulnerable population. This EU–Japan co-operation, however, has been limited so far, and it will be important to assess how to deepen areas for common action. There was little real progress at the April 2006 summit in Japan. President Barroso outlined the main priorities for EU–Japan relations: co-operation in environmental issues, energy, research and development. He also called for closer political co-operation with the aim of achieving convergence on international issues.[3]

The EU and Japan are both perceived as 'soft powers' on the international stage, promoting peace and security through economic assistance, development aid, non-military security co-operation. Contrary to the US under the Bush administration, the EU and Japan are both active in promoting alternative concepts of security as well as concepts of preventive diplomacy and conflict prevention. Again, in contrast to the US, the EU and Japan share common concepts and visions of global governance. Both the EU and Japan are strong supporters of multilateralism and have a shared interest in promoting Kyoto and the ICC. But relations were strained a little in 2003 when Japanese Prime Minister Koizumi fully backed the US-led invasion of Iraq and later sent Japanese troops to assist in the stabilisation of that country. Japan's newfound assertiveness in international security also raised some suspicions with its neighbours, notably China and South Korea. The scope for EU–Japan co-operation is thus wide, but to date both sides have been disappointed by the failure to achieve the goals set out in the Action Plan.

EU–South Korea relations are largely dominated by trade issues. While trade has boomed, there remain some difficulties concerning Korean subsidies to its shipbuilding industry and semiconductors. Despite these trade frictions, which will be settled at the WTO in Geneva, the EU and South Korea have been able to expand their bilateral relations significantly in recent years, and European FDI is growing every year. EU–South Korea relations are based on the 2001 EU–South Korea Framework Agreement, and last year the EU and South Korea celebrated forty years of diplomatic relations. The EU is committed to supporting South Korea's policy of 'Peace and Prosperity' (formerly 'Sunshine Policy'), South Korea–North Korea reconciliation and South Korea's efforts to find a peaceful solution to the nuclear crisis on the Korean peninsula. The EU is also involved directly in North Korea via the Korean Peninsula Energy Development Organisation (KEDO). The EU has a seat on KEDO's executive committee and has made significant contributions (money and manpower) to KEDO in recent years. Given North Korea's refusal, however, to dismantle verifiably its nuclear weapons programme, the KEDO process is on hold, and it remains unclear when (or indeed if) KEDO will continue its work providing North Korea with non-nuclear energy through the construction of two light-water reactors in North Korea. The political will on the US and Japanese side to continue work on KEDO any time soon remains limited at best. In the absence of US and, until recently, Japanese food and humanitarian aid, the EU remains, at least for the time being, the largest donor of food and humanitarian aid to North Korea and will continue its efforts to contribute to the resolution of the humanitarian and food crisis. The EU is deliberately separating security and nuclear issues on the Korean peninsula from humanitarian issues, but does nevertheless urge the North Korean regime to dismantle its nuclear weapons programme to enable the EU to implement its technical assistance programmes for North Korea. Since the nuclear revelations in North Korea in October 2006 the EU's technical assistance projects (significant in number and scope) are on hold, and the EU will only resume the execution of the programme when North Korea complies with its international obligations to dismantle its nuclear weapons programme.

SOUTH-EAST ASIA/ASEAN

The EU shares with South-East Asia many common features and interests. Both are seeking to deepen regional co-operation and integration between highly diverse member states through the EU and the ASEAN respectively. Countries from both regions enjoy cultural, religious and linguistic diversity. Both regions are committed to strong multilateral international institutions. These common interests and values should form the basis of a new partnership between the two regions. The two regions also enjoy very strong commercial links. On trade, the EU is now the ASEAN's third-largest trading partner, accounting for 14 per cent of ASEAN trade. Total EU–ASEAN trade in 2005 was over €100 billion. Significantly, the EU is the ASEAN's second-largest export market after the US. On investment, EU investors put nearly €2 billion in 2005 into the ASEAN region, which was about one-third of total FDI. ASEAN countries are again displaying impressive growth figures, and the ASEAN region is set to become one of the most dynamic growth engines for the world economy. With its growing export-led economies and a quickly developing domestic market of 530 million people, the ASEAN is a region of global economic importance that the EU cannot afford to neglect. while still we it? · ·

Established in 1967, the ASEAN has made relatively little progress in achieving its own proclaimed goals. There has been some limited progress on the reduction of customs barriers and the abolition of tariffs. The ASEAN summit in 2003 agreed to set up an Economic Community (AEC) with the aim of achieving an ASEAN internal market by 2020. In this regard, the ASEAN has indicated that it sees the EU as a role model for its economic integration and to be interested to learn from EU experiences. However, the ASEAN's 'principle of non-interference in the internal affairs of its member states' formulated in the ASEAN charter still remains an obstacle to closer regional integration. Perhaps some progress could be made on the trade front. In 2005 several Asian countries agreed to establish an Asian Free Trade Agreement (AFTA) within a decade. The ASEAN has also agreed to work towards a customs union for most industrial products by 2012.

In its turn, the EU sees a stable and prosperous ASEAN as a fundamental ingredient of stability in the wider Asia region. For more than two decades the 1980 ASEAN–EC Co-operation Agreement 'between equal partners' governed relations. The failure of the ASEAN side to meet its declared goals, and disputes over East Timor and Burma, meant that relations did not develop as hoped. This led to a rethink on the European side, and in July 2003 the Commission launched its communication with the aim of reinvigorating relations with the region and with the ASEAN.[4] The paper identified the following main priorities: supporting regional stability and the fight against terrorism; promoting human rights, democratic principles and good governance; mainstreaming Justice and Home Affairs issues; injecting a new dynamism into regional trade and investment relations; supporting the development of less prosperous countries; intensifying dialogue and co-operation in specific policy areas

It also intends to engage the ASEAN on a wider and modern policy agenda. It offers regional dialogues on trade matters (the TREATI initiative) and non-trade matters (the READI initiative). The dialogue process will be closely co-ordinated with the ASEAN secretariat and will be organised around the ASEAN's own policy and expert meetings and agenda. A fundamental issue in this respect will be to increase mutual awareness and the EU's profile in South-East Asia. South-East Asia's political agenda is driven by both regional and international concerns. The terrorist attack carried out in October 2002 in Bali demonstrated the threat to the region and spurred efforts to develop co-operation on security issues both within the ASEAN and with the international community. The EU–ASEAN ministerial meeting in January 2003 issued a joint declaration on co-operation to combat terrorism, and there have been regular meetings at official level. The dramatic rise in the political and economic importance of China has also helped push the ASEAN countries closer together, and there is now a new determination to achieve long-forgotten deadlines in economic integration. As the ASEAN advances it is increasingly challenged to take more political responsibility. The critical statement on Burma/Myanmar, the creation of a Security Community and the setting up of a dispute-settlement mechanism, all in 2003, are signs of a maturing political will within the ASEAN. For the ASEAN a key priority remains to deal with the development gap between its richer and poorer members after the enlargement with Vietnam, Cambodia, Laos and Burma/Myanmar in the 1990s. Average per capita income in South-East Asia is €1,217, ranging from €215 in Cambodia to €3,900 in Malaysia and €23,500 in Singapore. This enormous disparity between the poorest and the richest ASEAN members places a direct restraint on economic and social integration. The substantial differences between the EU and the ASEAN in terms of political and economic integration as well as GDP also set parameters to the relationship.

SOUTH ASIA (SAARC)

As regards South Asia and the SAARC (Bangladesh, Bhutan, India, the Maldives, Nepal, Pakistan, Sri Lanka), this was accorded a lower priority by the EU, and the focus was largely on trade matters and development assistance. South Asia has significant development potential, but also faces profound political and economic challenges. The region is home to some of the world's most difficult political crises: the ongoing tensions between India and Pakistan, the Maoist armed insurgency in Nepal and the civil war in Sri Lanka. There have, however, been positive developments in all these situations. Developments in Afghanistan also influence the political situation in the SAARC, even though Afghanistan is not a member of the organisation. The EU takes an active interest in supporting the resolution of these tensions, recognising that a stable South Asia is important for global security. Most of these problems require national-level solutions. However, as indicated above, regional frameworks like the SAARC can make a contribution to conflict solution and prevention, in particular by promoting intra-regional economic links.

Seven countries set up the South Asian Association for Regional Co-operation (SAARC) in 1985: Bangladesh, Bhutan, India, the Maldives, Nepal, Pakistan and Sri Lanka. It is much less developed than the ASEAN – a situation that reflects underlying tensions between its members (e.g. India and Pakistan). It has very few concrete achievements, even in the areas of its eleven action programmes (i.e. agriculture; communications; education, culture and sport; environment and meteorology; health and demography; prevention of drug trafficking and drug abuse; rural development; science and technology; tourism; transport; women's position in society).

The cooling of tensions between India and Pakistan led to a more productive summit in Islamabad in January 2004 when the SAARC adopted three important documents on free trade, the financing of terrorism and social affairs. With the results of the summit, the SAARC has given itself a clear economic-integration agenda, which could provide the basis for closer co-operation with the EU. One idea would be an EU–South Asia summit in the near future to signal the EU's interest in a region with the world's largest democracy and to counter the previous EU concentration elsewhere in Asia. In economic terms, South Asia has an enormous resource in its population of some 1.4 billion people. Although it only represents 1.6 per cent of world exports and imports, it has significant growth potential. For example, growth reached 8 per cent in 2003 in the region's largest country, India, and India's GDP is expected to match Italy's within a decade. India, however, remains way behind China in both trade and FDI. In 1978 the merchandise exports of China and India were similar; but, by 2004, Chinese exports had jumped to over $400 billion, while India was just over $60 billion. Inter-regional trade is ten times higher in East Asia than in South Asia. Very importantly, from an EU point of view, the EU plays a significant role for the region and its individual economies. On average, over the last few years, the EU was destination or origin for 20 per cent to 25 per cent of SAARC exports and imports. The EU is the largest trading partner for all South Asian countries except Nepal, accounting for up to 30 per cent of their exports.

Despite progress, South Asia still has a significant trade liberalisation agenda to address. Most countries continue to have a high anti-export bias in their trade regimes, and in general national economies remain highly protected. While South Asia's intra-regional trade has doubled since 1990, it remains far below its potential. The recent agreement to establish a South Asian Free Trade Area is a major step in boosting regional trade and integration. On investment, India is now a growing destination for investors, especially in the modern high-tech sector, but other countries in the region attract relatively little FDI. South Asia needs to dismantle trade barriers further, improve its human skills and technological base, and engage fully in regional and multilateral trade arrangements.

Realising its potential is restrained by chronic and pervasive levels of poverty, with more than a third of its citizens living on less than a dollar a day. Despite significant growth over the last decade, mostly in India, it is no surprise that Bangladesh, Bhutan and Nepal remain classified by the UN as least-developed countries. Hitherto the EU has paid most, albeit still modest, attention to India, which ranks only eighteenth among the EU's trading partners. In June 2004 the Commission proposed a strategic partnership with India that covered co-operation on conflict prevention, the fight against terrorism, non-proliferation and human rights; strengthening economic ties through sectoral and regulatory policy dialogues; co-operation in development policies in order to help India meet the Millennium Development Goals; increasing intellectual and cultural exchanges.[5]

EU TECHNICAL ASSISTANCE FOR ASIA

The EU has many development and technical assistance programmes for Asia. At present, the EU is operating eighteen multi-country programmes including Asia-wide programmes, and sub-regional programmes for the ASEAN and the SAARC. There is a €380 million budget for these programmes covering specific themes such as trade, energy, the environment, health, transport and agriculture. The most important Asia-wide programmes include: Asia Invest, which aims to support economic co-operation between the EU and Asia through business-to-business matchmaking opportunities, partnership-building and capacity-strengthening activities; Asia Urbs, which aims to promote local government partnerships to undertake urban development projects; Asia Pro Eco, which aims to improve environmental performance through EU–Asia technology partnerships that promote more sustainable products, processes and services; Asia IT&C, which aims to improve the quality of Europe–Asia partnerships and to link the two regions in the search for innovative and compatible solutions and standards in IT&C; Asia-Link, which aims to promote sustainable partnerships between higher education institutions in Europe and Asia. In general, the Asia-wide programmes benefit from a high visibility in Asia and Europe and are unique in that they directly address key target groups of civil society. The EU–Asia-wide programmes provide added value to member states' initiatives in that they promote multi-lateral partnerships involving typically institutions from at least two different European countries, thus encouraging a 'European dimension'.

CONCLUSION

Given the diversity of states in Asia, it is impossible to construct a monolithic EU–Asia relationship, a single policy or approach, equally valid across the whole region. With this caveat in mind, and having regard to the changes within both regions as well as changes in international affairs, it is important that the two regions seek to deepen their relations. Both regions face similar political and economic challenges, ranging from terrorism and failed states to health scares and the challenges posed by globalisation. Both share a commitment to multilateralism and a desire to strengthen the institutions of global governance. Both have to deal with an American hyperpower that pursues its own and often different agenda from that of Asia and Europe.

But an EU focused on its own internal affairs, enlargement, and its prob-lematic neighbourhood and transatlantic relations too often ignores Asia's rising political and economic importance. The EU's efforts to play a more active global role require closer engagement, co-operation and dialogue with the rapidly changing and increasingly dynamic countries of Asia. At the same time it is necessary for Asians to pay more attention to developments within the EU, to support efforts to improve educational and cultural exchanges and to try to overcome differences on human rights and other issues. A meeting of minds between Europe and Asia would be of enormous benefit in helping to resolve many global problems.

KEY QUESTIONS

What are the main EU interests in Asia?
Is ASEM a satisfactory forum for EU–Asia relations?
EU attention is now focused overwhelmingly on China. Discuss.
What are the prospects of Asia moving down the integration path like the EU?

FURTHER READING

There are not many studies on EU–Asia relations. In book form, there are Bridges (1999), Dent (1999), and Connors, Davidson and Dosch (2004). The website of the Asia Europe Foundation (www.asef.org) is very useful as are the European Institute for Asian Studies (www.eias.org/asiaguide.html), the *Far Eastern Economic Review* (www.feer.com) and the Institute for Southeast Asian Affairs (www.iseas.ac.sg).

10 Development policy

SUMMARY

The EU has close relations with most of the developing world and is a strong supporter of the Millennium Development Goals (MDGs). It is the major provider of development and humanitarian assistance, and the largest market for goods from the developing world. Yet there is considerable criticism of the EU for its lack of coherence and its failure to open further its markets, particularly to agricultural products from developing countries. There is also some tension resulting from Europe's colonial legacy and the post-9/11 focus on terrorism. Developing countries have also been concerned at the EU's concentration on its immediate neighbourhood. The Cotonou agreement that replaced the Lomé agreement is the main contractual relationship between the EU and the African, Caribbean and Pacific (ACP) countries. The EU also provides substantial assistance to non-ACP developing countries, including in Asia and Latin America. In recent years Africa has become a main focus for the EU, given the enormity of the problems that the continent faces. In December 2005 the EU agreed a new strategy towards Africa.

INTRODUCTION

EU development policy began when France insisted on preferential treatment for its ex-colonies and overseas territories in the Treaty of Rome. Many EU policies, such as agriculture, the customs union and the single market, had a major impact on the developing world and led to demands for a more structured relationship. When Britain joined the EU in 1973 there was an expansion of countries, especially in the Caribbean and the Pacific, involved in the EU's development agenda. The ACP group now has seventy-one members, of which more than half are designated least-developed countries (LDCs) by the UN. They all benefit from the EU's preferential trade system (GSP) and since 2001 from the 'everything but arms' initiative that grants tariff-free entry to the EU for almost all goods from the ACP countries. About two-thirds of all aid goes to the ACP states and consists of grants from the European Development Fund

(EDF) and low-interest loans from the European Investment Bank (EIB). Development policy is an area of mixed competence, with responsibility shared between the EU and the member states. Article 130 of the TEU states that:

> Community policy in the sphere of development cooperation, which shall be complementary to the policies pursued by the Member States, shall foster:
>
> - the sustainable economic and social development of the developing countries and more particularly the most disadvantaged among them;
> - the smooth and gradual integration of the developing countries into the world economy;
> - the campaign against poverty in the developing countries.

The European Security Stratetgy (ESS) also recognised the importance of development policy in tackling the root causes of terrorism. Increasingly the EU has sought to impose more conditions on aid including democracy and human rights, good governance and regional co-operation. Development policy also has other elements including trade policy, environmental policy, migration, humanitarian aid, technical assistance, combating infectious diseases, and crisis management. Given that nearly all member states have their own development policies, often focusing on areas of special interest, what is the added value of the EU's efforts? Proponents of EU development assistance argue that EU efforts are complementary to those of member states and allow the smaller member states to become involved in an important policy area without having to establish their own structures. There is some truth in this argument, as most of the new member states did not consider development aid a priority issue when they joined the Union. The question of balance between EU and member-state efforts in development assistance is likely to continue for some time.

EUROPEAN COLONIAL RULE

The colonial legacy still impacts on how developing countries view Europe. Many European states were involved in the scramble for colonies in Africa and elsewhere in the nineteenth century. One of the worst elements of European imperialism was the massive and destructive trade in slaves carried on by the Portuguese, the Dutch, the French, the British and others. In all, some 14 million Africans are estimated to have been transported to the Caribbean and the Americas or to have lost their life as a result of the trade. At the UN-sponsored Durban conference on racism in 2004 there were loud calls for compensation from European states that had been involved in the exploitation of colonies. In the spring of 2006 the Archbishop of Canterbury publicly apologised for the Church's role in the slave trade. Even before the main scramble for colonies began in the 1870s, the UK and France had been steadily increasing their commercial and political involvement in Africa, followed by

Belgium, the Netherlands, Portugal and Germany. The British were omnipresent on the continent; the French were mainly involved in West Africa, Belgium in the Congo, Portugal in Angola and Mozambique, and Germany in South-West Africa (now Namibia) and Tanganyika. The Europeans imposed artificial boundaries on their colonies, which often enclosed a varied assortment of societies (the Somali, for example, were split among British, French, Italian and Ethiopian administrations). The Second World War greatly weakened the colonial powers; and, partly under pressure from the US, the Europeans started to grant independence to their colonies. European rule ended mainly in the 1960s and 1970s, leaving the present patchwork of Africa as its political legacy. British, French and Dutch rule in Asia ended earlier, with the British, for example, leaving India in 1947 and France leaving Vietnam in 1954. The EU as such does not suffer any stigma of a colonial past; but, given the prominent role of several member states in colonial expansion, the tension remains just below the surface. Since 2004 the Commissioner for Development has been Louis Michel, the former Belgian foreign minister, who has been a strong advocate of the developing countries' interests. Given his background, it is not surprising that he takes a special interest in the Congo.

DEVELOPMENT POLICY

Since the Second World War vast sums of money have been spent on development, and entire professions have emerged concerned solely with poverty alleviation. The line of politicians who have declared poverty to be the world's most pressing issue stretches back through the decades. It is no wonder, therefore, that many have started to question the efficacy of development aid. For many years it seemed that many developing countries were making progress. But the 1970s and 1980s witnessed a slump in trade; collapsing commodity prices and the economic shock of successive oil crises undid the advances made. Unable to mitigate the effects of economic crisis themselves, developing countries were forced to turn more to external donors and international organisations. Under the so-called Washington consensus, international donors began to call for the public sector to downsize and to undo its network of controls over economy and society. The market was resurgent, and private investment held up as the solution to poverty and the new engine of development. The Structural Adjustment Programmes (SAPs) imposed upon governments called for the state to act as a manager of development and welfare, not the deliverer. The principles of the free market were to be adopted, and governments were encouraged to sell off state-owned enterprises, dramatically cut the number of civil servants and public officials, eliminate subsidies and price-supports, and open up their economies. But the hoped-for massive inflow of private capital following liberalisation and structural adjustment did not occur, and development indicators for much of sub-Saharan Africa during the 1990s seemed to go into reverse. As the HIV/AIDS pandemic swept across the continent, with debt levels increasing and many countries suffering from famine, it became increasingly clear that the power of the market alone was not sufficient to resolve development problems. Governance became the new watchword of development. There were increasing voices stating that simply increasing the level of aid was not sufficient, unless there was a guarantee that the money would be used effectively and efficiently, and not siphoned off by corrupt officials. Donors such as the US Millennium Challenge Fund began to call for more effective governance – defined as democratic, with an independent judiciary, transparent and open in its dealings, and a strong civil society able to participate fully in public life – as the vital framework in which developmental targets could be achieved. Development thus no longer means economic growth from which all else will flow: it incorporates broad social objectives; notions of people's right to certain opportunities, services and levels of care; and issues of sustainability and security. Development has come to mean the creation of an entirely different society, where absolute poverty is eradicated, where all people have access to the same opportunities, where all live without fear, and under a minimum of democratic standards.

For many development countries trade is as important as, if not more important than, aid. Improving the capacity of developing countries to trade and participate in the global market has been a fundamental objective of the EU and other major donors. However, Africa's share of world trade, for example, has fallen from 6 per cent in 1980 to just 2 per cent in 2005. Africa faces several constraints in expanding trade, promoting economic growth and feeding that growth into development, including internal barriers to trade and a lack of production capacity. The two critical factors, however, are the impact of subsidies paid to producers in the developed world, and the effect of tariffs and artificial barriers in limiting access of African commodities to the markets of OECD countries. Agriculture is the dominant productive sector across Africa, and agricultural subsidies in the developed world thus have a particularly large impact on African economies.

There is little argument at the international level over the perceived need to increase the scale of development assistance. During 2005 the US committed itself to granting $674 million worth of aid to Africa while the EU announced in May 2005 that it was to double its aid to poor countries over the next five years to US$14,000 million annually by 2010. The fifteen richest EU member states also committed themselves to meeting a target of spending 0.51 per cent of gross domestic product on Official Development Assistance (ODA) (with the poorer ten states agreeing to a target of 0.17 per cent), with the ultimate goal of meeting the 0.7 per cent target adopted by the UN General Assembly in 1970. However, although there is almost universal agreement on the need to provide increased levels of aid to Africa, not all governments are prepared to increase spending on such a huge scale in the immediate future. Germany, Italy and Portugal suggested that they may not be able to afford the announced EU aid target whilst the agreement was being announced. Furthermore, the US has refused to commit itself to meeting the 0.7 per cent target.

The issue of debt in the poorest countries has seen the most significant movement during recent years, with a major agreement by the G8 countries in June 2005 to cancel immediately the debt owed to the World Bank, the IMF and the African Development Bank by eighteen countries (fifteen of which are African). The agreement has removed US$40,000 million of debt, with the prospect of another twenty countries eligible to qualify if they meet targets on corruption and good governance, taking the package up to a potential US$55,000 million of debt cancellation. However, with Africa's total external debt at around US$300,000 million, equating to US$10,000 million of repayments due each year, and only fifteen sub-Saharan countries having benefited from this deal, critics have pointed out that the problem of debt is far from being resolved. Individual countries have agreed to cancel the debt owed to them. Britain, for example, has cancelled 100 per cent of debt from those countries that met the terms of the initiative for heavily indebted poor countries. Countries such as Germany and Japan, however, which are major creditors, have been less willing to move towards a universal cancellation of African debt. They argue that there are no guarantees that the money saved will be spent on poverty reduction, and that simply wiping the slate clean will not address the structural causes of Africa's poverty.

Didn't we cancel debt before? *True?*

THE MILLENNIUM DEVELOPMENT GOALS (MDGS)

At the UN Millennium Summit in 2000, 191 states undertook to achieve eight goals by 2015 to eradicate poverty and to reduce the inequalities in the world. As of mid-2006 there were severe doubts as to whether the MDGs could be met on target. In sub-Saharan Africa, at current rates of progress, the targets for universal primary education will not be met until 2130 (some 115 years late); the target of halving poverty until 2150; and that for reducing avoidable child deaths by 2165 (150 years after the MDG deadline). The slow progress towards meeting those targets is evidence of the deep-rooted problems in the continent. This was the background to the 'London agenda', which was most broadly outlined in the Commission for Africa report of March 2005, and the proposals put before the G8 at Gleneagles in July 2005. These debates have focused on three inter-related themes: promoting a fairer trade regime under which African producers are not penalised and are given fair prices for their produce; a massive expansion of aid (and a restructuring of how that aid is financed and disbursed); and measures to deal with the massive burden of debt owed by poor countries, and by African nations in particular (see section on Africa below).

Box 10.1: The Millennium Development Goals (MDGs)

- Cut by half, between 1990 and 2015, the proportion of people whose income is less than 1 US dollar a day.
- Cut by half, between 1990 and 2015, the proportion of people who suffer from hunger.
- Achieve Universal Primary Education.
- Promote Gender Equality and Empower Women.
- Reduce by two-thirds, between 1990 and 2015, the under-five mortality rate. Reduce by three-quarters, between 1990 and 2015, the maternal mortality ratio.
- Have halted by 2015 and begun to reverse the spread of HIV/AIDS. Have halted by 2015 and begun to reverse the incidence of malaria and other major diseases.
- Ensure Environmental Sustainability. Integrate the principles of sustainable development into country policies and programmes and reverse the loss of environmental resources; cut by half, by 2015, the proportion of people without sustainable access to safe drinking water and access to basic sanitation; by 2020, to have achieved a significant improvement in the lives of at least 100 million slum dwellers.
- Develop a Global Partnership for Development. Develop further an open trading and financial system that is rule-based, predictable and non-discriminatory. A commitment to good governance, development and poverty reduction – nationally and internationally.

THE COTONOU AGREEMENT

The Cotonou agreement, signed on 23 June 2000 and which came into force in April 2003, represented a new stage in co-operation between the ACP states and the EU, which began with the signing of the first co-operation convention (Yaoundé Convention) in 1964 and continued with the four Lomé conventions, the last one expiring on 29 February 2000. The agreement's main objectives are the reduction and eventual eradication of poverty and the gradual integration of ACP states into the global economy, whilst adhering to the aims of sustainable development. Given the limited success of the main approach of non-reciprocal trade preferences in the previous conventions and the need to adapt to international developments such as globalisation and technological advances, plus the far-reaching social changes in ACP states, the agreement established a new approach to co-operation in this field. The new approach of the agreement aims to strengthen the political dimension, provide more flexibility and entrust the ACP states with greater responsibilities. It recognises the substantial differences between the ACP states and allows for a more flexible approach. For example, for some very poor developing countries, trade preferences are only of minor importance compared to debt relief. The agreement has three main dimensions, namely politics, trade and development, and represents an approach that is both integrated and sectoral. The agreement has been concluded for twenty years, with a revision clause every five years. Political conditionality plays a bigger role under the Cotonou agreement, which provides for the establishment of a regular political dialogue, enhancing local capacities for peace-building and conflict resolution, respect for democracy and human rights, and good governance and regional co-operation. Article 96 of the agreement lays down the possibility of taking appropriate measures (usually sanctions or suspension of the agreement) in cases of violation by one of the parties of the requirements of essential elements of the agreement, namely respect for human rights, democratic principles and the rule of law. In the case of Fiji, for example, following the coup d'état of May 2000 the Commission decided to suspend parts of the aid package. The clause has also been used against other countries such as Zimbabwe, Liberia, Chad and Haiti.

The agreement envisages a substantial role for non-state actors in the design and implementation of development strategies and programmes, for example the private sector and economic and social partnerships. The integrated approach of the partnership stresses a number of key areas for co-operation. These include: economic development, with the focus on investment and private-sector development (e.g. enhancing export activities); macroeconomic and structural reforms and policies (e.g. liberalising trade regimes); and sectoral policies (e.g. developing the industrial, trade and tourism sectors). Second, social and human development with a focus on social-sectoral policies (e.g. improving education, health and nutrition systems, and population issues), youth issues (e.g. protecting the rights of children and particularly girls) and cultural development (e.g. recognising, preserving and promoting the value of cultural traditions and heritage). Two other priorities involved regional co-operation and cross-cutting issues. On regional co-operation the aim is to promote and expand inter- and intra-ACP trade and trade with third countries. The cross-cutting issues include gender equality, sustainable management of the environment, institutional development and capacity building.

The agreement provides for the negotiation of new trading arrangements with a view to liberalising trade between the two parties, putting an end to the system of non-reciprocal trade preferences from which the ACP states currently benefit. None the less, the current system will remain in force for a preparatory period, up to 2008 (the date envisaged for the new arrangements to come into force), with a transitional period of at least twelve years. Negotiations on the new regional economic partnership agreements began in October 2003 with the CEMAC (Economic and Monetary Community of Central Africa) and the ECOWAS (Economic Community of West African States). In order to simplify the process and make financing more flexible, provision was made for the rationalisation of co-operation instruments, especially of the EDF. In contrast to the previous conventions, the EDF will no longer be divided into several instruments with rigid allocation systems. All EDF resources will be channelled through two instruments:

- Grants; these total €11.3 billion under the ninth EDF, €1.3 billion of which is set aside for regional programmes. The Commission and the ACP states will administer them jointly. Each country will receive a lump sum.
- Risk capital and private-sector loans – investment facility: the EIB will administer this new instrument, allotted €2.2 billion from the ninth EDF. The Bank may provide loans, equity and quasi-capital assistance. It will also be able to provide guarantees in support of domestic and foreign private investment.

The financial resources include €13.5 billion from the EDF, €9.9 billion unspent from previous EDFs and €1.7 billion from the EIB. The ACP states now have greater responsibility for determining objectives, strategies and operations, and for programme management and selection. The main instrument used for programming grants is the country support strategy (CSS). The Commission and the country in question will draw up a CSS for each ACP state. The CSS will set out general guidelines for using the aid, which will be supplemented by an indicative operational programme containing specific operations and a timetable for their implementation. An annual review is provided for in order to adjust the CSS, the operational programme or the resources allocated. The joint institutions for co-operation established by the former Lomé conventions remain in force, namely: the Council of Ministers, the Committee of Ambassadors, the Joint Parliamentary Assembly. Decisions of the Council shall be arrived at on the basis of a consensus of its members.

FOCUS ON AFRICA

Given the enormity of the problems facing Africa, it is surprising that until 2005 there was no overall EU strategy for the continent. Africa was divided into those members of the ACP group, the North African states with association agreements with the EU, and South Africa. This changed in late 2005 with a Commission communication on Africa and then a contribution from the Council. The European Council endorsed both papers in December 2005. Many African diplomats wondered why there could not have been just one paper. These two papers reflected again the dysfunctional pillar system of the EU.

Without substantial additional political will and financial resources Africa will only be able to reach most of the MDGs, not by the target year of 2015, but by 2050. As the biggest donor of development aid and the biggest trading partner of Africa, the EU set out the principles of the strategy as *equality, partnership and ownership*. The strategy focuses on the key requirements without which sustainable development in Africa will not be possible: *peace, security and good governance*. It subsequently looks into action on key areas that create the necessary economic environment for development such as *economic growth, trade and infrastructure.* Finally, the strategy pushes for investing in areas with an important and direct impact on the fulfilment of the MDGs, such as *health and education, sanitation.*

The EU Strategy for Africa will depend on the member states coming up with the necessary resources and also on a more co-ordinated and coherent approach. The paper provides for:

- Finance: At least 50 per cent of the additional annual budget made available for development aid by 2010 will go to Africa. EU aid to Africa will increase by two-thirds from €17 billion in 2003 to a total of €25 billion in 2010 (approximate figures).
- Budgetary support will increasingly be used to implement development projects faster and strengthen African ownership.
- Co-ordination among EU donors should be strengthened through concrete initiatives proposed in the Strategy; in this sense, it proposes to elaborate an Action Plan in 2006 enabling progress on issues such as Joint Programming.
- Coherence with other policy areas such as trade, agriculture, fisheries and migration will be strengthened.

The EU strategy also proposes the following additional initiatives:

- Twinning partnerships between universities, schools, municipalities, businesses, parliaments and civil society.
- Creation of a pan-European voluntary service for young people with skills to share who are interested in Africa's development.
- Building on the experience and success of the Erasmus programme, a similar programme for student exchange between Africa and Europe will be examined.

The EU also established a Trust Fund in February 2006 for supporting infrastructure in Africa. The euros 60 Fund, financed by the Commission and the EIB, will be used for projects in transport, water supply, information and communications technology.

Box 10.2: Africa facts

- The country with the largest population is Nigeria, with 136.5 million people. It is followed by Ethiopia, with 68.6 million people; and by the Democratic Republic of Congo, with 53.2 million.

- The countries with the highest life expectancy, 73 years (2003), are the Seychelles and Mauritius.
- The country with the lowest total life expectancy, 36 years (2003), is Zambia, followed by Lesotho and Sierra Leone with 37 years.
- The countries with the greatest reduction in life expectancy over the past decade in SSA are Lesotho (–20 years), Botswana (–19 years), and Zimbabwe (–18 years).
- The country with the greatest HIV prevalence is Swaziland, where one out of every four adults has contracted the virus (38.8 per cent of people in the 15–49 age group). This is followed by Botswana; while the lowest is Mauritania (0.9).
- Nearly half the population of Uganda (49.8) and Niger (48.9) are under 14 years old (2002).
- The country with the highest level of child malnutrition is Angola: 53 per cent of children under 5 are stunted (small for their age). Mauritania has the lowest levels, with 10 per cent.
- The country with the highest adult literacy is Zimbabwe (90 per cent).
- The country with the lowest adult literacy is Niger (17 per cent).
- The country with the lowest percentage of population with access to safe water is Ethiopia, with 22 per cent.
- The country with the least access to safe sanitation is Ethiopia, with only 6 per cent of the population having access.
- The country that received the highest net aid per capita during 2002 was Cape Verde (€256), followed by São Tomé and Principe (€200) and the Seychelles (€92).
- The countries that received the lowest net ODA per capita in 2003 were Nigeria (€1.67), Togo (€7.50), Central Africa (€10.90) and South Africa (€11.70).
- Every 30 seconds, an African child dies of malaria.
- Malnutrition and unsafe drinking water are widespread throughout the continent.
- 40 per cent of all Africans are still living on less than €1 a day.
- Three out of every four persons who die from AIDS are Africans.
- One African out of five lives in a country affected by war or violent conflict.
- Eighteen out of the twenty poorest countries in the world are African (in terms of per-capita income).
- Africa is the only part of the developing world where life expectancy has been falling over the last 30 years.

AFRICAN DEVELOPMENTS

With the birth of the New Economic Partnership for Africa's Development (NEPAD) in 2001 and the African Union (AU) in 2002, Africa has equipped itself with a strategy and institutions capable of guiding Africa on the road towards political and economic integration. The Regional Economic Communities (RECs), the building blocks of the continental integration process, are committed to fostering economic growth and political stability. At national level, many countries are making progress in the field of governance. In the past five years, for example, more than two-thirds of the countries in sub-Saharan Africa have held multi-party elections. A number of countries, such as Ghana in West Africa, Kenya, Uganda and Tanzania in East Africa and the Republic of South Africa, Namibia, Botswana and Mozambique in southern Africa have proved that political stability and sustainable development are two sides of the same coin.

The African Union, formally established in July 2002, has rapidly developed into a strong and credible continental political organisation. The AU seeks to promote progressive political and economic integration, democratic societies and sustainable development on the basis of African-owned strategies. Only three years after its establishment, the AU has already made considerable progress and earned international respect as a credible and legitimate continental political actor and agent of change. Despite its limited resources, the AU was able to take responsibility and leadership for the African peace and security agenda, and it continues to play a crucial role in the ongoing Darfur crisis. The EU has provided considerable political and financial support to the African Union and supports its objectives. Building on its own experience with integration processes, the EC has considered itself a key ally in the AU's ambition to become a credible 'change actor' on the continent. The EU and the AU have identified three main ways of building an effective partnership: through political dialogue, existing agreements and the creation of a pan-African programme. The EU and the AU currently implement a number of joint projects, includ-ing the Peace Facility for Africa and a €50 million support programme for the AU's institutional and operational development. The EU's dialogue with the AU started in 2000 in Cairo. There are regular meetings to discuss issues such as human rights, democracy and good governance, conflict prevention, food security, HIV/AIDS and other pandemics, environment, regional integration and trade, external debt, return of illicitly exported cultural goods.

EU–LATIN AMERICA

The EU also provides substantial development assistance to other parts of the world, notably in Asia and Latin America. The EU's relations with Latin America were of a limited nature until the accession of Spain and Portugal in 1986. These two countries, with their long history of close ties to Latin America

(Portugal to Brazil, Spain with the other countries), ensured that the EU paid more attention to the continent. In the 1970s and 1980s the emphasis was on political issues, with European governments and civil society pushing for the restoration of democracy throughout the region. In the 1990s the emphasis turned to economic and trade issues. Since 1999 there have been regular summits, involving the EU, Latin America and the Caribbean, which have been held in Madrid, Guadalajara and Vienna (May 2006). In addition, the EU has a number of sub-regional dialogues, with the countries of Mercosur, the Andean pact and Central America. There has only been limited progress in EU–Latin American relations in the past decade; and this has led to disappointment for the Latino side, who complain that the EU only wishes to discuss its own interests and is unwilling to open its market. Negotiations with Mercosur for an FTA remain stalled. Many see an opportunity lost for the EU as the South Americans were keen to have an alternative model and partner to the US. The EU is now the largest provider of FDI and the leading provider of development co-operation ($2 billion a year). Support for regional integration and social inclusion remains the top priority for the EU. Latin America has the highest levels of income inequality in the word, and this distorts statistics about poverty. There are over 100 million living below the poverty line.

Cuba is a special case. During the 1960s and 1970s many Europeans had a romantic attachment to Fidel Castro's Cuba and sympathised with the regime that had stood up to the US for forty years. But, as the scale of human rights abuses became known, support for Castro diminished. The EU defined its common position on Cuba in 1996, stating that full co-operation depended on improvement of human rights on the island. Despite some attempts to change the policy, it has remained the official EU line. The new member states, mindful of their own recent struggle for human rights, have been powerful advocates of a tough line towards Cuba.

HUMANITARIAN AID

The EU is a major provider of humanitarian aid and is to the fore in crises such as the December 2004 tsunami in South-East Asia and the August 2005 earthquake devastation in Pakistan. The European Commission Humanitarian Aid Office (ECHO), with an annual budget of about €500 million, co-ordinates emergency assistance and relief to the victims of natural disasters or armed conflict outside the EU. The aid is intended to go directly to those in distress, irrespective of race, religion or political convictions. ECHO's task is to ensure goods and services get to crisis zones fast. Goods may include essential supplies, specific foodstuffs, medical equipment, medicines and fuel. Services may include medical teams, water-purification teams and logistical support. Goods and services reach disaster areas via ECHO partners. Since 1992, ECHO has funded humanitarian aid in more than eighty-five countries. Its grants cover emergency aid, food aid, and aid to refugees and displaced persons worth a total of more than €500 million per year. But ECHO does more than simply fund humanitarian aid. It carries out feasibility studies for its humanitarian operations; monitors humanitarian projects; promotes and co-ordinates disaster-prevention measures by training specialists, strengthening institutions and running pilot micro-projects; gives its partners technical assistance; raises public awareness about humanitarian issues in Europe and elsewhere; and finances network and training study initiatives in the humanitarian field

CONCLUSION

In the financial perspectives for 2007–13 there was a modest increase in funding for development. Financial aid is important, but many question the effectiveness of this aid. For all the effort, energy and words expended on development in Africa, what has been achieved? Life expectancy for someone living in sub-Saharan Africa was 58 years in 1960. By 1990 it had risen to 70 years, but has since declined to just 46 years in 2005. Today 203 million people in sub-Saharan Africa suffer from hunger (33 million more than a decade earlier). Every ten seconds a child dies from a preventable disease. One could be forgiven for assuming that development has achieved little on the continent. Certainly the levels of suffering are almost beyond imagination, reduced to statistics showing in stark numbers the realities of life for millions of people.

Development policy has not failed but it needs to be part of a wider and more coherent approach involving fair trade, debt relief and good governance. Ultimately the answers lie within the developing countries themselves. China and India have both taken millions of their citizens out of the poverty trap by high rates of economic growth. Despite the fads of the international donor community there are encouraging signs that many countries are making the necessary choices to tackle the horrendous problems they face. African governments have sought to address in concert some of the problems facing the continent. Through the establishment of NEPAD, the AU, the creation of an African peace-keeping force, through free trade zones and other institutional unions, Africa is gradually restoring a measure of control over its own destiny.

The EU's record is mixed. Food aid has been a means of reducing EU surpluses, while the aid programmes have benefited EU companies and enterprises, which have won most of the contracts awarded under the programmes. In addition the EU has not always adopted a coherent approach to development. EDF funds have often been diverted to help finance projects such as the UN AIDS fund and the African Peace Facility. As in other policy areas, the impact of the EU would be greater if all twenty-five member states and the European Commission pulled in the same direction and spoke with one voice. This may take some time to achieve.

KEY QUESTIONS

How coherent is EU development policy?
Should there be a common EU policy for development?
How would you evaluate the EU's Africa Strategy?
To what extent can conditionality be used in development policy?

FURTHER READING

There is a vast literature on development policy. Holland (2004) examines the EU's approach, as do Lister (1997), Cosgrove-Sachs (1999), and Arts and Dickson (2004).

The EU Strategy for Africa can be downloaded at: http://europa.eu.int/comm/development/index_en.htm. The various branches of the UN have good websites, e.g. www.undp.org. For the Commission on Africa, see www.commissionforafrica.org.

11 Conflict prevention and crisis management

SUMMARY

The EU is becoming more and more involved in conflict prevention and crisis management. To some extent this may be described as the 'new frontier' as regards an identity for EU foreign and security policy. It is also becoming one of the main driving forces of European integration, although an area bedevilled by disputes over competences. There is also a perception by third countries that the EU is becoming a major player in crisis management and has established a reputation as an honest broker. The EU has developed a mix of instruments to use in handling sensitive political and security situations. These instruments cover all three pillars, which sometimes creates problems of coherence in EU policy, and include political dialogue, trade and economic measures (including sanctions), development and humanitarian assistance. Some examples of EU action include its mediation in Macedonia, its support for UN peace-keeping in the Congo and its crisis-management operation in Aceh, Indonesia.

INTRODUCTION

In July 1995 the Bosnian Serb army forced its way past Dutch UN peace-keepers and took control of what had been declared a 'safe area' for Bosnian Muslims. Until then, Srebrenica had been just another place on the map of Yugoslavia. But since that day Srebrenica has symbolised the cruelty of man and the inadequacies of the international community. The Muslims were herded out of the town and as many as 8,000 were killed in the worst atrocity in Europe since the Second World War. How could Srebrenica happen? All armed conflicts can create conditions under which atrocities can happen. The early warning of conflicts is a complex issue, requiring analysis of the interaction of a wide range of political, economic, military, environmental and social factors. In recent years, largely as a result of events in the Balkans and in Africa, the EU has paid increasing attention to conflict prevention even though the development of effective early-warning systems and the utility of early warning are problematic. Early warning is of little value unless it is linked to policy formulation and results in timely and effective action. Many conflicts have been widely predicted, and the failure to prevent them has lain not so much in the lack of early warning as in the absence of political will to take effective action – Rwanda, Kosovo and Darfur being only a few of the most recent and obvious examples. In the EU there has been a growing recognition that effective conflict prevention requires a more comprehensive approach addressing the underlying causes of instability and conflict, not simply the more immediate causes or symptoms of violence. Peace-keeping, state-building, election support, disarmament, demobilisation, reintegration of combatants, human rights monitoring, humanitarian aid and long-term development co-operation are all needed. The EU, with a large number of instruments at its disposal, has a major role to play in this field. It is also reacting to a genuine need. For example, in 2001 the EU became involved in Macedonia (see below) and spent €68 million in that operation; in 2002 in Afghanistan (at a cost of €207 million); in 2003 it helped Iraq to the tune of €121 million; in 2004 it provided over €200 million in assistance following the tsunami; and since 2004 it has been involved in Sudan, the Great Lakes and many other trouble spots.

THE EU'S GROWING ROLE IN CONFLICT PREVENTION

Set against the background of modern European history, the European Union itself may be described as the best example of conflict prevention. One of the main motives of the Founding Fathers in establishing the EU in the early 1950s was the desire to prevent any further recurrence of conflict by creating a security community, defined by Karl Deutsch as a community where states do not threaten or use force to resolve their differences. The recent and continuing enlargement of the Union may also be seen in this context, namely as a massive conflict-prevention programme designed to spread the Union's values relating to democracy and the rule of law throughout the entire continent. By imposing strict conditions (Copenhagen criteria) for membership, the EU has been able to use its mix of carrots and sticks (essentially financial and technical assistance, trade concessions and political co-operation) to extend the Western European zone of peace, prosperity and stability towards the East. Rarely has there been such voluntary interference in the domestic affairs of individual countries as in the central and eastern European countries preparing for EU membership.

The EU's more traditional role in conflict prevention emerged parallel to the EU's growing international role. But the EU's political ambitions never matched its economic stature, hence the unkind description of the EU as 'an economic giant and political dwarf'. The EU was quite unprepared for the challenges emerging as a result of the ending of the Cold War. But the successive foreign policy crises of the 1990s brought a rapid maturing of the EU in terms of foreign and security policy. The EU accepted that its external policies should be tied to the promotion of democracy, the rule of law, and respect for human and minority rights. A number of treaty changes boosted the CFSP and paved the way for a military component (ESDP). Since the 2001 Swedish Presidency, there has been a major increase in the EU's awareness of the importance of conflict prevention. This has led to the development of policies and instruments that provide a comprehensive 'toolbox' to enable the Union to tackle the root causes of violent conflict. The 2001 Gothenburg programme for the prevention of violent conflict was a key landmark in this process, as was the 2003 ESS.

The ESS offers a number of guidelines of direct concern to conflict prevention. The emphasis is on extending the zone of security on the EU's periphery, supporting multilateral institutions (specifically the UN and regional organisations), and seeking a comprehensive approach to old and new security threats. The ESS stresses that priority security objectives (WMD proliferation and international terrorism) should be addressed through 'effective multilateralism'; in other words, by supporting the UN system, by strengthening national responses through EU synergies, and by addressing root causes such as poverty and weak governance by drawing upon community instruments and political dialogue. These characteristics, along with an emphasis upon 'preventive engagement' rather than 'pre-emption', are generally acknowledged to make the ESS stand apart from the US national security strategy. Yet the ESS recognises that the first line of defence lies beyond EU frontiers; acknowledging that inaction is not an option; understanding that a military response is not always appropriate but might form one element of a combined response. In this way, the EU can engage in the systematic political engagement of 'prevention'. The ESS also stresses that Europeans generate inadequate capability from their considerable defence spending. Member states must make better use of the €160 billion devoted annually to defence (the US spends around €400 billion).

THE GOTHENBURG PROGRAMME

At the Gothenburg European Council in 2001 the EU agreed an ambitious programme for the prevention of violent conflicts. The main points were:

a. Set clear political priorities for preventive actions. The Commission and the Council should co-operate more closely on conflict prevention: the Commission should provide assistance for the monitoring of potential conflict issues at the beginning of each Presidency and should also strengthen the conflict-prevention content of its country strategy papers. This is easier said than done. One of the main problems is the division of responsibilities ('competences', in EU jargon) between the Council and the Commission. Broadly speaking, the Council leads on the more political-security issues. It has far fewer resources than the Commission but it clearly feels in the ascendancy as a result of Solana's high profile and member-state support (see Chapter 3). The Commission has the human and financial resources and most of the instruments useful for conflict prevention but often finds itself on the defensive as a result of member states' reluctance to grant the Commission any powers in foreign and security policy. The tension between the Council and the Commission from 1999 to 2004 was often hidden because of the good personal relations between the SG/HR (Javier Solana) and the Commissioner for External Relations (Chris Patten). The relationship at the top level has not been the same with Benita Ferrero-Waldner as Commissioner. This is not to say that co-operation does not proceed; rather that it often relies more on informal contacts and relationships than on agreed structures.

Within the Commission, DG Relex and DG Development are the two most important DGs in terms of conflict prevention. The conflict prevention and crisis management unit in DG Relex is responsible for co-ordinating Commission conflict-prevention activities. It provides expertise and training to headquarters and field staff, and promotes conflict assessment methodologies within the Commission. Despite its extensive mandate, the unit, which was established only in 2001, has a very small staff. In close co-operation with the Council secretariat and the joint situation centre (SITCEN), the unit provides the Council with a watch-list of potential crisis states on which the EU should focus. This is based on a root-causes checklist and reports from Commission delegations and other sources. It is given to each presidency and periodically reviewed. However, there has been criticism that the reports overly stress the economic and financial issues contained in the checklist, while only super-ficially covering the questions on the existence of a civil society or the political legitimacy of the regime in place. There has been some success in integrating conflict-prevention concerns into Commission policies, particularly the pro-gramming of external assistance. This has also led to the progressive inclusion of conflict-prevention indicators in the country strategy papers.

b. Improve its early-warning, action and policy coherence. To help achieve this aim the Union agreed that there should be greater input (intelligence, assess-ments, political reporting) from member states into the institutions. Coherence among the different EU policy areas should continue to be ensured by Coreper, while the Political and Security Committee's role in supervising the EU's activities on the conflict-prevention front should be reinforced. There has been a steady increase in material flowing from member states, but it is patchy and sometimes provided with caveats. There is perhaps at least as much informa-tion provided informally to national diplomats serving temporarily in the Policy Unit of the Council. Language is another factor that inhibits free circu-lation of material. The establishment in early 2005 of the new civilian–military cell has helped improve coherence as it is mandated to conduct integrated civilian–military strategic planning. The creation in 2001 of the rapid reaction mechanism (RRM) has also helped increase effectiveness. The RRM is a flexible instrument and has been deployed usefully on numerous occasions (more than a dozen projects in 2005). The RRM has helped make EU assistance more responsive and is run by the conflict-prevention unit in DG Relex. It has an annual budget of around €30 million, to be spent on projects lasting no longer than six months. The RRM is intended to allow more flexible and rapid funding in crisis situations for primarily civilian initiatives. It has been used *inter alia* in Afghanistan, Macedonia, Nepal, Sri Lanka, Sudan, Liberia, Aceh, Moldova and Somalia.

c. Enhance its instruments for long- and short-term prevention. The Gothenburg programme proposed that all relevant EU institutions should mainstream conflict prevention in their areas of competence. The instruments for disarmament, non-proliferation and arms control, it was noted, should also play a vital role in the EU's conflict-prevention policy. Although the EU has managed to introduce the concept of conflict prevention into all its institutions, a strong discrepancy persists between long-term (structural) policy, aimed at addressing the root causes of conflict, and medium-/short-term early-warning and crisis management. Development issues have been effectively separated from external relations policy in the Commission. In DG Relex, attention to the root causes of a conflict is very limited and hinges largely on the geopolitical significance of the country considered. There is also very little attention paid to development issues at the Council level, which de facto undermines the co-ordination of ESDP/CFSP policy with longer-term conflict prevention. Another type of discrepancy affects the allocation of funds between civilian and military crisis management. Operations with a military component are more easily funded, as they are directly charged to member states. The financing of civilian operations is more intricate, as they are usually financed through the Community budget. Even the CFSP budget line is part of the EC budget.

d. Build effective partnerships for prevention. The EU should intensify its co-operation and exchange of information with the other relevant global institutions (the UN, the OSCE, NATO), as well as with the regional organisations competent for the regions of concern. With conflict prevention an increasingly visible external objective, the EU has expanded its contacts with and operational dealings with a number of international partners. The EU institutions are in regular contact with the UN, the OSCE, NATO and several relevant regional organisations such as the African Union (AU). In the western Balkans, and especially in Macedonia, co-operation between the EU and other multilateral organisations, primarily NATO but also the OSCE and the World Bank, was decisive during the critical phase of the conflict (see below). This concerted and successful action was underpinned by a common assessment of the situation and a consensus on the goals. The EU has also proved to be an influential actor in the building of international regimes, such as small-arms control (1988 Code of Conduct and 1999 Joint Action). The EU continues to seek to work with as many relevant international actors as possible. First and foremost, this means the UN, and the December 2003 European Council welcomed the EU–UN 'Declaration on Co-operation in Crisis Management'. Clearly, one of the goals of the effort to develop standardised ESDP training mechanisms is to allow EU forces to make meaningful and efficient contributions to UN operations. Relations with the UN have developed rapidly in the past few years and need to be further strengthened. The EU also plays an active if sometimes incoherent role in the OSCE and the Council of Europe as well as in the international financial institutions, notably the IMF and the World Bank, both key actors in conflict prevention. It has also tried to strengthen other international frameworks such as the UN Convention Against Corruption (UNCAC), the Financial Action Task Force (FATF), the Extractive Industries Transparency Initiative (EITI) and the Kimberley Process, which seeks to curb the illegal trade in diamonds.

Perhaps the EU's most ambitious support initiative for a regional organisation is its African Peace Facility (APF), established in April 2004 in response to a request from the AU's Maputo summit. It has made €250 million available from the European Development Fund (EDF) to promote African solutions to African crises by giving the AU financial muscle to back up its political resolve. This money will help pay for African-led, -operated and -staffed peace-keeping missions, though these need not be exclusively military; indeed, APF money cannot be used to buy arms. The January 2004 Common Position on conflict prevention, management and resolution in Africa (2001/374/ CFSP, 26 January 2004) identified a need for a longer-term, more integrated approach to conflict prevention. It stressed mainstreaming conflict-prevention perspectives in particular within development and trade policies to reduce the risk of fuelling conflicts and to maximise impact on peace-building. The necessity to support other international peace-building regimes and organisations has been recognised for some time. The EU has a strong interest in promoting these at both the regional and sub-regional level, such as the ASEAN, the OAS, the Community of Andean Nations, and Mercosur. In addition to the previously cited support for the African Union, the EU also works on that continent with regional bodies such as the ECOWAS (West Africa) and the SADC (southern Africa).

The Irish Presidency in 2004 reported positively on the implementation of the Gothenburg programme, and its conclusions were endorsed at the European Council in June of that year. The reform of EU external assistance that began in 2000 aimed to establish a closer match between development co-operation and the political commitment to address the root causes of conflict, while ensuring that high-quality standards were met. A main focus of the reform is the actual programming of assistance, which is supposed to lead to greater coherence between the EU's strategic priorities and to the right 'policy mix' for each country or region. The Commission can rightly claim some success here, although there are still in-house weaknesses in co-ordination and too few staff working on conflict prevention and crisis management. The reorganisation of the Commission DGs in 1999 and the transfer of conflict-prevention competences from DG Development to DG Relex was regarded by some as limiting the EU's capabilities in terms of long-term conflict-prevention policy. There is little interaction between the two DGs apart from preparation of the country papers, which are meant to help the desk officers, and delegations of the Commission, to target the Community aid better by increasing their awareness and knowledge of the root causes of conflicts. A more substantive issue is the need to assess the match between development co-operation and conflict-prevention objectives. There is no in-house system for reviewing the overall impact of EU assistance on local and regional conflicts.

An additional difficulty is represented by the internal fragmentation of competences within the Commission and within Directorate Generals. DG Relex, DG Development and Aidco, within DG Development, all have separate responsibilities, while the Commission's delegations have been given responsibility for project and aid management. This fragmentation has not helped raise the profile of conflict prevention within the Commission. The websites of DG Relex and DG Development devote little space to conflict prevention, and speeches by Commissioners have paid little more than lip-service to the concept. The Commission is also struggling to find the right balance between security and development. While it was recognised in the ESS, in the Cotonou agreement and in the Africa strategy that both go hand in hand, it is also clear that strategies to reduce poverty will not necessarily contribute to strengthening democracy and preventing conflict. Economic and social development meant to alleviate poverty may fuel conflict in communities, depending on which social, sectoral or ethnic groups are the beneficiaries of this aid.

The majority of EU external assistance is delivered through long-term instruments and intended to support structural conflict prevention and peaceful resolution of disputes through targeted programmes that promote the rule of law, good governance and poverty reduction. Humanitarian aid delivered through ECHO can also help mitigate crises or prevent conflicts, as witness efforts in the Congo (DRC), Liberia and Sudan. As best it can, ECHO seeks to insulate its humanitarian mission from the political decisions and policies pursued by other elements of the EU and by its member states. Critics have suggested that highly developed participants in the global economy such as the EU and the US could provide substantially more benefits to many under-developed countries by eliminating trade subsidies, particularly in agriculture, than they do through foreign aid (see Chapter 10).

Case study 11.1: The EU's role in the Former Yugoslav Republic of Macedonia (FYROM)

Macedonia gained independence from Yugoslavia in 1991. In a dispute between Greece and Macedonia over its name a stalemate was reached in 1993 when Greece gave its acquiescence to Macedonia joining the United Nations under the provisional name 'Former Yugoslav Republic of Macedonia' instead of 'Republic of Macedonia'. The disagreement over the name remains to be resolved. The conflict in Macedonia broke out in 2001, a decade after the country's secession from Yugoslavia. Macedonia has a multi-ethnic population of about 2 million. The two largest groups are the Slav Macedonians (64 per cent of the population) and the ethnic Albanians (25 per cent). The latter live mostly in the western and north-western part of the country, but also in Skopje which makes a separation impossible. Tensions between Macedonians and Albanians had already been simmering in the Yugoslav era. Smaller uprisings in 1995 and 1998 could be contained. The Albanian grievances began to gain political currency in late 2000 as Albanians demanded better minority protection under the constitution and greater participation in the government. Open hostilities broke out in February 2001 when the Albanian National Liberation Army (NLA) took up armed attacks against government forces. The insurgency spread through northern and western Macedonia during the first half of 2001, resulting in EU and international mediation. In July 2001, a cease-fire was brokered and the government coalition was expanded to include the major opposition parties. The agreement formed the basis of the subsequent peace negotiations between the four main Macedonian and Albanian political parties.

The peace agreement could not have been concluded without the EU's and other international actors' active involvement. In spring 2001 the shuttle diplomacy of EU High Representative for CFSP, Javier Solana, and External Relations Commissioner Chris Patten, together with NATO Secretary General, Lord George Robertson, had only mixed results. Therefore, the EU in June 2001 nominated the retired French politician François Léotard, who, together with his US counterpart James Pardew, brought the negotiations to a successful ending. At a critical moment in the talks, Solana visited Ohrid and managed to put the negotiations back on track. On 13 August 2001 the Ohrid Framework Agreement could be signed and brought an end to the fighting. It provided for constitutional and legislative changes to improve minority rights in Macedonia, e.g. with respect to the Albanian language and a multi-ethnic police force. NATO also played a key role by deploying around 4,500 peace-keeping forces to Macedonia. These troops were replaced later by an EU force. The EU also provided funding under its RRM for restoring electricity, rebuilding houses, mine clearance and media and police training.

Since the conclusion of the Ohrid Agreement the EU has maintained its efforts to assist Macedonia on its path towards peace and democracy and European integration. On 31 March 2003 the EU took over from NATO and launched an eight-month military mission to further stabilise the country. EUFOR Concordia comprised 400 troops from 26 countries.

continued

From 15 December 2003 the EU also maintained a police mission called EUPOL-Proxima with 170 international staff supported by 150 local staff. Its objective is to support the development of an efficient and professional police service based on European standards. Its task is to monitor, mentor and advise the Macedonian police. It was replaced by a small EU Police Advisory Team (EUPAT) on 15 December 2005. EUPAT consists of 30 personnel, both EU police officers and civilian experts assisted by 20 national staff. EUPAT will build on Proxima's achievements and focus its activities on four different sectors: public peace and order, organised crime/criminal police, border police, and police-judiciary co-operation.

Between 1992 and 2005 the EU provided some €76 million in aid to Macedonia. The indicative programme for Macedonia for 2005–6 focuses on strengthening the administrative capacity of the country with particular emphasis on the rule of law, support of economic development (improvement of business environment, SMEs development) and strengthening social cohesion. The priority sectors for Macedonia within the EU's Community Assistance for Reconstruction, Development and Stabilisation (CARDS) programme are democratic stabilisation (implementation of the Ohrid Peace Agreement), public administration reform, justice and home affairs, investment climate, trade and infrastructure, education and employment, and environment. Macedonia has benefited from other EU funding sources, such as the European Investment Bank for transport, SME, and energy projects. EC humanitarian assistance (ECHO) activities came to an end in 2003.

On 9 April 2001, Macedonia became the first south-east European country to conclude a Stabilisation and Association Agreement (SAA) with the EU, which came into force on 1 April 2004. Macedonia applied for EU membership on 22 March 2004 and was granted candidate status (albeit with no date for starting accession negotiations) at the December 2005 European Council. The EU played a substantial role in settling the conflict in Macedonia and preventing further outbreaks of violence. Its representatives significantly contributed to the achievement of the Ohrid Peace Agreement with their intense diplomatic efforts and peace-keeping forces. The timely release of funds under the RRM also helped stabilise the country. But probably the most important factor was the EU's offer of membership to Macedonia, providing the country with a vision for the future as well as incentives to agree reforms.

IMPROVING THE CIVILIAN RESPONSE CAPABILITY

While much attention has been paid to the need for the EU to improve its military capabilities there has been parallel pressure to improve its civilian capabilities and to ensure more attention for human security. Solana has taken a strong interest in the whole human security agenda and commissioned a report in 2004 that urged greater EU resources to deal with conflict prevention and crisis management. The report urged more attention to be paid to human rights and proposed a mainly civilian, 15,000-strong Human Security Response Force.[1] Member states, however, showed little interest in taking this idea further. The EU had already sought to increase its civilian capabilities, and the member states agreed at the Feira European Council in June 2000 to provide by 2003: a minimum of 5,000 police officers, 1,000 of whom can be deployed within thirty days; 200 rule-of-law experts, including prosecutors, lawyers and judges and a rapid response group capable of deployment within thirty days; a pool of civilian administration experts; and two or three civil protection assessment teams of ten experts each, capable of dispatch within hours of a disaster, with a 2,000-strong civil protection intervention contingent available for later deployment. The Feira decision was important because there was nothing specific in the TEU about crisis management and these commitments thus provided essential targets for the Union.

The EU has done a fair job in meeting these goals. The civilian capabilities commitment conference on 22 November 2004 declared that member states had volunteered 5,761 police, 631 rule-of-law specialists, 562 civilian administrators and 4,988 civil protection personnel. Proxima in Macedonia and the EUPM in Bosnia were police missions, as was the Europol mission to the Democratic Republic of Congo ('Kinshasa'); and, in response to an invitation from Georgia, the EU decided in June 2004 (Joint Action 2004/523/CFSP of 28 June 2004) to send its first ever ESDP Rule of Law Mission (Themis) to Tbilisi for one year. In December 2004 the European Council agreed on an integrated police, rule-of-law and civilian administration mission for Iraq. The EU also agreed a new Civilian Headline Goal (2008) that runs parallel to the Military Headline Goal (2010). The aim is to improve the EU's capacity to act in terms of both quantity and quality of resources. There is a need to have a roster of experts with language skills and areas of expertise and have them trained with other nationalities. There is also likely to be a demand for increased integrated packages involving rapidly deployable civilian response teams.

In the longer term, the EU's added value in conflict management should be its ability to deploy mixed civilian and military missions rapidly. But, just as this requires new thinking about the function of armed forces, it also requires new seriousness about civilian capabilities as, in many situations, at least an equal complement to military capabilities. To date, the EU has trained over one thousand people for possible civilian deployment. As this has been mainly done at the national level, it is crucial to ensure more coherence in national training programmes, so that personnel deployed from different member states can work together effectively from day one. There is currently no link between training courses and deployment, and mechanisms need to be introduced to ensure that those trained are also willing and able to take part in EU operations. Recruitment, the responsibility of member states, is procedurally diverse, which makes it quite difficult to identify qualified personnel to deploy at short notice. The newly adopted standard EU training concept in ESDP has the potential to improve inter-operability between civilian officials from different member states and spread a common ESDP culture based on lessons learned from past operations. However, it is clear that EU civilian capabilities have not yet come near their potential. The problem is one of co-ordination between both political priorities and Council and Commission competences. There has been pressure from some NGOs to create a European peace-building agency, while others have proposed a European civil peace corps, but member states are yet to be persuaded of the viability or desirability of these proposals.[2]

Case study 11.2: The EU and Aceh

The EU carried out a successful crisis-management mission in Aceh, Indonesia, in 2005–6. Why did the EU become involved and what did it do? Indonesia, the world's largest Muslim nation, is a key player in South-East Asia, accounting for half of the ASEAN's population and economy. It is rich in resources and an active partner and participant in the ASEM, the ASEAN and other regional organisations. Indonesia only made the transition from authoritarian rule to democracy in the late 1990s, and the EU had a major interest in helping to support the democratic forces in the country. The EU also wants Indonesia to be a reliable partner in terms of promoting regional security. After the October 2002 Bali bombings, Indonesia and the EU had a shared interest in combating terrorism. The 1999 vote for East Timor independence, however, sent a shockwave through the Indonesian political elite and froze successive government initiatives regarding Aceh for several years.

The region of Aceh had struggled to achieve independence for many years, even during the Dutch and Japanese imperial occupations. From 1945 the Acehnese actively supported Indonesia's independence, but unrest resurfaced in the early 1950s. Aceh became one of the archipelago's most profitable areas for international investment (liquid natural gas), but little of the revenues was to benefit the province. The armed resistance group Gerekan Aceh Merdeka (GAM), established in 1976, was able to gather broad popular support but met with violent repression. Its leadership fled to Sweden in 1979 and created a government in exile.

In December 2002 the Cessation of Hostilities Agreement (CoHA) was signed by the government of Indonesia and GAM but it failed to hold. President Yudhoyono, who took up office in 2004, seized the opportunity provided by the tsunami disaster that killed close to 180,000 Acehnese, to relaunch efforts for a cease-fire. The former Finnish president, Maarti Ahtisaari, emerged as a mediator and he secured the support of the EU for a mediating and monitoring mission. After Ahtisaari helped secure a comprehensive memorandum of understanding, the EU agreed in August 2005 to an Aceh monitoring mission (AMM) comprising some 80 monitors from EU member states, Norway, Switzerland and ASEAN countries. From 15 September 2005 the AMM functioned as a civilian ESDP mission and was the first ESDP mission to include human rights monitors.

The reason for the successful deal lay in a combination of factors. The tsunami was Indonesia's most serious catastrophe in living memory. Post-disaster uncertainty, poverty and hopelessness changed the picture, with both sides ready to compromise and accept an agreement that provided for considerable autonomy for Aceh. The EU was able to react swiftly with financial assistance and the monitoring mission. The deal was also strongly supported by the ASEAN states, which contributed qualified personnel to the AMM. As regards the EU, the Council and Commission worked smoothly together to set up and run the AMM. The newly established Civil–Military Cell within the Council Secretariat contributed substantially to the planning and launching of the AMM, which had as its main tasks:

- Monitor the demobilisation of GAM and monitor and assist with the decommissioning and destruction of its weapons, ammunition and explosives.
- Monitor the relocation of military forces and police troops.
- Monitor the reintegration of active GAM members.
- Monitor the human rights situation and provide assistance in this field in the context of the tasks set out above.
- Monitor the process of legislative change.
- Rule on disputed amnesty cases.
- Deal with complaints and alleged violations of the MoU.
- Establish and maintain liaison and good co-operation with the parties.

continued

At its peak AMM deployed some 230 monitors from the EU, Norway, Switzerland and ASEAN member states, in four mobile decommissioning teams, operating from 11 district offices. The AMM was financed from the CFSP budget line (€9 million) and by contributions from member states and other participating countries (€6 million). In addition the Commission provided €24.4 million to address structural issues beyond the AMM mandate. This provided support for reintegration of GAM combatants, local elections, capacity building of police, access to justice, promotion and protection of human rights and enhancing local government.

The success of the Aceh mission helped to raise the profile of the EU in Indonesia and throughout Asia. It provided an opportunity to strengthen relations with the government of Indonesia and to support the domestic reform process. It also helped strengthen the EU's relations with the ASEAN, which had been feeling neglected as the EU had spent so much time and energy dealing with China. Both sides hoped to expand their dialogue on political and security issues including conflict prevention and crisis management. Overall, therefore, the Aceh mission was a considerable success story for the EU.

CONDITIONALITY, DEMOCRACY AND HUMAN RIGHTS

Conditionality entails the EU linking perceived benefits to another state, such as financial assistance, trade concessions, co-operation agreements, political contacts or even membership, to the fulfilment of certain conditions. These normally relate to the protection of human and minority rights, the advancement of democratic principles and, in some cases, willingness to engage in regional co-operation. Negative conditionality would lead to the withholding or withdrawal of such benefits and could also involve a visa ban and targeted sanctions. Conditionality, however, is not an easy instrument to use. There are no scientific rules covering democracy, and there remain different interpretations of human rights. In December 1991, Croatia was recognised even though it had not met the (Badinter) conditions, whilst recognition of Macedonia was withheld even though it had met the conditions. In 1992 the EU turned a blind eye as the military intervened after the first round of voting in the Algerian election. Indeed, the EU has never invoked the articles allowing for suspension in the Association Agreements with the Mediterranean partners if there is evidence of human rights abuses. Although the use of conditionality by the EU has increased steadily in recent years it is difficult to assess its effectiveness. A preliminary conclusion may be that the bigger the EU carrot on offer, the greater the likelihood of EU pressure bringing results. There is little doubt that the carrot of EU membership has acted as an incentive to all central and eastern European countries to improve their democratic structures. There is also some evidence that geographical proximity to the EU is an important factor, as is the size of the country. It is easier to influence Albania than China or Russia.

Election observation is a significant component of the EU's policy of promoting human rights and democratisation throughout the world, and thus part of its overall conflict-prevention strategy. This is an area where the Commission has asserted leadership. The legal basis for EU election observation missions consists of Council regulations 975/99 and 976/99. The decision to provide electoral assistance and to send EU observers must be taken on the basis of a Commission proposal.

Case study 11.3: EU election observation missions

In recent years there has been a considerable expansion of the EU's involvement in third-country elections. This support is twofold: technical assistance to electoral authorities and the deployment of EU Election Observation Missions (EOM). These are organised by the European Commission with the Community budget and are made up of experts and observers from the member states.

In 2000 the Commission developed a standard methodology for election observation. This covers all phases of the election cycle: pre-election, election day, and immediate post-election. EOMs do not interfere in the organisation of the election itself, but collect and analyse factual information concerning the election process, and provide an independent public assessment. Since then, and with a total budget of over €77 million, the EU has deployed forty-seven missions in thirty-five countries involving the participation of over 4,000 experts and observers.

EOMs do not just serve to assess election day but observe the whole process and thus also assess the state of democratic development in a given country at a particular point in time. In addition to observing and reporting on the elections, the presence of EU observers can enhance transparency and confidence in the process, serve as a conflict-prevention mechanism by deterring violence and possibly preventing fraud.

EOMs are carefully selected on the basis of complementarity with other human rights and democratisation activities and the added value that such a mission can bring to the election process. A final decision is only taken after an exploratory mission has visited the country to

continued

determine whether an EU EOM would be useful, advisable and feasible. The EU does not observe elections where they can be credibly or systematically observed by other international organisations or local stakeholders. This is the case of the OSCE area where the OSCE/ODIHR leads in election observation.

The EU also has to be invited by the local government; and then a number of conditions should be met:

- Franchise is genuinely universal.
- Political parties and individual candidates are able to enjoy their legitimate right to take part in the election.
- There is freedom of expression allowing possible criticism of the incumbent government and the right to free movement and assembly.
- All contesting parties and candidates have reasonable access to the media.

Finally, a Memorandum of Understanding detailing rights and responsibilities of observers and the host government and the adequate co-operation between both parties has to be signed between the European Commission and the Election Commission as well as the Foreign Ministry of the host country.

The EOM not only have the ambitious task of observing and reporting on elections, they also enhance the transparency of the process and the confidence of voters. They can serve as a conflict-prevention mechanism, providing an impartial assessment of the election process, defusing tension and, by their presence, deterring or reporting fraud. The Chief Observer returns to the country to present the final report and its recommendations, sometimes during a roundtable with all players involved in the election process. The record that is left behind by an EOM can be of value to those who will support the country's capacity building and democracy in the future. National and international stakeholders may use the conclusions and recommendations to promote election reform, including through projects of capacity building for the election administration or other aspects of the process. At a political level, the EU EOM final report may be the basis for specific discussions on elections in the framework of the EU's political dialogue with the country concerned. Most observer missions have been in developing countries as the OSCE tends to monitor elections in its member countries. EOMs have been involved in countries such as Zimbabwe, Haiti, East Timor, Palestine, Uganda and Cambodia.

AFRICA SECURITY

In recent years the EU has paid more attention to Africa and especially to the strengthening of an indigenous peace-keeping force for the continent. Although it might not be apparent from the popular press, in recent years there have been important changes in the commitment of African leaders to manage crises on the continent. Institutionally, the inauguration of the Peace and Security Council on Africa Day, on 25 May 2004, in the Ethiopian capital, Addis Ababa, was the most concrete manifestation of this readiness to commit more attention and resources to the quest for greater stability. Much work has gone into the establishment of the Africa Standby Force (ASF), composed of a brigade on standby for peace-keeping duties in each of Africa's five regions and a complement of observers, military police and civilian personnel on standby at the continental level for deployment in Africa, following the provision of an appropriate political mandate from the Peace and Security Council. The EU has been a principal supporter of the ASF and its parent organisation, the African Peace Facility. For example, in June 2004 the EU agreed to provide €12 million to support observers monitoring a ceasefire between the Sudanese government and two rebel groups in Darfur. The twelve-month funding was requested by the AU, which led the international mission of 120 observers and a protection force of 270 soldiers. Overall the EU has provided €250 million to support peace-keeping in Africa. The EU has also sent its own missions to the continent. For example, in summer 2006, Germany led an ESDP mission to provide security for elections in the Congo.

Much of Africa's lack of development and instability is a result of poor governance. For the AU to engage in a situation before the eruption of widespread violence requires a political determination to address internal policies and practices against the wishes of the governing elite. Perhaps no African countries bear greater testimony to how difficult it is for the Union to engage in these matters than Zimbabwe, where the ruinous policies of President Robert Mugabe have severely damaged the economic base, and Sudan, where the complicity of the government has been alleged in what some have likened to genocide by Arab militias in the Darfur region. The situation in Zimbabwe has yet to be debated at any level within the AU, despite ample public evidence of the extent of human rights abuses, executive excess and economic policies that compound hunger and increase poverty. As regards the AU, its controversial finding that the March 2002 presidential election in Zimbabwe was legitimate, despite substantial evidence to the contrary, compounds its complicity. In the case of Sudan, the AU only responded through the token deployment of a handful of observers under intense donor and other pressure, and only after the displacement and death of substantial numbers of the local population.

Although significant progress has been achieved, anything more than token observer missions will continue to depend on 'framework' or capable 'lead' nations such as South Africa, Nigeria and Kenya (rather like the situation within the EU!). For the moment, the contribution of the ASF will, at most, lie in the support that could be provided to peace-making through the deployment of small observer missions, verification teams and monitoring units that can build confidence between protagonists. Africa has, of course, experienced many strategies for conflict mitigation in the past. However, current developments involve important changes to previous situations. African leaders themselves recognise that the continent cannot develop without greater stability and an end to the conflicts that deny it investment. The slow and messy process of improving governance and advancing democracy remains the principal requirement of stability and development in Africa.

CONCLUSION

Q - Sudan - Why so long?

Since 2000 there has been a step-change in the EU's approach to conflict prevention and crisis management. It is more active and has developed significant new capabilities. It is clear that mainstreaming – the process of establishing an in-house culture of prevention – has become more and more embedded in EU bodies. But it is not an easy task to assess its strengths and weaknesses at this stage. The EU has had a number of modest achievements, but paradoxically this has raised new questions on the limits of its role. Had Macedonia been devoid of any hope of future EU membership, could the EU still have been successful in its intervention? Is it likely that the institutional constraints inherent to the EU conflict-prevention policy (pillarisation, dispersal of bodies and complexity of decision-making) would condemn it to a more modest policy agenda, covering only crises in regional proximity and horizontal issues of a limited range; international crime, the diamond trade, drug trafficking, child soldiers? Or could it overcome these barriers and draw on its entire range of instruments – trade policy, trade and co-operation agreements, experience of security sector reform, or tools derived from areas such as justice and home affairs, migration, social or environmental policy? A coherent preventive approach to conflict and crisis depends on three factors: a clear definition of objectives, capacity to act, and the political will to act.

Although the EU has moved steadily into the field of conflict prevention, there are a number of ways in which it might expand and enhance its role. There is a continuing need to develop ways in which conflict prevention is integrated, including gender sensitivity and awareness, more fully into existing programmes and policies; and to develop new frameworks through which women's conflict prevention and peace-building activities are supported. More sophisticated conflict-impact assessments could assist in the development of a strategic framework. The Union also needs to have clearer guidelines as regards financing for its external actions in order to avoid confusion and delays. It should also reflect more on how to maximise use of its growing array of Special Representatives. Perhaps the major obstacle facing the EU and other international actors is the lack of political will to take effective action at an early enough stage in the process. But what does 'political will' really entail?

Much depends on the building of a political consensus to act as well as ensuring the necessary capabilities. There are sometimes differences between the twenty-five EU member states on the use of instruments to deal with potential conflicts, and some may also have specific interests in a region. There are also the oft-cited rivalries between those responsible for Community instruments and those responsible for the CFSP/ ESDP. It is thus not always easy to secure a common vision of the desired outcome of a crisis, and there are limitations on the EU's use of its well-stocked toolbox. Some member states may also prefer to operate through NATO in high-risk areas, e.g. Afghanistan. Partly as a result, there are also doubts about the future of the Anglo-French partnership in the ESDP. Practitioners need to recognise that these constraints are likely to inhibit the EU's potential in conflict prevention for some considerable time.

KEY QUESTIONS

What have been the EU's main achievements in conflict prevention?
What are its principal weaknesses in this area?
How has it related to the UN in terms of conflict prevention?
Examine the EU efforts at crisis management in either Macedonia or Aceh.
How would you explain the difference between hard and soft security?

FURTHER READING

Youngs (2001) looks at democracy promotion, and Telò (2005) examines the EU as a civilian power. There are not many books on the EU and conflict prevention, and here it is useful to consult websites such as www.conflictprevention.net.

12 Tackling terrorism

SUMMARY

Since 9/11 terrorism has become a major foreign as well as domestic policy issue. The international dimension of terrorism is well known, and the European Security Strategy (ESS) identified terrorism as one of the main security threats facing the Union. Terrorists may plan an attack in one country, ensure financing from a second country, conduct the crime in a third country and seek refuge in a fourth. Mainly under US pressure, the EU has had to develop its own policies to tackle terrorism. Inevitably these have had an external dimension, as the EU has had to negotiate with international partners and seek their co-operation for counter-terrorist policies. In addition the EU has provided increasing technical assistance to third countries in an effort to tackle terrorism at source. The EU has much to offer the international community, from police and judicial co-operation to border management, from enhanced information exchange to data protection, from legislation to policy funding, from national to regional co-operation. Some eighty countries benefit from EU-financed assistance programmes. The EU is also active at the UN seeking to build consensus on tackling terrorism. It is also engaged in efforts to tackle the root causes of terrorism.

INTRODUCTION

Terrorism, sometimes referred to as the world's second-oldest profession, has moved to the top of the international political agenda. It has replaced the Cold War as one of the main security threats – at least in the perception of many in the developed world. Several EU member states have a long history of dealing with terrorism. These include the UK and the IRA, Spain and ETA, and Italy and the Red Brigade. But with the Al Qaeda attack on the New York twin towers on 11 September 2001 the threat of international terrorism rose to the top of the agenda in the EU as well as in the US. The Madrid bombings of February 2004 and the London bombings of July 2005 were a grim reminder that nowhere in Europe was safe from terrorism. While many member states have had years of experience in fighting national terrorism, they have had to adjust to fighting a new type of international terrorism, which is not conducted as a way of achieving a clearly defined aim, such as Basque independence, nor is it confined to one particular country. The international dimension of terrorism has increased significantly as a consequence of globalisation, the worldwide reach of the media, international banking systems, the ease of foreign travel and the cyber revolution. These developments had led to significant changes in the EU itself. The interplay between domestic and foreign policy is particularly striking in the context of the third pillar of the EU that deals with justice and home affairs (JHA). Border controls, transnational crime, illegal migration and asylum are all sensitive issues; but, above all, it has been terrorism that has propelled the Union to greater co-operation in the JHA field. New institutions such as Europol, Eurojust and the European Police College (CEPOL) have been established, while pressure from the US has also been an important catalyst in the EU agreeing new measures to tackle terrorism.

The EU agenda in fighting terrorism is based on prevention, protection, prosecution and consequence management. Preventive measures include tackling money-laundering as well as the root causes of terrorism. Protection is concerned with critical infrastructure. Prosecution involves closer judicial co-operation, including the European arrest warrant. Consequence management involves minimising the risk of a terrorist attack and limiting the damage if one was to occur. On the external front the EU provides technical assistance to over eighty countries in fighting terrorism. The EU has found it easy to draw up action plans but less easy to translate these into action. After the Madrid bombings the EU appointed a counter-terrorist co-ordinator, the Dutch MEP Guy de Vries, but he has very limited powers. His principal role is to improve co-ordination within the EU and between the EU and third countries. He also ensures that texts and decisions adopted by member states are implemented but he is not responsible for co-ordinating individual member states' national counter-terrorism structures or operations. According to de Vries himself, the basic problem with his job is that 'everybody says they are in favour of co-ordination but nobody is in favour of being co-ordinated'.[1] The reflex of interior ministers is jealously to protect their powers at the national level, even though the fight against terrorism is a global one. There are also continuing concerns about possible abuses of human rights in tackling terrorism. European public opinion has been highly critical of US methods in Guantanamo Bay, the Abu Ghraib prison in Iraq and alleged CIA torture flights. At the same time the EU has had to accede to US requests to tighten container security and to provide advance passenger data on all those travelling to the US.

How the EU deals with its own large Muslim communities also has foreign policy implications as their treatment is watched closely by many Islamic states. The publication of cartoons about the prophet Muhammad in Denmark sparked widespread demonstrations against European embassies in many Muslim countries in February 2006, prompting a hurried mission by Solana to the region.[2] Danish Prime Minister Anders Rasmussen described the situation as 'the worst foreign policy crisis for Denmark since 1945'. Rioting Muslim youths in France or the arrest of extremist Imams in Britain can also provoke unrest abroad. What is the cause of the new terrorism? There are a number of extra-European aspects including corruption and lack of democracy in the Islamic world, deficient socio-economic development, the perception of Western support for corrupt regimes, drawn-out armed conflicts, alleged hypocrisy of the West concerning the Israeli–Palestinian dispute – and Iraq. Security experts also speak of the widespread feeling of despair that is often a motive for terrorist attacks. Overall the EU approach has been to emphasise a comprehensive approach to tackling terrorism. Its leaders have avoided the black-and-white rhetoric of the US and preferred to talk of a 'fight against terrorism' instead of a 'war on terror'. The EU has also given more emphasis to international institutions and co-operation. Although terrorism has become one of the EU's greatest challenges, one of the problems of EU efforts is that not all member states, and certainly not all citizens, have the same perception of the threat. This may be partly because there is a wide variation in the number and location of attacks. Between 1968 and 2005 there were over 1,200 attacks in Spain, over 800 in the UK but only one in Finland and Slovenia. Ninety per cent of all incidents in this period were carried out in just six member states – the UK, France, Germany, Spain, Italy and Greece. This has led to wide differences in how citizens view terrorism. In the new member states, not more than 3 per cent view terrorism as the major threat compared to 46 per cent in Spain. Overall, in the list of threats facing Europe, polls show terrorism at number eight on the list. In short, in many member states there is no perception of terrorism as a pan-European threat. Yet in the ESS it was stated that 'terrorism poses a growing strategic threat to the whole of Europe' and that 'Europe is both a target and a base for terrorism'.

TACKLING TERRORISM

The anti-terrorist measures and intensified co-operation between the EU member states that followed the 9/11 attacks were already agreed during the European Council meeting in Tampere, Finland, in 1999. Thus, 9/11 was not exactly an impetus for a change; it rather provided an environment which speeded up the implementation of adopted measures and shifted the priority of the security policy towards the fight against terrorism. Immediately after 9/11 the EU agreed an action plan and roadmap containing some seventy measures to be taken, including:

- enhancing police and judicial co-operation – introduction of the European arrest warrant; adoption of a common definition of terrorism
- drawing up of a common list of terrorist organisations
- improving co-operation and exchange of information between all intelligence services

- setting up of joint investigation teams
- sharing with Europol all useful data regarding terrorism
- establishing special anti-terrorist teams within Europol
- developing international legal instruments – and agreeing that all existing international conventions on the fight against terrorism were to be implemented as quickly as possible
- stopping the funding of terrorism – directive on money-laundering and the framework decision on freezing assets were to be adopted
- strengthening air security – classification of weapons, technical training for crew, checking and monitoring of hold luggage, protection of cockpit areas, quality control of security measures applied by member states
- co-ordinating the EU's global action – concentrating on prevention and stabilisation of regional conflicts, especially in the Middle East.

In March 2004, shortly after the terrorist attacks in Madrid, the EU revised the action plan and agreed an ambitious Declaration on Combating Terrorism, which included the creation of a counter-terrorism co-ordinator to oversee European anti-terrorist activities, the integration of an intelligence structure on terrorism within the Council Secretariat, a reinforced role for Europol, Eurojust and the Police Chiefs' Task Force. The EU also agreed on two further measures: a 'solidarity clause' (taken from the draft constitutional treaty), which provides for mutual assistance in the event of a terrorist attack; and the creation of a European Borders Agency. On the external front, the EU agreed a raft of measures including a strengthening of the UN bodies dealing with terrorism, new money-laundering policies, protection of airports, closer co-operation with NATO and other international organisations in consequence management. EU leaders also agreed on the need:

> to identify the factors which contribute to recruitment to terrorism, both within the EU and internationally, and develop a long-term strategy to address these. It also calls for a continued investigation into the links between extreme religious or political beliefs, as well as socio-economic and other factors, and support for terrorism, building on work already undertaken in this area, and identifying appropriate response measures.

Finally, the EU agreed on the need to enhance capabilities to evaluate third-country activities in counter-terrorism and to insert counter-terrorism clauses in agreements with priority countries. These were deemed to be Pakistan, Iran, India, Afghanistan and countries of Central Asia.[3]

In comparison with the original action plan from September 2001, the 2004 plan stressed the need for international co-operation and consensus. The EU was ready, willing and able to help third countries enhance their capabilities in counter-terrorism. More difficult was the aim of developing a long-term strategy to address the factors which contribute to radicalisation and recruitment for terrorist activities. Another difficult area in which to secure EU-wide agreement was the call for common visa rules. Less controversial were plans to upgrade the Schengen system that covers passport-free travel among its members. One of the problems for the EU is the very different capabilities of member states in being able to provide credible threat assessments. The ESS states that 'common assessment of threats is the basis for common actions and this requires improvement in the exchange of intelligence information among Member States and partners', but there is a reluctance of member states to share sensitive information (see below). At first glance it would seem that the EU is particularly suited to playing a central role in developing international and cross-agency intelligence co-operation because it is the only international organisation that has its own agencies for the exchange and production of military intelligence (decision of the EU military staff – EUMS), imagery (EU satellite centre – EUSC), criminal and security (Europol) and external intelligence (Joint Situation Centre – SITCEN). However, these bodies have limited capacities, and their work is often handicapped because they depend largely on national contributions.

EU STRUCTURES

One of the difficulties in co-ordinating counter-terrorism efforts at the EU level is that there is no one single body that deals with all matters related to terrorism. The structures that the EU has established to tackle terrorism are highly complicated and reflect again the lack of coherence between the different pillars. The Justice and Home Affairs Council (JHA Council) and the GAERC both play leading roles, but other bodies such as ECOFIN also play a role when it comes to issues such as money-laundering. In the roadmap for the fight against terrorism the JHA Council was designed to be the responsible body for adoption of a number of legislative and operational measures. The JHA Council also had a number of responsibilities concerning co-operation in the field of justice and home affairs with the US. This concerned especially the assessment of all aspects of terrorist threat, co-operation between Europol and the US law enforcement agencies and co-operation on mutual assistance in criminal matters. Within the Council there are two working groups dealing with terrorism. The Terrorism Working Group (TWG), which is composed of representatives of member states' ministries of the interior/law enforcement agencies, deals with internal threat assessments, practical co-operation and co-ordination among EU bodies and meets three times per Presidency. The Working Party on Terrorism (COTER) deals with external aspects and is mainly composed of representatives of members states' ministries of foreign affairs. It meets monthly and deals with implementation of UN conventions and threat assessments as regards third countries and regions. There is a certain rivalry between these two working groups, partly because of the very different working cultures and objectives of the parent bodies – the ministries of foreign affairs and ministries of the interior. There are many other working groups that deal with some aspects of terrorism, but TWG and COTER are the two main ones. Both Solana and de Vries have called for more coherence in tackling terrorism, but so far member states have been reluctant to cede more powers to the EU in this field. Under the constitutional treaty, the decision-making process would be significantly improved. There would be more qualified majority voting (QMV) in justice and home affairs, a stronger role for Europol and Eurojust, and the creation of a new standing committee 'to ensure that operational co-operation on internal security is promoted and strengthened within the Union'. This proposal was regarded as dangerous by some human rights observers who considered that the new body would become the de facto 'EU Interior Ministry' and erode the traditional division of powers between legislative, executive and judicial functions which is the hallmark of the first pillar. While the fate of the treaty is in abeyance, and to gain practical experience with co-ordination in the mean time, the Council organises a joint meeting every six months between the chairpersons of the Strategic Committee on Immigration, Frontiers and Asylum (SCIFA) and the Article 36 Committee (CATS) and representatives of the Commission, Europol, Eurojust, the European Business Association (EBA), the Police Chiefs' Task Force, and the SITCEN.

Set up by the Maastricht Treaty, and accountable to the JHA Council, Europol was originally a clearing house for the exchange of intelligence on drugs trafficking. After all member states ratified the Europol Convention in 1998 its mandate was extended to deal with all serious forms of international crime, including terrorism. Europol serves as a central databank on terrorism and maintains a computerised information system for consultation by member states. It also has a special counter-terrorism taskforce that specialises in the profiling of Islamic terrorists. But, like the FBI, it is handicapped by a lack of Arabic speakers. It also has very limited human and financial resources. Europol has an annual budget of about €58 million (in comparison Britain's MI5 security service has a budget of €450 million) and some 350 employees (compared to over 3,000 in MI5). Even though Europol is one of the most relevant EU structures for the fight against terrorism, its role has remained limited to the collection, transmission and analysis of data provided by national police forces. Different legal systems in the member states also make co-operation difficult. Eurojust was set up in February 2002 to improve the effectiveness of the prosecuting and investigating authorities in the member states by promoting co-operation between its members, providing information on judicial cases and liaising with third countries, especially the US. Each member state is represented in Eurojust by senior, experienced prosecutors or judges. Eurojust is the first permanent network of judicial authorities in the world and handled about 300 cases in 2005 ranging from co-ordinating house searches in different countries to police requesting access to bank accounts outside their own jurisdiction. The European Commission in the guise of its DG on Justice and Home Affairs also plays a growing role in fighting terrorism as it has direct or shared responsibility for issues such as container security, data protection and biometric identifiers. Although not part of the EU, the Bern

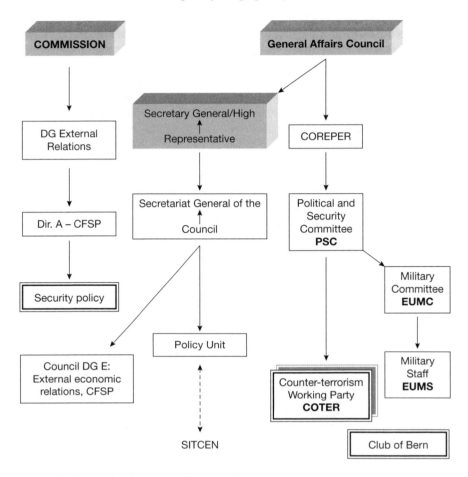

Figure 12.1 CFSP structures against terrorism

Club is an informal meeting of the heads/chiefs of foreign intelligence service agencies from EU member states plus Norway, Switzerland and the US. It has been meeting annually since 1971, and after 9/11 it set up a counter-terrorism group which is a useful forum for intelligence exchange between the EU and the US. As can be seen from Figure 12.1 the EU structures dealing with terrorism in the CFSP area are highly complicated.

INTELLIGENCE SHARING

There have been several calls, including a proposal by the Belgian prime minister, Guy Verhofstadt, to create a European central intelligence agency. But most member states do not seem to be ready for such a step, and many

EU officials argue that it would be better to improve the functioning of the existing institutions and relations before creating new structures. There are several obstacles to closer intelligence co-operation. One is the very different legal frameworks in the member states. Intelligence services are by definition reluctant to share information, stressing the importance of source protection. Traditionally there is a high level of distrust between intelligence services. They prefer to work on a bilateral level and to exchange the minimum amount of information. Some member states who have privileged intelligence relations with other countries, i.e. with the US, fear that they might jeopardise receiving information if information is shared within the Union's framework. Those that do have good intelligence services question why they should pay for the free-riders. After the Iraq 2003 war, there is another fear – the manipulation of intelligence for political purposes. There is also a trend towards an informal directoire in this field. The interior ministers from five of the larger member states – Germany, France, Spain, the UK and Italy – met for an informal meeting on terrorism in July 2004 and decided to deepen security co-ordination and intelligence-sharing among them. French Interior Minister Nicolas Sarkozy defended the meeting, stating that it was unrealistic to expect to share sensitive data with twenty-five nations (Reuters, 19 March 2004).

The lack of effective co-operation between the intelligence agencies has been criticised by the Spanish investigative judge Baltasar Garzon who, in the aftermath of the Madrid bombings, stated that:

> there is an enormous amount of information, but much of it gets lost because of the failures of co-operation. We are doing maybe one-third of what we can do within the law in fighting terrorism in Europe. There is a lack of communication, a lack of co-ordination, and a lack of any broad vision. (*The New York Times*, 22 March 2004)

The problem with intelligence-sharing in Europe is that there are too many bureaucratic, institutional and also linguistic burdens, which in fact give the advantage to the terrorists.

INTERNATIONAL CO-OPERATION

Like the US, the EU is aware that terrorism cannot be defeated by any one state and hence has steadily increased its support for international efforts. At the UN, the EU has played an important role in securing support for the Convention Against Nuclear Terrorism and continues to promote agreement on a General Convention Against Terrorism. EU experts have joined UN teams on counter-terrorism fact-finding missions to Algeria, Albania, Kenya and Morocco. The EU has agreed counter-terrorism assistance projects with Morocco and Algeria, partly financed from the EU budget. In addition, the CFSP budget is being used to finance EU non-proliferation policy and to reduce the risks of weapons of mass destruction falling into terrorists' hands. The largest funding goes to reduce nuclear and chemical stockpiles in Russia. Terrorism is also top of the agenda in nearly all political dialogue meetings with third countries, notably with the US, Russia, India and Pakistan. A counter-terrorism declaration and a five-year work programme have been agreed between the EU and the Euro-Med countries. In addition, counter-terrorism co-operation has been included in the action plans which the EU has negotiated with Algeria, Morocco, Jordan, Israel, the Palestinian Authority and Ukraine. With the US four agreements have been negotiated: on container security, airline passenger name records, extradition, and mutual legal assistance. A high-level dialogue has been set up to discuss border and transport security. American and EU experts on terrorist financing work closely together, as do European and American customs officials. The US Secret Service and the FBI have agreed to post liaison officers at Europol. Co-operation between Europol and Russia is also expected to intensify now that Russia has accepted the necessary data-protection rules.

As a result of 9/11, the US has been the principal third-country actor pushing the EU to strengthen its defences against terrorism. However, 9/11 did not have the same impact on Europe, given its decades-long experience with terrorism. Even the Madrid attacks, while leading to closer co-operation in the fight against terrorism, did not fundamentally alter European perceptions. The terminology used to describe the response to the terrorist threat further highlights the difference in approach by the EU and the US. The US was slow at first to recognise the importance of the EU in helping the fight on terror, but now the Department of Homeland Security is one of the strongest supporters of an effective EU policy in this area. Both Tom Ridge and Michael Cherthoff, the first two heads of the department, were fulsome in their praise of the EU contribution in tackling terrorism (speeches available on www.theepc.be). Transatlantic co-operation in the entire JHA field is now very extensive and covers transport issues, data protection, money-laundering, customs, border controls, police and intelligence co-operation. The issue of data protection remains a difficult area, especially the new tough requirements for visitors to the US which include storage of fingerprint and biometric data. The European Parliament and human rights groups have vigorously protested against such measures. Other measures taken include the Extradition and Mutual Legal Assistance Agreements signed on 25 June 2003 at the US–EU summit in Washington.

The EU has struggled to uphold its commitment to human rights around the world and engage in the fight against terrorism. Public opinion is overwhelmingly opposed to US incarceration of prisoners without trial at Guantanamo Bay and quickly aroused by issues such as rendition, when the CIA allegedly transported suspects to third countries for torture. Striking a fair balance between fighting against terrorism and protecting human rights can be difficult, but torture cannot be justified, as Cherie Booth, Tony Blair's wife, pointed out in a *Financial Times* article on 2 March 2006. As Secretary-General Kofi Annan stated at the Security Council on 6 March 2003, 'Our responses to terrorism, as well as our efforts to thwart it and prevent it, should uphold the human rights that terrorists aim to destroy. Respect for human rights, fundamental freedoms and the rule of law are essential tools in the effort to combat terrorism – not privileges to be sacrificed at a time of tension.' Furthermore, in order to tackle root causes of terrorism, including a reduction in the gap between rich and poor, the focus cannot just be on terrorism. Many governments give financial priority to the fight against terrorism, while simultaneously neglecting the equally important sector of development policy in achieving global stability. Developed countries spend $900 billion on defence and $340 billion in agricultural subsidies but give only $68 billion in developing assistance (OECD figures). These numbers speak for themselves. But perhaps the biggest root cause is the continuing Israel–Palestine dispute. If the West, and principally the US, was really to engage with both parties, and if necessary force a deal, it would undercut one of the principal grievances throughout the Middle East.

The impact on minorities in Europe

The development of anti-terrorist policies not only affects public perceptions of Islamic groups in Europe, but also has a direct impact on Europe's large Muslim minority groups who have been most affected by recent changes in counter-terrorism laws. Without properly understanding this effect, Western policies may in fact increase the threats they seek to counter. Whether expatriate engineers studying in Germany or young second-generation Arab men living in the suburbs of Paris, they find companionship and dignity in religious ideologies. As noted in the ESS, 'the most recent wave of terrorism is global in scope and is linked to violent religious extremism. It arises out of complex causes. These include the pressures of modernisation, cultural, social and political crises, and the alienation of young people living in foreign societies.' The terrorist attacks of 11 September 2001 arguably had the greatest impact on shaping public opinion of Islam. They reinforced perceived linkages of Islam with terror and violence as well as the view of Islam as a problem for the West. As a result there has been growing distrust from non-Muslims, which triggered an intense debate on the role of Muslims in European society. The looming threat of future terrorist attacks in Europe further fuels this already volatile situation. Despite politicians seeking to assure Muslims that the fight against terrorism is not a war on Islam, the popular media often preach a different story. European intelligence services have noted an increase in polarisation and radicalisation in recent years, with some European converts to Islam engaging in terrorist acts.

A further concern is that the countries of origin still seek to exert control over the major Muslim institutions in Europe, e.g. through the financing of major mosques. Countries like Saudi Arabia and Egypt regularly send Muslim scholars to Europe who have been known to preach radical messages. The Dutch government has sought to counter these radical elements by setting up a programme in which Muslim clerics attend courses on Dutch values.

Case study 12.1: The EU and Iran

The EU3 (France, Germany and the UK) have taken the lead in seeking a diplomatic solution to the Iran nuclear crisis. This has become a highly sensitive issue involving the US, Russia and China as well as the UNSC. The origins of the crisis may be traced back to 1979 when the pro-Western Shah was overthrown and a revolutionary Islamic regime under Ayatollah Khomeini took power. The US broke off diplomatic relations with Iran after revolutionary guards stormed the US embassy and held several diplomats hostage. The US also employed economic sanctions against Iran and later, under George W. Bush, described it (together with North Korea and Libya) as part of the 'axis of evil'.

The EU, in contrast, preferred a different policy of engagement with Iran. It began a 'critical dialogue' with Iran in 1993, partly as a response to the Salman Rushdie affair (the British author who had written a novel that led to calls for his death in the Islamic community) and partly because Europe recognised Iran's importance in the Middle East, including as an energy supplier. The EU was prepared to offer Iran a trade and co-operation agreement if Iran stopped funding terrorism, improved its human rights record and lifted the death threat (*fatwa*) on Rushdie. In 1998, after the dialogue had been suspended for a year as a result of alleged Iranian involvement in a terrorist attack in Berlin, the EU resumed its offer to Iran and added an extra condition: Iran should give up plans to develop nuclear weapons. The EU argued that such an agreement would bring major benefits to both sides: the EU would gain enormously from Iran's reserves of oil and natural gas, and Iran would profit from EU trade and investment.

Negotiations have made little progress as a result of the stalemate on the nuclear issue. Iran maintains that it has the right to develop civilian nuclear technology and that it has no intention of developing nuclear weapons. The EU is worried at a possible 'domino effect' if Iran acquires nuclear weapons, and would like to see international safeguards, through the IAEA, applied to Iran's nuclear programme. Another motive for the European policy is demonstrating to the US that the EU is serious about preventing proliferation of WMD.

The EU3 diplomatic initiative on Iran, which was launched in 2004, was partly due to the need to find an issue on which France, Germany and the UK could agree after the splits over Iraq and partly due to concerns that a nuclear device could fall into the hands of a terrorist group. It was also clear at last to these countries that they had more credibility on nuclear issues than any other EU member states. But their initiative sparked resentment among other member states such as Italy, the Netherlands and Sweden, and it was soon agreed that Javier Solana should join the EU3 to provide an essential EU institutional presence.

The EU3's efforts to contain the Iranian nuclear threat were initially successful, with Iran suspending some aspects of its enrichment activities for up to 18 months. However, when Tehran reneged on its agreement with the Europeans in August 2005 by restarting its nuclear fuel cycle programme, it claimed that the Europeans had not implemented their part of the bargain (progress on the trade and co-operation agreement and access to civilian nuclear technology). The Europeans then offered to implement these, but were rebuffed by the Iranians, and the talks broke down. The election of the hard-line Mahmoud Ahmadinejad as president in late 2005 (as opposed to the more moderate Rafsanjani) made Iran even less willing to compromise, especially as they perceived that the US was bluffing in its threat of a military strike in light of the situation in neighbouring Iraq.

The US had initially opposed the EU negotiations, then moved to accepting them and finally came around to supporting the EU. In June 2006 the EU3, with the tacit support of the US – and Russia and China – made a major offer to Iran promising help with their civilian nuclear effort plus economic and financial assistance if Tehran stopped the enrichment process that could lead to the production of weapons-grade plutonium.

While the EU offer was considered by Tehran, it became clear that it was really only the US that could offer Iran its main wish, a credible security guarantee. Iran also wants the US to lift the current economic sanctions and support Iran's bid to join the World Trade Organisation. Iran's negotiating position is also based on the calculation that US air strikes would be very unlikely if Iran had nuclear weapons – a lesson they must have drawn from the North Korea experience.

It remains to be seen whether Tehran will accept the EU offer or a modified version that would allow Iran to develop civilian nuclear energy under safeguards and thus benefit from financial, economic and trade benefits. But, if it did, it would demonstrate to the world – including the US – that the EU3's approach of critical engagement was more fruitful than threats of a military strike. Certainly the EU's efforts have helped to contain and slow down the Iranian drive towards uranium enrichment. It has helped restore credibility to the IAEA, and it has raised the level of the foreign policy debate and engagement in European countries. It has also raised the EU's profile in the Middle East and in the US. The EU's handling of the Iran crisis was thus in marked contrast to its lack of coherence over the Iraq crisis.

CONCLUSION

Terrorism is a threat that will continue to preoccupy the EU for many years. It will colour relations with third countries and also impact on domestic policy. Indeed, the interplay between domestic and external policy is well illustrated in the policy options facing the EU and the member states in responding to terrorism. The cartoon issue in Denmark is a good example of such interplay as it necessitated a swift tour of the Middle East by Javier Solana to try to cool tensions and to minimise the consequences for European foreign and trade policy. The EU will also need to maintain and increase its engagement in regional conflicts and in failed states as both can lead to a breakdown in order and thus become breeding grounds for organised crime and terrorism. The lack of co-ordination at EU level also needs to be addressed. If and when the constitutional treaty is ratified, there could be an improvement in internal EU co-operation, but much could be done under the present arrangements to improve co-operation if the member states were really committed. The counter-terrorist co-ordinator could be given increased powers, there could be greater sharing of intelligence and a new willingness to work through a stronger Europol and stronger Eurojust. There must also be more attention to regional conflicts because, as Solana wrote in the *Financial Times* on 25 March 2004, 'there is a fanatical fringe who are beyond political discourse. But it is nourished by a pool of disaffection and grievance. Where these grievances are legitimate they must be addressed, not just because this is a matter of justice but also because "draining the swamp" depends on it.' The EU will thus have to use its existing instruments such as the European Neighbourhood Policy (ENP) to develop a broader comprehensive concept that helps win the battle for the hearts and minds of the people in Muslim countries as well as of Europe's large Muslim minorities. In this context it is worth noting that terrorism is not just an Islamic problem or a problem of the Middle East; its history is as much European as Middle Eastern, and as much secular as religious. Europe also holds responsibility for this phenomenon and, more importantly, not only Europeans and Americans are the victims of terrorism. The victims are also all people in the Middle East and elsewhere who stand against this totalitarian and fanatical, but determined and patient, enemy. How Europe tackles the problem could be decisive in preventing any 'clash of civilisations'.

KEY QUESTIONS

To what extent is terrorism a top priority for all member states?
Who are the EU's principal foreign interlocutors in tackling terrorism?
Discuss the interplay between developments in member states and EU efforts
to deal with the terrorist threat.

FURTHER READING

Halliday (2003) and Lewis (2003) examine the nature of the links between Islam and terrorism. Sageman (2005) looks at terrorist networks, while Clarke (2004) attacks the Bush administration's approach to terrorism. The centre for the study of terrorism and political violence at St Andrews University is a good resource in this area: http://www.st-andrews.ac.uk/academic/intrel/research/cstpv/

Q – Form EU intelligance
→ Bureaucrag better
than no teeth?

Q – New Treaty's effect?

13 Future prospects

INTRODUCTION

It should be evident from the above that the EU has developed steadily as an international actor during the past decade. More and more the EU operates as a political entity in dealing with terrorism, the Balkans, the proliferation of weapons, the Middle East peace process, African development and many other issues. Much has been achieved, but critics argue that much more could have been achieved with strengthened institutions. This is not obvious because without the political will to endow institutions with authority there would be little real difference in policy output. Foreign policy remains a sensitive area, and member states retain their *amour propre*. Foreign ministries are also reluctant to negotiate themselves into oblivion, not least because there remain unanswered questions about legitimacy. There also remain significant differences of foreign policy culture, experiences and expectations within the member states, let alone the Council and the Commission. At the end of the day the CFSP depends on the political will of its member states, and there are inevitable limitations in the conduct of foreign policy where national independence and identity rides high. In some important areas the EU finds itself hamstrung, but these areas are growing fewer as the member states come to accept the advantages of working together. Most member states recognise the limits of operating alone and were prepared to strengthen the CFSP and the ESDP through some innovative provisions in the constitutional treaty. As the proposals in the treaty are likely to resurface at some stage, it is worth taking a closer look at them as well as at other reform ideas.

THE EU'S FOREIGN POLICY RECORD

Javier Solana remains very upbeat about the EU's developing role in foreign and security policy. In an interview with the *ESDP Newsletter* in December 2005, he stated that 'foreign and security policy is probably the area where the EU has advanced most in recent years. And such progress is all the more relevant as it takes place in a fast-moving environment which has altered the very nature of international security.' Solana also said in Stockholm on 17 March 2006 that 'the EU had become a more rounded political actor and less a campaigning NGO'. External Relations Commissioner Benita Ferrero-Waldner was slightly less positive when she gave an overview of EU foreign policy in Brussels on 2 February 2006. She said there was room for improvement in strengthening coherence, effectiveness and visibility.[1] Most observers would not share Solana's positive assessment. It is not easy to find accepted measures to judge the EU's performance in foreign policy. Views will vary depending on whether one is looking at the CFSP from the perspective of the Commission, the Council, the Parliament, the member states, third countries or the general public. Israelis and Palestinians, Serbs and Albanians may have very different views of the EU's role in the Middle East and the Balkans. Like other policy areas, the CFSP reflects the 'multiple realities' that make up the EU. But, given the sensitive nature of foreign and security policy, there are additional tensions between the member states (not just between large and small), between the institutions, and between the CFSP machinery and the growing influence of the NGO world. The CFSP is also a moving target. One week's failure to prevent the outbreak of conflict may lead to next week's success in arranging a ceasefire. Furthermore, many successes in the field of conflict prevention often pass unnoticed. As argued above, it is also difficult, if not impossible, to isolate the CFSP from other external policies of the EU. Projecting stability may be achieved as much by association agreements and the prospect of membership, liberal trade policies and generous development assistance, contributing to improved living standards, than by any number of CFSP Declarations, Joint Actions, Common Positions or Common Strategies.

The development of the EU as an international actor is a tale of steady growth, of agreement on treaties that provided for progress in strengthening the institutional framework, of stronger capabilities, and of an increasing number of crisis-management operations. We have seen in Chapter 1 how there is a constant interplay between the internal and external developments of the Union, and how the development of new policy areas in the Union has had far-reaching external consequences. There is no reason to doubt that this interplay will continue in future as the world continues to shrink as a result of globalisation. The development of the CFSP, originating from European Political Co-operation (EPC), was described in Chapter 2 and the complexities arising out of the pillar system analysed. In Chapter 3 we examined the complexity of the institutional structures underpinning the CFSP and the ESDP and noted a trend towards 'Brusselisation' of European foreign policy. The role and influence of the member states, the key stakeholders in European foreign and security policy, was discussed in Chapter 4. We noted here the various formations such as the EU3 that had arisen in recent years to deal with specific situations. Chapter 5 considered the modest achievements in the defence field, notably the progress in developing EU military and civilian capabilities for crisis management. The most important external partner of the EU is the US, and the transatlantic relationship was the focus of Chapter 6. The change in attitude of the second Bush administration towards the EU was noted as well as the continuing suspicion of US foreign policy among European public opinion. The EU's relations with its neighbours were discussed in Chapter 7, which also assessed the prospects for the European Neighbourhood Policy. Chapter 8 reviewed the Union's very difficult experience in dealing with the Balkans and with Turkey. Relations with Asia were then discussed in Chapter 9, with particular focus on the blossoming relationship between the EU and China. Chapter 10 covered EU development policy and noted the increasing attention of the EU on Africa. The EU's growing involvement in conflict prevention and crisis management was reviewed in Chapter 11 and the growing number of ESDP operations described. Terrorism has risen to the top of the global foreign and security policy agenda, and Chapter 12 assessed the Union's response to the upsurge in political violence in recent years.

The increasing scope and range of EU foreign policy actions demonstrate that the EU has become more and more active as a global actor. It has inevitably given greater priority to its immediate neighbourhood but it is also active literally around the world. It will never be in the business of power projection like the US. There will be no EU marines being transported halfway around the world to undertake regime change. But the EU will continue to develop its soft-power capabilities tinged with a hard-power edge. What, then, are the prospects for the future, especially in light of the failure to ratify the constitutional treaty with its innovative provisions to strengthen further European foreign and security policy?

REFORMING THE CFSP

There have been many proposals to strengthen the CFSP; to make the EU a more effective, coherent, consistent actor and thus enhance its role on the world stage. These ideas range from a full-scale 'communitarisation' of foreign policy, i.e. giving the Commission a similar role as under the first pillar and introducing qualified majority voting (QMV), to modest tinkering with the existing machinery. Many proposals can only be viewed as part of the wider debate on institutional issues that were discussed in the Convention on the Future of Europe and which found expression in the constitutional treaty. These include the proposal to have an elected President of the European Council and the question of a democratic mandate for the Commission (Cameron, 2005). While there was widespread agreement in the Convention on the need to change the six-monthly rotating Presidency in the CFSP, there was less agreement on what should replace it. At present, each Presidency sets its own priorities, often in response to domestic concerns. The Swedes emphasise the Baltic region, the Belgians Africa, the Spanish Latin America, and so on. It is useful that Presidencies find the energy to organise meetings on these 'priority' issues, but there is an obvious problem of lack of continuity. Solutions put forward included an elected chair for two-and-a-half years and team Presidencies. Another variation would allow the High Representative to concentrate exclusively on foreign and security policy by relieving him of the post of Secretary General of the Council. The implications of these proposals for meetings of subsidiary bodies, such as the Political and Security Committee (PSC) and the large number of CFSP and ESDP committees, have not been fully discussed. In the much simpler Western European Union (WEU) setting, the Secretary General chaired the meetings of ministers and often of ambassadors, with his support staff chairing meetings at lower levels. The same is true of NATO. But what role would remain for Presidencies if such a system were adopted? And how would the Council Secretariat/Commission roles be disentangled? A related problem is the massive expansion in the number of political dialogue meetings, which doubled between 1995 and 2005. This imposes a huge burden on all Presidencies but especially for the smaller ones, even though there is now an effort to distribute the meetings over a range of Presidencies.

During the Convention many asked what lessons could be drawn from the relative effectiveness of the Community's external trade policy. The answer is not difficult. When the Union speaks with one voice in bilateral or multilateral trade negotiations it is a powerful voice representing in excess of 450 million citizens with a combined GDP roughly similar to that of the US. The Union could be as effective in other policy areas if it wanted to, simply by providing for a single representation. Reflecting on his own experience, former Trade Commissioner Pascal Lamy, when he gave evidence to the Convention, proposed that the Commission be given a mandate to negotiate and represent the Union in all international economic forums. As noted in Chapter 1, despite the advent of the euro there is still no EU seat or common EU voice at IMF or World Bank meetings. Indeed, the situation at these and other international economic meetings is extremely confusing in terms of 'who speaks for the EU'. There is certainly a strong case for granting the Commission this role, but an interim solution would at least provide for more debate and prior consultation between member states with a view to reaching common positions in advance of international meetings.

The external representation of the EU is a complicated process and likely to undergo further changes as and when there is the political will to implement some or all of the proposals in the constitutional treaty. The EU is gradually increasing its profile in the world, and more and more countries are looking to Brussels for a lead on global issues. Yet there are clear challenges to more effective EU participation in international bodies. First, how to develop effective and coherent EU representation within bodies that were set up for a membership comprising only states. Some argue that an EU seat at the UN would not be possible under present international law. Second, there are challenges for reaching common EU positions. This applies on the economic and financial front as well as on the political front. For example, the EU has been largely invisible in international efforts to deal with the recurrent financial and banking crises caused by the sharp swings in capital flows to emerging markets. No coherent EU position has ever been developed and defended, even in cases where Europe's strategic interests are clear, e.g. Turkey. In contrast, the US usually has well-defined positions and is highly effective at influencing multilateral bodies such as the IMF.

Foreign and security policy is a sensitive area as regards an increased role for the Commission. The solution put forward in the constitutional treaty was a merger of the positions of the High Representative and the External Relations Commissioner so that he (Solana was foreseen as the first EU foreign minister) could speak and negotiate for the EU where there was an agreed policy or common strategy. Member states would thus continue to enjoy bilateral relations with third countries but they would not discuss EU energy policy towards Russia, for example, if this were an area of agreed EU policy. The main argument for such a merger is that it would hopefully improve the coherence, consistency and visibility of EU policy. (The US would have its telephone number!) The argument against, put forward by some members of the Convention, is that it would put too much power in the hands of one person (and lead to his further undermining the opportunities for national foreign ministers to shine). An additional complication might arise if there was a semi-permanent president of the European Council as he could then overshadow the EU foreign minister. It was foreseen that the EU foreign minister would have been 'double-hatted', i.e. he would simultaneously chair the GAERC and be a vice-president of the European Commission. This would allow him to play a major role in bringing together all the various EU instruments available in external relations and thus promote greater coherence. The foreign minister would of course need to ensure that he enjoyed a good working relationship with the President of the Commission and the new chairman of the European Council, both of whom would have their own foreign policy responsibilities. As vice-president of the Commission, the foreign minister would chair meetings of the Relex Commissioners (Trade, Development, and Enlargement) and thus be able to steer Community action towards supporting overall EU foreign policy goals.

He would be supported by an EU external action service (equivalent to an EU diplomatic service) based on the 129 Commission delegations around the world that would be transformed into EU missions. A mix of Commission and Council staff as well as diplomats from member states on secondment would staff these missions. Some missions might even have political heads such as former Irish Prime Minister John Bruton, who became head of the Washington delegation in 2004. There were fears among the Commission staff that representatives from member states and the Council would take the plum jobs such as head of delegation and political counsellor. Certainly the delegations need to increase and improve their political reporting capabilities, which are highly variable. One of the problems is that the Commission never recruited staff for traditional diplomatic tasks and never put adequate resources into training. The transformation of the Commission delegations towards true EU embassies should improve the Union's capacity to develop more of its own internal assessments rather than being forced to rely on member states. One could imagine the Commission delegations being far more proactive than hitherto in providing an early-warning mechanism where potential conflicts affect EU interests and in co-ordinating a European response to political issues. The analysis of conflicts around the world is one obvious example, where continuity and permanent updating of information could arguably be co-ordinated better by the Commission than by rotating presidencies. EU missions would also be competent to implement specific policies in a range of fields – CFSP as well as justice and home affairs co-operation – that hitherto have been mostly beyond the scope of the delegations (Cameron and Grevi, 2005).

Even without a new treaty, there is considerable scope for member states and Commission delegations to co-operate more effectively in third countries. Too often member states, especially in major third countries, pay lip-service to EU co-ordination and co-operation. For the foreseeable future, bilateral and EU foreign policy will continue to co-exist; but there is pressure, especially after the 2004 enlargement, to increase sharing of premises and other facilities as well as more joint reporting. If foreign ministries do not ask the question, finance ministries will certainly ask why there needs to be twenty-five separate EU member state missions, plus a Commission delegation, in countries x, y and z, when the EU is supposed to operate a CFSP. The answer is a mixture of lack of political will and the vanity of diplomats and foreign ministers. How is Washington going to regard the EU when it often fails to speak with one voice on routine political issues? Member states send their brightest and best diplomats, who want to make a name for themselves, to Washington. There are supposed to be regular consultations between the twenty-five member states and the Commission delegation, but these usually amount to little more than a limited exchange of information about forthcoming visits. It is not uncommon for two or three EU foreign ministers to be visiting Washington in the same week. It is little wonder that the US has difficulty accepting the EU as a coherent actor when the member states do so much to undermine it.

The institutional problems noted above also affect attempts to ensure the benefits of conflict-prevention mainstreaming in most EU policy areas. In addition to the problems between the 'first' and 'second' pillars, a complexity arises when policing is involved, as this requires activation of the 'third' pillar. The different procedures under the pillar system thus serve to complicate matters and often delay decisions. Despite its limited role in the second pillar, the management of the EU budget gives the Commission considerable influence. Its comparative advantage in conflict prevention and management lies in areas closely linked to long-term structural issues or immediate humanitarian needs. It controls many of the resources for EU action and has numerous instruments at its disposal, from election monitoring to the rapid reaction mechanism. This contrasts with the Council and the SG/HR, who deal with the more classical security issues but have many political constraints and fewer instruments they can use to influence situations. The Commission will continue to be the main, sometimes exclusive, purveyor of EU foreign policy in those regions of the world member states do not consider strategic priorities. There will still be hesitations from some member states, anxious about their 'sovereignty', to overcome; but, whatever structure is agreed in future, the Commission will continue to hold considerable competences in the external field. The Commission has a clear interest in promoting a comprehensive vision of external relations, and in moving to a more proactive stance, where its ability and experience lend themselves to policy proposals. This means promoting a foreign policy culture amongst Commission staff, and ensuring that training and career development encompass the resulting needs in terms of human resources.

The constitutional treaty also contained provisions for some member states to act in the name of the Union on the defence front and the creation of an EU armaments agency. The proposal for a leading group on defence was simply recognition of the reality that some member states bring more capabilities to the table than others. The defence agency has already been established outside the treaty; but moving ahead on other issues, such as the EU foreign minister, despite widespread support, would be politically difficult. There are, however, a number of measures the EU could take without any treaty changes to strengthen its external representation and internal coherence. These include more high-profile missions for Solana, including speaking at the UN on behalf of the EU, inviting Solana to attend discussions on external relations at Commission meetings and creating a joint Council–Commission planning staff. There is also much that could be done to improve co-operation between Council and Commission, including sharing of facilities and resources. For example, a joint spokesman would make sense. Solana and Mrs Benita Ferrero-Waldner could also make joint appearances before the European Parliament. There should be increased sharing of intelligence and a greater exchange of diplomats and officials between the member states and the EU institutions. The time is overdue for the establishment of a European diplomatic academy that would provide the nucleus of a common training programme for diplomats from the EU institutions and the member states. There is also much preparatory work that could be done to ease the transition of the Commission delegations to EU missions. With moves to establish a common EU judicial space, there could also be a common EU visa provided by a lead member state in third countries.

COMMISSION PROPOSALS

In June 2006 the Commission issued a communication with some practical proposals to improve external relations.[2] President Barroso, introducing the paper, said that EU foreign policy suffered from a lack of visibility and coherence as well as continuity of external representation. In order to improve matters under the existing treaties, he proposed a series of pragmatic steps, including:

- *Better strategic planning.* There should be a six-monthly meeting of the main institutional actors to review external priorities. The SG/HR should be invited to meetings of the Relex commissioners, which should be extended to include other relevant commissioners. There should be more Council–Commission joint papers for policy discussions.
- *Improved effectiveness.* There should be a single EU message put forward by EU member states' missions, the Commission delegations and the EU special representatives. There should be increased efforts to obtain common EU positions in advance of key international meetings. There should be more flexible financial procedures to ensure quicker and more effective support for crisis management operations.
- *Greater co-operation between EU institutions and member states.* The paper proposed more exchange of personnel between EU institutions and the diplomatic services of member states, including for training. There should be greater co-operation in sharing of premises and support services in third countries; and in visa and consular assistance. More 'double-hatting' of Council–Commission representatives could be envisaged.
- *Improved accountability and visibility.* There should be more exchanges between EU special representatives, heads of Commission delegations and the European Parliament. There should be more resources for public diplomacy in third countries and within the EU.

WAITING FOR GODOT

It is difficult to assess the likely impact of the delay in establishing the new post of EU foreign minister and the external service. Foreign and security policy remains a very sensitive area for the member states, and even with the creation of a post of foreign minister he would still be dependent ultimately on the goodwill and support of the member states, especially the larger ones. But the proposals for an EU foreign minister and an external action service were not controversial and, according to *Eurobarometer*, enjoyed wide public support. There are those who believe that it would be possible to 'cherry-pick' these (and other) parts of the Constitution, but it is unlikely that there will be the necessary political will to undertake such a move until there is some clarity about the fate of the treaty. The new structures should have led to greater harmony and fewer bureaucratic turf wars. The delay in ratifying the treaty means that there is a danger of continuing Brussels in-fighting and, perhaps more serious, a danger of the larger member states moving to form a directoire in foreign policy. There were many concerns when the EU3 launched their diplomatic initiative on Iran. Several member states thought this could set a pattern leading to their semi-permanent exclusion from EU foreign policy. The inclusion of Solana in the EU3 team, however, helped to smooth some very ruffled feathers. The Iran model is likely to be used again. Indeed, one likely trend will be the further development of smaller groups dealing with specific

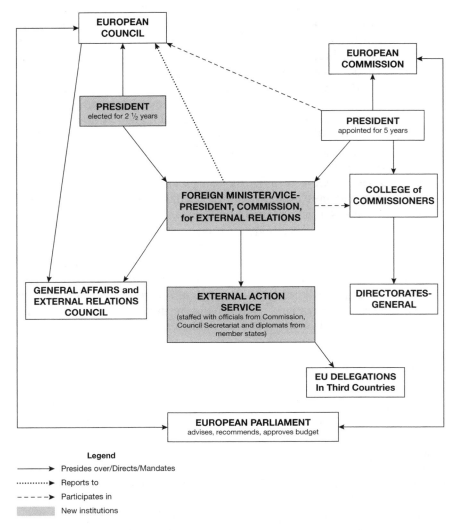

Figure 13.1 Proposed structures under the new constitution

issues. It does not make sense for all twenty-five member states to become involved in the details of every issue. What is likely to happen, therefore, is that there will be mini-groups that lead on certain issues. They would operate under a mandate from the Council and report back to the Council at the end of the negotiations or when the particular issue had been resolved.

It is unlikely, given the sensitivities of member states, that changes in the CFSP beyond what was agreed in the constitutional treaty would be acceptable in the foreseeable future. Most member states appear comfortable with present arrangements, although there are several that recognise the importance of changes on the external representation front in light of enlargement. While CFSP reform figured prominently on the agenda at the Convention and at the subsequent Inter-governmental Conference, change is likely to be incremental in nature. The CFSP approaches puberty after a difficult childhood with little sign that its parents have overly high ambitions for its future. As Patten has recognised, 'if the CFSP is to grow to maturity, it needs the nurture of both its parents, the Member States and the Community institutions. And – as any psychologist will tell you – the child is more likely to be happy and healthy if those parents love one another' (Patten, 2005).

BUDGET

A major increase in the CFSP budget is also necessary if the EU is to make any progress towards fulfilling its global ambitions. The CFSP budget was a very modest €30 million in 2005 and just over €100 million in 2006. This needs to be substantially increased if the EU is to play a genuine global role. At the same time, there needs to be clarity as to responsibility for different budget lines. Too much time is still wasted on inter-institutional squabbles over financing of operations such as de-mining in the Balkans or paying for the police mission in Bosnia.

PARLIAMENTARY AND PUBLIC SUPPORT

It will be important to enlist the support of the European public, through the involvement of the European Parliament (EP) and national parliaments as well as the media and NGOs, for the goals of the CFSP. This should involve not only a greater role for the European Parliament, but also perhaps a six-monthly debate in all national parliaments simultaneously on the CFSP's goals and achievements. This could be based on a report by Solana and would ensure that each member state's foreign minister was actively involved in explaining and defending the CFSP. There might also be regular forums for discussions on CFSP aims with NGOs. At present they tend to lobby, often noisily, on single issues. If they were confronted with the full range of problems facing the CFSP, it might help them better understand the limitations of CFSP.

ENERGY

A key area for the future of EU external policy will be energy. Concern over Russian tactics towards Ukraine in January 2006 and the uncertainty over future gas and oil supplies have catapulted energy security to the top of the EU's foreign policy agenda. At the spring 2006 European Council, Solana was given a mandate to produce a paper outlining EU priorities in this field. The background to the sudden urgency was not just Russian pressure but the realisation that Europe would be importing over 70 per cent of its energy needs by 2025 compared to just 50 per cent now. Reserves were also concentrated in only a few countries and regions not known for their stability – Russia, Central Asia, the Middle East and West Africa. There was also rapidly increasing demand from China and India which was affecting the geopolitics of several regions (the Middle East, Africa and Latin America). These considerations should offer the EU the opportunity to define a common external policy on energy, providing the member states agree. Some member states are more dependent on Russian gas and oil supplies than others, but all have a shared interest in security of supplies. This would need to be translated into concrete action concerning upgrading of pipelines and infrastructure, transit agreements and a new energy agreement with Russia and perhaps other suppliers. The June 2006 European Council endorsed an orientation paper by Solana, and he was charged with continuing his work, together with the Commission, to prepare proposals for discussion during the German Presidency in 2007.

EFFECTIVE MULTILATERALISM

Directly related to the ambition often stated at the Convention on the Future of Europe that the EU should play a stronger and more effective role on the world stage was the desire to strengthen the institutions of global governance. One of the central tenets of the European Security Strategy (ESS) was support for 'effective multilateralism'. This was never defined in the ESS, although there were references to the importance of strengthening the UN. Nevertheless, given the necessary political will, there is much the EU can do now to realise its ambition to speak with a united voice and to strengthen the institutions of global governance. For example, despite its obvious divisions over reform of the UN Security Council, the EU has played a prominent role in supporting the proposals of the Kofi Annan high-level panel that were the subject of discussion at the September 2005 Millennium Summit. The EU has played an important role in the establishment of the Peace-building Commission and the new Human Rights Council.

Partly because of its own history of sharing sovereignty and constant inter-governmental negotiations, the EU has been more willing than the US and many other countries to work through multilateral institutions. It will be a major challenge for the EU to build support for effective multilateralism amongst its partners. These include its strategic partners (Russia, China, India, Japan and Canada) and, above all, the United States. But it is the US that has appeared to reject the very idea of an international order. It has a poor record in recent years with regard to UN financing, the rejection of the Kyoto Protocol, the efforts to undermine the International Criminal Court (ICC) and the refusal to ratify a host of arms-control treaties, notably the Comprehensive Test Ban Treaty (CTBT). In the spring of 2005, the nominations of two leading neo-conservatives, Paul Wolfowitz to head the World Bank, and John Bolton to be the US ambassador to the UN, caused considerable consternation in Europe and renewed doubts about Washington's commitment to strengthening international institutions. There are, however, some small signs of a changed approach under the second Bush administration. There has been less hostile rhetoric about the UN, although right-wing republicans have strongly attacked Kofi Annan for his alleged laxity in the 'oil for food' scandal. John Bolton also attacked UN Deputy Secretary General Mark Malloch Brown for daring to criticise the lack of US public support for the UN in a June 2006 speech.[3] At the same time an important Congressional commission (Gingrich–Mitchell) has been broadly supportive of many proposals in the high-level panel report. Overall the US attitude may best be described as 'à la carte multilateralism'. It will be a difficult but necessary task for the EU to continue to press the US to support fully the multilateral system. US failure in Iraq may bring about a change in US attitudes.

THE EU AS A MODEL

The EU is also increasingly respected as a model for regional integration elsewhere in the world and has made an impact in terms of developing alternative concepts of security. The many attempts to imitate parts of the EU system around the world are perhaps the sincerest form of flattery even though the prospects for deepening any of these regional organisations is not very bright. The EU supports these efforts through a mix of political, financial, economic and technical measures. In Africa there is the increasingly important African Union, as well as a number of regional and sub-regional organisations. In Latin America there is the Andean Pact and Mercosur as well as the Central American Free Trade Association (CAFTA). In the Middle East there is the Gulf Co-operation Council (GCC). In Asia there is the Association of South-East Asian Nations (ASEAN) and the Asian Regional Forum (ARF). There is also much talk of an East Asian community involving China, Japan and South Korea.

The EU has also been to the fore in promoting a wider concept of security. The ESS adopted a holistic approach in stressing the importance of human security and soft power but at the same time recognising that the EU had to improve its military and non-military capabilities in order to deal with new threats and in particular the problem of failed states. The EU has also been a strong supporter of the concept of 'global public goods', and its input and influence on the UN reform debate was also significant. Yet when it comes to a values-based foreign policy the EU is better at rhetoric than at action. It has done remarkably little to press forcefully the question of human rights with China, Russia or even the US.

At some stage in the future, the EU will also have to confront the issue of power. This is a difficult task in the absence of firm, accepted borders. To be effective, the concept of European power must meet with public approval. This would seem to exclude any 'euro-nationalist' model trying to rival the superpower projection capabilities of the US, and equally exclude the civil power or Swiss power model favoured by some observers. A sustainable concept of a European power may require a new paradigm that redefines the specific European contribution in an increasingly interdependent and globalised world. As one analyst suggested, 'it is perhaps a paradox that the continent which once ruled the world through the physical impositions of imperialism is now coming to set world standards in normative terms'.[4] The EU has indeed developed almost by stealth a new model for international relations, a model based on the values of democracy, human and minority rights, the rule of law and support for diplomacy over force and a strengthened multilateral system. There are many states in the world that appreciate this model.

CONCLUSION

Despite the complicated structures for external relations the EU can take credit for some modest successes, especially in terms of crisis management and enlargement. There are few, however, who purport to see in the EU's enlargement policy evidence of the vitality of the CFSP itself. Indeed, one of Solana's senior officials has lamented that the EU's options seemed limited 'to speaking softly and carrying just one big carrot'. Leaving aside institutional changes, political will to agree common positions (and then implement them) remains the key factor. There will remain areas of disagreement, but the trend of the past decade is for the member states to agree increasingly on common policies towards third countries, and regions, and on functional issues. Enlargement has not altered this trend, although agreeing common policies at twenty-five as opposed to fifteen member states is undoubtedly more difficult. The bottom line, however, is that all foreign ministers recognise the value of the EU speaking with one voice. In the end, a Union with over 450 million citizens, the largest trading bloc in the world, with a single currency, the largest provider of development aid and humanitarian assistance, cannot escape from playing a greater role in world affairs. But it will be some time before it speaks with one voice in all international forums.

Appendix One
Consolidated Treaty on European Union, Title V

Provisions on a Common Foreign and Security Policy (extracts)

ARTICLE 11

1. The Union shall define and implement a common foreign and security policy covering all areas of foreign and security policy, the objectives of which shall be:

— to safeguard the common values, fundamental interests, independence and integrity of the Union in conformity with the principles of the United Nations Charter,
— to strengthen the security of the Union in all ways,
— to preserve peace and strengthen international security, in accordance with the principles of the United Nations Charter, as well as the principles of the Helsinki Final Act and the objectives of the Paris Charter, including those on external borders,
— to promote international cooperation,
— to develop and consolidate democracy and the rule of law, and respect for human rights and fundamental freedoms.

2. The Member States shall support the Union's external and security policy actively and unreservedly in a spirit of loyalty and mutual solidarity.

The Member States shall work together to enhance and develop their mutual political solidarity. They shall refrain from any action which is contrary to the interests of the Union or likely to impair its effectiveness as a cohesive force in international relations.

The Council shall ensure that these principles are complied with.

ARTICLE 12

The Union shall pursue the objectives set out in Article 11 by:

— defining the principles of and general guidelines for the common foreign and security policy,

— deciding on common strategies,
— adopting joint actions,
— adopting common positions,
— strengthening systematic cooperation between Member States in the conduct of policy.

ARTICLE 13

1. The European Council shall define the principles of and general guidelines for the common foreign and security policy, including for matters with defence implications.

2. The European Council shall decide on common strategies to be implemented by the Union in areas where the Member States have important interests in common.

Common strategies shall set out their objectives, duration and the means to be made available by the Union and the Member States.

3. The Council shall take the decisions necessary for defining and implementing the common foreign and security policy on the basis of the general guidelines defined by the European Council.

The Council shall recommend common strategies to the European Council and shall implement them, in particular by adopting joint actions and common positions.

The Council shall ensure the unity, consistency and effectiveness of action by the Union.

ARTICLE 14

1. The Council shall adopt joint actions. Joint actions shall address specific situations where operational action by the Union is deemed to be required. They shall lay down their objectives, scope, the means to be made available to the Union, if necessary their duration, and the conditions for their implementation.

3. Joint actions shall commit the Member States in the positions they adopt and in the conduct of their activity.

ARTICLE 15

The Council shall adopt common positions. Common positions shall define the approach of the Union to a particular matter of a geographical or thematic nature. Member States shall ensure that their national policies conform to the common positions.

ARTICLE 16

Member States shall inform and consult one another within the Council on any matter of foreign and security policy of general interest in order to ensure that the Union's influence is exerted as effectively as possible by means of concerted and convergent action.

ARTICLE 17

1. The common foreign and security policy shall include all questions relating to the security of the Union, including the progressive framing of a common defence policy, which might lead to a common defence, should the European Council so decide. It shall in that case recommend to the Member States the adoption of such a decision in accordance with their respective constitutional requirements.

The policy of the Union in accordance with this Article shall not prejudice the specific character of the security and defence policy of certain Member States and shall respect the obligations of certain Member States, which see their common defence realised in the North Atlantic Treaty Organisation (NATO), under the North Atlantic Treaty and be compatible with the common security and defence policy established within that framework.

The progressive framing of a common defence policy will be supported, as Member States consider appropriate, by cooperation between them in the field of armaments.

2. Questions referred to in this Article shall include humanitarian and rescue tasks, peacekeeping tasks and tasks of combat forces in crisis management, including peacemaking.

ARTICLE 18

1. The Presidency shall represent the Union in matters coming within the common foreign and security policy.

2. The Presidency shall be responsible for the implementation of decisions taken under this title; in that capacity it shall in principle express the position of the Union in international organisations and international conferences.

3. The Presidency shall be assisted by the Secretary-General of the Council who shall exercise the function of High Representative for the common foreign and security policy.

4. The Commission shall be fully associated in the tasks referred to in paragraphs 1 and 2. The Presidency shall be assisted in those tasks if need be by the next Member State to hold the Presidency.

5. The Council may, whenever it deems it necessary, appoint a special representative with a mandate in relation to particular policy issues.

ARTICLE 19

1. Member States shall coordinate their action in international organisations and at international conferences. They shall uphold the common positions in such forums. In international organisations and at international conferences where not all the Member States participate, those which do take part shall uphold the common positions.

2. Without prejudice to paragraph 1 and Article 14(3), Member States represented in international organisations or international conferences where not all the Member States participate shall keep the latter informed of any matter of common interest. Member States which are also members of the United Nations Security Council will concert and keep the other Member States fully informed. Member States which are permanent members of the Security Council will, in the execution of their functions, ensure the defence of the positions and the interests of the Union, without prejudice to their responsibilities under the provisions of the United Nations Charter.

ARTICLE 20

The diplomatic and consular missions of the Member States and the Commission delegations in third countries and international conferences, and their representations to international organisations, shall cooperate in ensuring that the common positions and joint actions adopted by the Council are complied with and implemented. They shall step up cooperation by exchanging information, carrying out joint assessments and contributing to the implementation of the provisions referred to in Article 20 of the Treaty establishing the European Community.

ARTICLE 21

The Presidency shall consult the European Parliament on the main aspects and the basic choices of the common foreign and security policy and shall ensure that the views of the European Parliament are duly taken into consideration. The European Parliament shall be kept regularly informed by the Presidency and the Commission of the development of the Union's foreign and security policy.

The European Parliament may ask questions of the Council or make recommendations to it. It shall hold an annual debate on progress in implementing the common foreign and security policy.

ARTICLE 23

1. Decisions under this title shall be taken by the Council acting unanimously. Abstentions by members present in person or represented shall not prevent the adoption of such decisions.

2. By derogation from the provisions of paragraph 1, the Council shall act by qualified majority:

— when adopting joint actions, common positions or taking any other decision on the basis of a common strategy,
— when adopting any decision implementing a joint action or a common position,
— when appointing a special representative in accordance with Article 18(5).

If a member of the Council declares that, for important and stated reasons of national policy, it intends to oppose the adoption of a decision to be taken by qualified majority, a vote shall not be taken. The Council may, acting by a qualified majority, request that the matter be referred to the European Council for decision by unanimity.

The votes of the members of the Council shall be weighted in accordance with Article 205(2) of the Treaty establishing the European Community. For their adoption, decisions shall require at least 62 votes in favour, cast by at least 10 members.

This paragraph shall not apply to decisions having military or defence implications.

3. For procedural questions, the Council shall act by a majority of its members.

ARTICLE 24

1. When it is necessary to conclude an agreement with one or more States or international organisations in implementation of this title, the Council may authorise the Presidency, assisted by the Commission as appropriate, to open negotiations to that effect. Such agreements shall be concluded by the Council on a recommendation from the Presidency.

ARTICLE 25

Without prejudice to Article 207 of the Treaty establishing the European Community, a Political and Security Committee shall monitor the international situation in the areas covered by the common foreign and security policy and contribute to the definition of policies by delivering opinions to the Council at the request of the Council or on its own initiative. It shall also monitor the implementation of agreed policies, without prejudice to the responsibility of the Presidency and the Commission.

Within the scope of this title, this Committee shall exercise, under the responsibility of the Council, political control and strategic direction of crisis management operations.

The Council may authorise the Committee, for the purpose and for the duration of a crisis management operation, as determined by the Council, to take the relevant decisions concerning the political control and strategic direction of the operation, without prejudice to Article 47.

ARTICLE 26

The Secretary-General of the Council, High Representative for the common foreign and security policy, shall assist the Council in matters coming within the scope of the common foreign and security policy, in particular through contributing to the formulation, preparation and implementation of policy decisions, and, when appropriate and acting on behalf of the Council at the request of the Presidency, through conducting political dialogue with third parties.

ARTICLE 27

The Commission shall be fully associated with the work carried out in the common foreign and security policy field.

ARTICLE 27A

1. Enhanced cooperation in any of the areas referred to in this title shall be aimed at safeguarding the values and serving the interests of the Union as a whole by asserting its identity as a coherent force on the international scene. It shall respect:

— the principles, objectives, general guidelines and consistency of the common foreign and security policy and the decisions taken within the framework of that policy,
— the powers of the European Community, and
— consistency between all the Union's policies and its external activities.

ARTICLE 27B

Enhanced cooperation pursuant to this title shall relate to implementation of a joint action or a common position. It shall not relate to matters having military or defence implications.

ARTICLE 28

2. Administrative expenditure which the provisions relating to the areas referred to in this title entail for the institutions shall be charged to the budget of the European Communities.

3. Operating expenditure to which the implementation of those provisions gives rise shall also be charged to the budget of the European Communities, except for such expenditure arising from operations having military or defence implications and cases where the Council acting unanimously decides otherwise.

Appendix Two
The European Security Strategy
(December 2003)

INTRODUCTION

Europe has never been so prosperous, so secure nor so free. The violence of the first half of the 20th Century has given way to a period of peace and stability unprecedented in European history. The creation of the European Union has been central to this development. It has transformed the relations between our states, and the lives of our citizens. European countries are committed to dealing peacefully with disputes and to co-operating through common institutions. Over this period, the progressive spread of the rule of law and democracy has seen authoritarian regimes change into secure, stable and dynamic democracies. Successive enlargements are making a reality of the vision of a united and peaceful continent.

The United States has played a critical role in European integration and European security, in particular through NATO. The end of the Cold War has left the United States in a dominant position as a military actor. However, no single country is able to tackle today's complex problems on its own. Europe still faces security threats and challenges. The outbreak of conflict in the Balkans was a reminder that war has not disappeared from our continent. Over the last decade, no region of the world has been untouched by armed conflict. Most of these conflicts have been within rather than between states, and most of the victims have been civilians.

As a union of 25 states with over 450 million people producing a quarter of the world's Gross National Product (GNP), and with a wide range of instruments at its disposal, the European Union is inevitably a global player. In the last decade European forces have been deployed abroad to places as distant as Afghanistan, East Timor and the DRC. The increasing convergence of European interests and the strengthening of mutual solidarity of the EU makes us a more credible and effective actor. Europe should be ready to share in the responsibility for global security and in building a better world.

45 million people die every year of hunger and malnutrition. Aids contributes to the breakdown of societies. Security is a precondition of development.

THE SECURITY ENVIRONMENT: GLOBAL CHALLENGES AND KEY THREATS

The post Cold War environment is one of increasingly open borders in which the internal and external aspects of security are indissolubly linked. Flows of trade and investment, the development of technology and the spread of democracy have brought freedom and prosperity to many people. Others have perceived globalisation as a cause of frustration and injustice. These developments have also increased the scope for non-state groups to play a part in international affairs. And they have increased European dependence – and so vulnerability – on an interconnected infrastructure in transport, energy, information and other fields.

Since 1990, almost 4 million people have died in wars, 90% of them civilians. Over 18 million people world-wide have left their homes as a result of conflict. In much of the developing world, poverty and disease cause untold suffering and give rise to pressing security concerns. Almost 3 billion people, half the world's population, live on less than 2 Euros a day. 45 million die every year of hunger and malnutrition. AIDS is now one of the most devastating pandemics in human history and contributes to the breakdown of societies. New diseases can spread rapidly and become global threats. Sub-Saharan Africa is poorer now than it was 10 years ago. In many cases, economic failure is linked to political problems and violent conflict. Security is a precondition of development. Conflict not only destroys infrastructure, including social infrastructure; it also encourages criminality, deters investment and makes normal economic activity impossible. A number of countries and regions are caught in a cycle of conflict, insecurity and poverty.

The last use of WMD was by the Aum terrorist sect in the Tokyo underground in 1995, using sarin gas. 12 people were killed and several thousand injured. Two years earlier, Aum had sprayed anthrax spores on a Tokyo street.

Competition for natural resources – notably water – which will be aggravated by global warming over the next decades, is likely to create further turbulence and migratory movements in various regions. Energy dependence is a special concern for Europe. Europe is the world's largest importer of oil and gas. Imports account for about 50% of energy consumption today. This will rise to 70% in 2030. Most energy imports come from the Gulf, Russia and North Africa.

KEY THREATS

Large-scale aggression against any Member State is now improbable. Instead, Europe faces new threats which are more diverse, less visible and less predictable.

Terrorism: Terrorism puts lives at risk; it imposes large costs; it seeks to undermine the openness and tolerance of our societies, and it poses a growing strategic threat to the whole of Europe. Increasingly, terrorist movements are well resourced, connected by electronic networks, and are willing to use unlimited violence to cause massive casualties. The most recent wave of terrorism is global in its scope and is linked to violent religious extremism. It arises out of complex causes. These include the pressures of modernisation, cultural, social and political crises, and the alienation of young people living in foreign societies. This phenomenon is also a part of our own society. Europe is both a target and a base for such terrorism: European countries are targets and have been attacked. Logistical bases for Al Qaeda cells have been uncovered in the UK, Italy, Germany, Spain and Belgium. Concerted European action is indispensable.

Proliferation of Weapons of Mass Destruction is potentially the greatest threat to our security. The international treaty regimes and export control arrangements have slowed the spread of WMD and delivery systems. We are now, however, entering a new and dangerous period that raises the possibility of a WMD arms race, especially in the Middle East. Advances in the biological sciences may increase the potency of biological weapons in the coming years; attacks with chemical and radiological materials are also a serious possibility. The spread of missile technology adds a further element of instability and could put Europe at increasing risk. The most frightening scenario is one in which terrorist groups acquire weapons of mass destruction. In this event, a small group would be able to inflict damage on a scale previously possible only for States and armies.

Regional Conflicts: Problems such as those in Kashmir, the Great Lakes Region and the Korean Peninsula impact on European interests directly and indirectly, as do conflicts nearer to home, above all in the Middle East. Violent or frozen conflicts, which also persist on our borders, threaten regional stability. They destroy human lives and social and physical infrastructures; they threaten minorities, fundamental freedoms and human rights. Conflict can lead to extremism, terrorism and state failure; it provides opportunities for organised crime. Regional insecurity can fuel the demand for WMD. The most practical way to tackle the often elusive new threats will sometimes be to deal with the older problems of regional conflict.

State Failure: Bad governance – corruption, abuse of power, weak institutions and lack of accountability – and civil conflict corrode States from within. In some cases, this has brought about the collapse of State institutions. Somalia, Liberia and Afghanistan under the Taliban are the best known recent examples. Collapse of the State can be associated with obvious threats, such as organised crime or terrorism. State failure is an alarming phenomenon, that undermines global governance, and adds to regional instability.

Organised Crime: Europe is a prime target for organised crime. This internal threat to our security has an important external dimension: cross-border trafficking in drugs, women, illegal migrants and weapons accounts for a large part of the activities of criminal gangs. It can have links with terrorism. Such criminal activities are often associated with weak or failing states. Revenues from drugs have fuelled the weakening of state structures in several drug-producing countries. Revenues from trade in gemstones, timber and small arms, fuel conflict in other parts of the world. All these activities undermine both the rule of law and social order itself. In extreme cases, organised crime can come to dominate the state. 90% of the heroin in Europe comes from poppies grown in Afghanistan – where the drugs trade pays for private armies. Most of it is distributed through Balkan criminal networks, which are also responsible for some 200,000 of the 700,000 women victims of the sex trade world wide. A new dimension to organised crime, which will merit further attention, is the growth in maritime piracy.

Taking these different elements together – terrorism committed to maximum violence, the availability of weapons of mass destruction, organised crime, the weakening of the State system and the privatisation of force – we could be confronted with a very radical threat indeed. In an era of globalisation, distant threats may be as much a concern as those that are near at hand. Nuclear activities in North Korea, nuclear risks in South Asia, and proliferation in the Middle East are all of concern to Europe. Terrorists and criminals are now able to operate world-wide: their activities in central or southeast Asia may be a threat to European countries or their citizens. Meanwhile, global communication increases awareness in Europe of regional conflicts or humanitarian tragedies anywhere in the world.

Our traditional concept of self-defence – up to and including the Cold War – was based on the threat of invasion. With the new threats, the first line of defence will often be abroad. The new threats are dynamic. The risks of proliferation grow over time; left alone, terrorist networks will become ever more dangerous. State failure and organised crime spread if they are neglected – as we have seen in West Africa. This implies that we should be ready to act before a crisis occurs. Conflict prevention and threat prevention cannot start too early. In contrast to the massive visible threat in the Cold War, none of the new threats is purely military; nor can any be tackled by purely military means. Each requires a mixture of instruments. Proliferation may be contained through export controls and attacked through political, economic and other pressures while the underlying political causes are also tackled. Dealing with terrorism may require a mixture of intelligence, police, judicial, military and other means. In failed states, military instruments may be needed to restore order, humanitarian means to tackle the immediate crisis. Regional conflicts need political solutions but military assets and effective policing may be needed in the post conflict phase. Economic instruments serve reconstruction, and civilian crisis management helps restore civil government. The European Union is particularly well equipped to respond to such multi-faceted situations.

Enlargement should not create new dividing lines in Europe. Resolution of the Arab/Israeli conflict is a strategic priority for Europe.

BUILDING SECURITY IN OUR NEIGHBOURHOOD

Even in an era of globalisation, geography is still important. It is in the European interest that countries on our borders are well-governed. Neighbours who are engaged in violent conflict, weak states where organised crime flourishes, dysfunctional societies or exploding population growth on its borders all pose problems for Europe.

The integration of acceding states increases our security but also brings the EU closer to troubled areas. Our task is to promote a ring of well governed countries to the East of the European Union and on the borders of the Mediterranean with whom we can enjoy close and cooperative relations. The importance of this is best illustrated in the Balkans. Through our concerted efforts with the US, Russia, NATO and other international partners, the stability of the region is no longer threatened by the outbreak of major conflict. The credibility of our foreign policy depends on the consolidation of our achievements there. The European perspective offers both a strategic objective and an incentive for reform. It is not in our interest that enlargement should create new dividing lines in Europe. We need to extend the benefits of economic and political cooperation to our neighbours in the East while tackling political problems there. We should now take a stronger and more active interest in the problems of the Southern Caucasus, which will in due course also be a neighbouring region.

Resolution of the Arab/Israeli conflict is a strategic priority for Europe. Without this, there will be little chance of dealing with other problems in the Middle East. The European Union must remain engaged and ready to commit resources to the problem until it is solved. The two state solution, which Europe has long supported, is now widely accepted. Implementing it will require a united and cooperative effort by the European Union, the United States, the United Nations and Russia, and the countries of the region, but above all by the Israelis and the Palestinians themselves.

The Mediterranean area generally continues to undergo serious problems of economic stagnation, social unrest and unresolved conflicts. The European Union's interests require a continued engagement with Mediterranean partners, through more effective economic, security and cultural cooperation in the framework of the Barcelona Process. A broader engagement with the Arab World should also be considered.

Our security and prosperity increasingly depend on an effective multilateral system. We are committed to upholding and developing International Law. The fundamental framework for international relations is the United Nations Charter.

AN INTERNATIONAL ORDER BASED ON EFFECTIVE MULTILATERALISM

In a world of global threats, global markets and global media, our security and prosperity increasingly depend on an effective multilateral system. The development of a stronger international society, well functioning international institutions and a rule-based international order is our objective. We are committed to upholding and developing International Law. The fundamental framework for international relations is the United Nations Charter. The United Nations Security Council has the primary responsibility for the maintenance of international peace and security. Strengthening the United Nations, equipping it to fulfil its responsibilities and to act effectively, is a European priority.

We want international organisations, regimes and treaties to be effective in confronting threats to international peace and security, and must therefore be ready to act when their rules are broken. Key institutions in the international system, such as the World Trade Organisation (WTO) and the International Financial Institutions, have extended their membership. China has joined the WTO and Russia is negotiating its entry. It should be an objective for us to widen the membership of such bodies while maintaining their high standards.

One of the core elements of the international system is the transatlantic relationship. This is not only in our bilateral interest but strengthens the international community as a whole. NATO is an important expression of this relationship. Regional organisations also strengthen global governance. For the European Union, the strength and effectiveness of the OSCE and the Council of Europe has a particular significance. Other regional organisations such as ASEAN, MERCOSUR and the African Union make an important contribution to a more orderly world.

It is a condition of a rule-based international order that law evolves in response to developments such as proliferation, terrorism and global warming. We have an interest in further developing existing institutions such as the World Trade Organisation and in supporting new ones such as the International Criminal Court. Our own experience in Europe demonstrates that security can be increased through confidence building and arms control regimes. Such instruments can also make an important contribution to security and stability in our neighbourhood and beyond. The quality of international society depends on the quality of the governments that are its foundation. The best protection for our security is a world of well-governed democratic states. Spreading good governance, supporting social and political reform, dealing with corruption and abuse of power, establishing the rule of law and protecting human rights are the best means of strengthening the international order.

Trade and development policies can be powerful tools for promoting reform. As the world's largest provider of official assistance and its largest trading entity, the European Union and its Member States are well placed to pursue these goals. Contributing to better governance through assistance programmes, conditionality and targeted trade measures remains an important feature in our policy that we should further reinforce. A world seen as offering justice and opportunity for everyone will be more secure for the European Union and its citizens.

A number of countries have placed themselves outside the bounds of international society. Some have sought isolation; others persistently violate international norms. It is desirable that such countries should rejoin the international community, and the EU should be ready to provide assistance. Those who are unwilling to do so should understand that there is a price to be paid, including in their relationship with the European Union.

We need to develop a strategic culture that fosters early, rapid and, when necessary, robust intervention.

III. POLICY IMPLICATIONS FOR EUROPE

The European Union has made progress towards a coherent foreign policy and effective crisis management. We have instruments in place that can be used effectively, as we have demonstrated in the Balkans and beyond. But if we are to make a contribution that matches our potential, we need to be more active, more coherent and more capable. And we need to work with others.

More active in pursuing our strategic objectives. This applies to the full spectrum of instruments for crisis management and conflict prevention at our disposal, including political, diplomatic, military and civilian, trade and development activities. Active policies are needed to counter the new dynamic threats. We need to develop a strategic culture that fosters early, rapid, and, when necessary, robust intervention. As a Union of 25 members, spending more than 160 billion Euros on defence, we should be able to sustain several operations simultaneously. We could add particular value by developing operations involving both military and civilian capabilities. The EU should support the United Nations as it responds to threats to international peace and security. The EU is committed to reinforcing its cooperation with the UN to assist countries emerging from conflicts, and to enhancing its support for the UN in short-term crisis management situations. We need to be able to act before countries around us deteriorate, when signs of proliferation are detected, and before humanitarian emergencies arise. Preventive engagement can avoid more serious problems in the future. A European Union which takes greater responsibility and which is more active will be one which carries greater political weight.

More Capable. A more capable Europe is within our grasp, though it will take time to realise our full potential. Actions underway – notably the establishment of a defence agency – take us in the right direction. To transform our militaries into more flexible, mobile forces, and to enable them to address the new threats, more resources for defence and more effective use of resources are necessary. Systematic use of pooled and shared assets would reduce duplications, over-heads and, in the medium-term, increase capabilities. In almost every major intervention, military efficiency has been followed by civilian chaos. We need greater capacity to bring all necessary civilian resources to bear in crisis and post crisis situations. Stronger diplomatic capability: we need a system that combines the resources of Member States with those of EU institutions. Dealing with problems that are more distant and more foreign requires better understanding and communication. Common threat assessments are the best basis for common actions. This requires improved sharing of intelligence among Member States and with partners. As we increase capabilities in the different areas, we should think in terms of a wider spectrum of missions. This might include joint disarmament operations, support for third countries in combating terrorism and security sector reform. The last of these would be part of broader institution building. The EU–NATO permanent arrangements, in particular Berlin Plus, enhance the operational capability of the EU and provide the framework for the strategic partnership between the two organisa-tions in crisis management. This reflects our common determination to tackle the challenges of the new century.

Acting together, the European Union and the United States can be a formidable force for good in the world.

More Coherent. The point of the Common Foreign and Security Policy and European Security and Defence Policy is that we are stronger when we act together. Over recent years we have created a number of different instruments, each of which has its own structure and rationale. The challenge now is to bring together the different instruments and capabilities: European assistance programmes and the European Development Fund, military and civilian capailities from Member States and other instruments. All of these can have an impact on our security and on that of third countries. Security is the first condition for development. Diplomatic efforts, development, trade and environmental policies, should follow the same agenda. In a crisis there is no substitute for unity of command. Better co-ordination between external action and Justice and Home Affairs policies is crucial in the fight both against terrorism and organised crime. Greater coherence is needed not only among EU instruments but also embracing the external activities of the individual member states. Coherent policies are also needed regionally, especially in dealing with conflict. Problems are rarely solved on a single country basis, or without regional support, as in different ways experience in both the Balkans and West Africa shows.

Working with partners. There are few if any problems we can deal with on our own. The threats described above are common threats, shared with all our closest partners. International cooperation is a necessity. We need to pursue our objectives both through multilateral cooperation in international organisations and through partnerships with key actors. The transatlantic relationship is irreplaceable. Acting together, the European Union and the United States can be a formidable force for good in the world. Our aim should be an effective and balanced partnership with the USA. This is an additional reason for the EU to build up further its capabilities and increase its coherence. We should continue to work for closer relations with Russia, a major factor in our security and prosperity. Respect for common values will reinforce progress towards a strategic partnership. Our history, geography and cultural ties give us links with every part of the world: our neighbours in the Middle East, our partners in Africa, in Latin America, and in Asia. These relationships are an important asset to build on. In particular we should look to develop strategic partnerships, with Japan, China, Canada and India as well as with all those who share our goals and values, and are prepared to act in their support.

CONCLUSION

This is a world of new dangers but also of new opportunities. The European Union has the potential to make a major contribution, both in dealing with the threats and in helping realise the opportunities. An active and capable European Union would make an impact on a global scale. In doing so, it would contribute to an effective multilateral system leading to a fairer, safer and more united world.

Appendix Three
Some key figures in EU foreign policy

The foreign ministers of the Big Three always play an important role in EU foreign policy. In the UK **Robin Cook** was Foreign Secretary in the first Blair government (1997–2001) and attempted to introduce an ethical dimension to British diplomacy. **Jack Straw**, who was previously Home Secretary, succeeded him in 2001. He had little foreign policy experience when he took office and tended to adopt a pragmatic approach knowing that major issues, such as relations with the US, are handled by the Prime Minister's Office. **Margaret Beckett**, the UK's first female foreign secretary, replaced him in 2006. France has changed its foreign minister several times in recent years. Perhaps the most well known is **Dominique de Villepin**, who famously contradicted Colin Powell during a UNSC debate on Iraq in February 2005. Tall and handsome, he looks as if he could have walked out of Hollywood central casting for the role of France's top diplomat. He was succeeded by **Michel Barnier**, a confidant of President Chirac and a former French Commissioner, but he was blamed for the French 'no' in the May 2005 referendum on the constitutional treaty and was forced to resign. He in turn was succeeded by **Philippe Douste-Blazy**, a strange choice as he was a medical doctor with no previous foreign policy experience. For many years Germany had perhaps the most flamboyant foreign minister in **Joschka Fischer**, the leader of the Greens and former student revolutionary. He managed to change his party's traditional pacifist outlook to one of support for humanitarian interventions, e.g. Kosovo in 1999, but he was also critical of US policy on Iraq. In February 2003 he confronted US Secretary of Defense Donald Rumsfeld at a conference: 'If you cannot convince me about Iraqui WMD how do you expect me to convince my fellow citizens?' With the formation of a grand coalition in Germany in November 2005 the SPD regained the foreign ministry for the first time since Willy Brandt over 30 years ago. The new minister was **Frank-Walter Steinmeier** who had been chief of staff to former Chancellor Gerhard Schroeder. He, too, had little foreign policy experience but had been at Schroeder's side at many summits and bilateral meetings. Born in 1956 and the son of a carpenter, Steinmeier is a lawyer by training. But he made his career in the SPD and gained a reputation as a capable fixer of complex problems.

Few other foreign ministers have made a real mark on the European scene with the exception of Sweden's **Anna Lindh**, who was tragically killed in 2002. In 2006, Carl Bildt, the former prime minister, became foreign minister, thus raising Sweden's profile in foreign policy. In the EU the spotlight usually falls on **Javier Solana**, the gregarious Spanish socialist. On the Commission side, two former foreign ministers have prominent roles, **Benita Ferrero-Waldner** (Austria) in charge of external relations and neighbourhood policy; and **Louis Michel**, the motorcycling Belgian in charge of development policy. There is also much attention on **Peter Mandelson** (UK), a close ally of Tony Blair and responsible for trade policy; and **Olli Rehn**, the Finnish Commissioner for Enlargement.

Overall, foreign policy tends to be made in the offices of prime ministers and presidents, leaving foreign ministers with a less glamorous and less exciting job than in the past. When it comes to the really big decisions, then, it is **Tony Blair**, **Jacques Chirac** and **Angela Merkel** who have the decisive say.

Glossary

CFSP Councillors. These are officials based in the Permanent Representations of the member states in Brussels and the Commission. They examine horizontal problems concerning the CFSP, in particular legal, institutional and financial aspects of CFSP actions (notably Joint Actions, Common Positions), which they finalise before approval by the PSC, Coreper and the Council.

Committee of Permanent Representatives ('Coreper'). Permanent Representatives of member states to the EU and the Commission Deputy Secretary General meet once a week to prepare Council meetings and decisions. Coreper has overall responsibility for preparing the work of the Council in all its compositions. Coreper can attach comments and recommendations to opinions and proposals submitted to the Council by the PSC but in practice it rarely has the time or expertise to do so.

Common Positions are designed to make co-operation between the EU and member states on foreign policy more systematic and co-ordinated. The member states are required to comply with and uphold such positions, which are adopted unanimously by the Council.

Common Strategy. The European Council decides Common Strategies to be implemented by the Union in fields where the member states have important interests in common, e.g. Russia, Ukraine, the western Balkans, the Mediterranean.

COREU network. The COREU telex network (Correspondant Européen) is a network allowing transmission of enciphered messages used for all aspects of information exchange between capitals and with the Commission, and by the Presidency in the everyday management of the CFSP. The Council may act on CFSP matters by simplified written procedure using the COREU network.

Council CFSP Working Groups. CFSP working groups (or parties) are composed of experts from EU member states and the Commission meeting along geographical and horizontal lines to elaborate policy documents and options for the consideration of the PSC (see list in Chapter 3).

Council of Ministers. EU foreign ministers meet at least once a month as the General Affairs and External Relations Council (GAERC) in which the Commission is represented by the External Affairs Commissioner. According to the Treaty (Art. 13), the Council 'shall take the decisions necessary for defining and implementing' the CFSP 'on the basis of the general guidelines defined by the European Council', it shall 'recommend Common Strategies to the European Council and implement these, in particular by adopting joint actions and common positions' and 'ensure the unity, consistency and effectiveness of action by the Union' in the field of the CFSP. The Council is the general forum for information and consultation on CFSP matters among member states (Art. 16 TEU). In addition to its permanent role in ensuring the smooth operation of the Community and the Union and its specific responsibility under the CFSP, the GAERC has overall responsibility for all preparatory work for the European Council; consequently matters to be submitted to the European Council must first be submitted to the GAERC. The Council and the Commission are jointly responsible for the 'consistency of the Union's external activities as a whole, in the context of its external relations, security, economic and development policies' and 'shall cooperate to this end' (Art. 3 TEU).

Declarations. This is an instrument for which there is no treaty provision but which was a feature of European political co-operation (EPC). It is still frequently used under the CFSP. There were several such declarations at the June 2006 European Council.

Double-hatting. This concept relates to the proposed EU foreign minister being simultaneously the chair of the GAERC and a Vice-President of the Commission. This would allegedly improve coherence. It has also been used in third countries, e.g. Macedonia, where the Commission head of delegation doubles as the Council representative.

European Correspondents. European Correspondents are mid-level officials from member states and the Commission who ensure co-ordination of the input into the CFSP. They assist the PSC and prepare and participate in meetings within the CFSP structures, including political dialogue meeting with third countries. In addition European Correspondents co-ordinate daily CFSP communications, notably through the COREU network (see above).

European Council. The European Council is composed of heads of state and government and the Commission President who meet four times a year. It 'shall provide the Union with the necessary impetus for its development and shall define the general policy guidelines thereof' (Art. 4 TEU). In the CFSP in particular, its role is to 'define the principles and general guidelines including for matters with defence implications' (Art. 13 TEU). Furthermore the European Council is 'to decide on common strategies to be implemented by the Union in areas where the Member States have important interests in common'. The direct involvement of the European Council in the CFSP adds political weight and commits the highest political authorities in member states to the CFSP.

European Parliament. According to the Treaty (Art. 21), 'the Presidency shall inform and consult the European Parliament on the main aspects and the basic choices of the common foreign and security policy and shall ensure that the views of the European Parliament are duly taken into consideration. The European Parliament may ask questions of the Council or make recommendations to it. It shall hold an annual debate on progress in implementing the common foreign and security policy.' The Presidency and/or the Commission, when considered useful and necessary, attends the meetings of the Parliament's Committees on Foreign Affairs and Security and participates, if need be, in Parliament's debates in plenary session. At Council meetings the Presidency informs the Council of Parliament's reactions, communications, questions, recommendation or resolutions concerning the CFSP.

High Representative (Mr CFSP). The Amsterdam Treaty introduced the new office of a High Representative (HR) for the CFSP. He is also the Council Secretary General. The HR 'shall assist the Council in matters coming within the scope of the CFSP, in particular through contributing to the formulation, preparation and implementation of policy decisions, and, when appropriate and acting on behalf of the Council at the request of the Presidency, through conducting political dialogue with third countries' (Art. 26). The HR will also 'assist the Presidency' in the external representation of the EU and in the implementation of decisions in CFSP matters (Art. 18).

Joint Action refers to a legal instrument under Title V of the Treaty on European Union and means co-ordinated action by the member states whereby resources of all kinds (human resources, know-how, financing, equipment, etc.) are mobilised to attain specific objectives fixed by the Council on the base of general guidelines from the European Council.

Petersberg tasks. These tasks involve the use of military forces provided by EU member states for 'humanitarian and rescue tasks; peacekeeping tasks; tasks of combat forces in crisis management, including peacemaking'.

Policy Planning and Early Warning Unit (PPEWU). Situated in the Council, its mandate includes monitoring, analysis and assessment of international developments and events, including early warning on potential crises. It also includes drafting, upon Council request or on its own initiative, of policy options, which may contain recommendations and strategies for presentation to the Council under the responsibility of the Presidency as a contribution to policy formulation. PPEWU staff come from the Council Secretariat, member states and the Commission.

Political and Security Committee (PSC). The PSC is composed of ambassadors from the member states and a representative from the Commission. The PSC is more commonly known as COPS from the French (comité politique et securité) and meets twice a week, Tuesdays and Fridays. Its main tasks include: monitoring the international situation in the areas covered by the CFSP; contributing to the definition of policies by delivering opinions to the Council at the request of the Council or on its own initiative; monitoring the implementation of agreed policies, 'without prejudice to the responsibility of the Presidency and the Commission'; and overseeing crisis-management operations.

Presidency/Troika. The Amsterdam Treaty modifies rules on external representation and responsibility for implementation of decisions in the area of the CFSP. The Presidency remains in charge and represents the Union in matters coming within the CFSP as well as being responsible for implementation of decisions. In its tasks it is assisted by a troika – the High Representative for CFSP and 'if need be' by the next member state to hold the Presidency. As before, the Commission is fully associated in these tasks. There are thus usually four actors in the troika.

Notes

3 THE EU FOREIGN POLICY MACHINERY

1 *External Relations: Demands, Constraints and Priorities*, SEC (2000) 922.
2 See Patten's speeches in Paris in June 2000 and in Dublin in March 2001.

5 THE DEFENCE DIMENSION

1 See the Foreign and Commonwealth Office joint declaration issued at the British–French summit, St-Malo, France, 3–4 December 1998.
2 See European Council, Presidency Conclusions of the European Council in Helsinki, 10–11 December 1999.
3 http://www.securityconference.de/
4 See also speeches at the Munich Security Conference in February 2006.
5 See also speech by Guenther Verheugen on 9 February 2006 calling for more collaboration between EU and national space and defence industrial research.
6 See note 1.

9 THE EU AND ASIA

1 See the 2001 Commission communication, *Europe and Asia: A Strategic Framework for Enhanced Partnerships*.
2 Commission communication, *A Maturing Partnership: Shared Interests and Challenges in EU–China Relations*, COM(03) 533, Brussels, 10 September 2003.
3 Speech in Tokyo, 21 April 2006.
4 *A New Partnership with South-East Asia*, COM (2003) 399 final, 9 July 2003.
5 The June 2004 Commission communication, *EU–India Strategic Partnership*.

11 CONFLICT PREVENTION AND CRISIS MANAGEMENT

1 *A Human Security Doctrine for Europe*, Barcelona, 15 September 2004.
2 Solana produced a paper on 3 March 2006 on how to improve the EU's response to disasters and three days later came out with proposals at a meeting of EU defence ministers in Innsbruck to improve civil–military co-ordination. Both papers are available on the Council website.

12 TACKLING TERRORISM

1 Conversation with the author.
2 See Council website for meeting between Solana and the secretary-general of the Islamic Conference in Jeddah on 13 February 2006.
3 The latest action plan is available as Council document 5771/1/06 of 13 February 2006.

13 FUTURE PROSPECTS

1 Speech at the European Policy Centre.
2 *Europe in the World: Some Practical Proposals for Greater Coherence, Effectiveness and Visibility*, COM (2006) 278, 8 June 2006.
3 *Le Monde*, 6 June 2006. Bolton was unable to secure a second term after the Democrats captured Congress in the November 2006 elections.
4 Richard Rosecrance, *Paradoxes of European Foreign Policy*, EUI Working Papers, RSC 97/64.

Bibliography

There are a vast number of sources for the external relations of the EU, and this review is by no means comprehensive. It is designed more as a guide to help students by highlighting some of the principal books on the subject. Inevitably I have had to be selective; and, given the fast-changing nature of foreign policy, the list is biased towards the most recent publications. Many good articles on the external relations of the EU are published in academic journals such as the *Journal of Common Market Studies*, the *European Foreign Affairs Review*, *Foreign Affairs*, *Foreign Policy*, the *International Spectator*, *Internationale Politik* and *Politique étrangère*. The Paris-based EU Institute for Security Studies also produces a very good series called the Chaillot Papers. They are available at www.iss-eu.org. The weekly newspaper *European Voice* also contains good coverage of EU external affairs. Another very useful source is the academic foreign policy network www.fornet.info.

BOOKS AND ARTICLES

Aliboni, R. (2005) 'The geopolitical implications of the European neighbourhood', *European Foreign Affairs Review*, vol. 10, no. 1.

Arts, K. and Dickson, A.K. (eds) (2004) *EU Development Cooperation: From Model to Symbol*, Manchester: Manchester University Press.

Balfour, R. et al. (2005) 'The challenges of the European Neighbourhood Policy', *The International Spectator*, vol. 40, no. 1.

Barbé, E. and Herranz, A. (eds) (2005) *The Role of Parliaments in European Foreign Policy*, Observatory of European Foreign Policy, Institut Universitari d'Estudis Europeus, Barcelona.

Bildt, C. (1998) *Peace Journey*, London: Weidenfeld & Nicolson.

Biscop, S. (2005) *The European Security Strategy*, Brussels: Belgian Royal Institute of International Affairs.

Bretherton, C. and Vogler, J. (2006) *The European Union as a Global Actor*, 2nd edn, London: Routledge.

Bridges, B. (1999) *Europe and the Challenge of the Asia–Pacific: Change, Continuity and Crisis*, London: Edward Elgar.

Buchan, D. (1993) *Europe: The Strange Superpower*, Aldershot: Dartmouth,

Buzan, B., Waever, O. and de Wilde, J. (1998) *Security: A New Framework for Analysis*, Boulder, Colo.: Lynne Rienner.

Cameron, F. (1999) *The Foreign and Security Policy of the European Union: Past, Present and Future*, Sheffield: Sheffield Academic Press.

Cameron, F. (2005) *US Foreign Policy after the Cold War*, London: Routledge.

Cameron, F. (2006) *The ENP as a Conflict Prevention Tool*, EPC issue paper no. 47.

Cameron, F. and Grevi, G. (2005) *Towards an EU Foreign Service*, EPC issue paper no. 29.

Carlsnaes, W., Sjursen, H. and White, B. (eds) (2004) *Contemporary European Foreign Policy*, London: Sage.

Chaban, N. and Holland, M. (eds) (2005) *The EU through the Eyes of the Asia-Pacific*, NCRE Research Series no. 4, New Zealand: University of Canterbury.

Christiansen, T. and Tonra, B. (eds) (2004) *Rethinking EU Foreign Policy*, Manchester: Manchester University Press.

Clarke, R. (2004) *Against All Enemies*, London: Simon & Schuster.

Connors, M. K., Davidson, R. and Dosch, J. (eds) (2004) *The New Global Politics of the Asia-Pacific*, London: Routledge.

Cooper, R. (2003) *The Breaking of Nations: Order and Chaos in the Twenty-First Century*, New York/London: Atlantic Monthly Press/Atlantic Books.

Cosgrove-Sachs, C. (ed.) (1999) *The European Union and Developing Countries: The Challenges of Globalization*, Basingstoke: Macmillan.

Dannreuther, R. (ed.) (2004) *European Union Foreign and Security Policy: Towards a Neighbourhood Strategy*, London: Routledge.

de Schoutheete de Tervarent, P. (1980) *La coopération politique européenne*, 2nd edn, Brussels: F. Nathan Editions Labor.

Deighton, A. (ed.) (1997) *Western European Union, 1954–97: Defence, Security, Integration*, Oxford: St Antony's College.

Dent, C. M. (1999) *Europe and East Asia: An Economic Perspective*, London: Routledge.

Deutsch, K. (1968) *The Analysis of International Relations*, Englewood Cliffs, NJ: Prentice-Hall.

Doyle, M. and Ikenberry, J. (eds) (1997) *New Thinking in International Relations Theory*, Boulder, Colo.: Westview Press.

Eeckhout, P. (2005) *External Relations of the European Union: Legal and Constitutional Foundations*, Oxford: Oxford University Press.

Elsig, M. (2002) *The EU's Common Commercial Policy: Institutions, Interests and Ideas*, Aldershot: Ashgate.

Emerson, M. et al. (2005) *The Reluctant Debutante: The European Union as Promoter of Democracy in Its Neighbourhood*, Brussels: Centre for European Policy Studies.

Fukuyama, F. (1992) *The End of History and the Last Man*, New York: Maxwell Macmillan International,

Galloway, D. (2002) *The Treaty of Nice and Beyond: Realities and Illusions of Power in the EU*, Sheffield: Sheffield Academic Press.

Gillespie, R. (ed.) (1997) *The Euro-Mediterranean Partnership*, Ilford: Frank Cass.

Ginsberg, R. (2001) *The European Union in International Politics: Baptism of Fire*, Lanham, Md: Rowman & Littlefield.

Gordon, P. and Shapiro, J. (2004) *Allies at War: America, Europe, and the Crisis over Iraq*, New York: McGraw-Hill.

Goulard. S. (2004) *Le Grand Turc et la République de Venise*, Paris: Fayard.

Haas, E. (1958) *The Uniting of Europe*, Stanford, Calif.: Stanford University Press.

Halliday, F. (2003) *Islam and the Myth of Confrontation*, London: Tauris.

Hamilton, D. and Quinlan, J. (2004) *The Changing Geography of the Transatlantic Economy*, Washington, DC: Johns Hopkins University Press.

Hannay, D. (2004) *Cyprus – the Search for a Solution*, London: Palgrave.

Hill, C. (1993) 'The Capability–Expectations Gap, or Conceptualizing Europe's International Role', *Journal of Common Market Studies*, vol. 31, no. 3.

Hill, C. (ed.) (1996) *The Actors in Europe's Foreign Policy*, London: Routledge.

Hill, C. (2003) *The Changing Politics of Foreign Policy*, Basingstoke: Palgrave.

Hill, C. and Smith, K. E. (eds) (2000) *European Foreign Policy: Key Documents*, London: Routledge.

Hill, C. and Smith, M. (eds) (2005) *International Relations and the European Union*, Oxford: Oxford University Press.

Hocking, B. and Spence, D. (eds) (2002) *Foreign Ministries in the European Union: Integrating Diplomats*, Basingstoke: Palgrave.

Holbrooke, R. (1998) *To End a War*, New York: Random House.

Holland, M. (ed.) (1997) *Common Foreign and Security Policy: The Record and Reforms*, London: Cassell Academic.

Holland, M. (2002) *The European Union and the Third World*, Basingstoke: Palgrave.

Holland, M. (2004) *Common Foreign and Security Policy: The First Decade*, Continuum, London.

Howarth, J. and Keeler, J. (eds) (2003) *Defending Europe: The EU, NATO, and the Quest for European Autonomy*, New York: Palgrave/Macmillan.

Kagan, R. (2003) *Paradise and Power: America and Europe in the New World Order*, London: Atlantic Books.

Keohane, R. (1983) *International Institutions and State Power: Essays on International Relations*, Boulder, Colo.: Westview Press.

Kronenberger, V. and Wouters, J. (eds) (2004) *The European Union and Conflict Prevention: Legal and Policy Aspects*, The Hague: TMC Asser Press.

Kupchan, C. (2002) *The End of the American Era*, New York: Knopf.

Larsen, H. (1997) *Foreign Policy and Discourse Analysis*, London: Routledge.

Leonard, M. (2005) *Why Europe Will Run the 21st Century*, London: Fourth Estate.

Lewis, B. (2003) *The Crisis of Islam*, London: Weidenfeld & Nicolson.

Lister, M. (1997) *The European Union and the South*, London: Routledge.

Lord, C. and Winn, N. (2001) *European Foreign Policy Beyond the Nation State: Joint Actions and Institutions Analysis of the CFSP*, Basingstoke: Palgrave.

Lynch, D. (2004) *The Russia–EU Partnership and the Shared Neighbourhood*, European Union Institute for Security Studies, July.

Mair, P., Zielonka, J. and Hill, C. (eds) (1996) *The Actors in Europe's Foreign Policy*, London: Routledge.

Manners, R. and Whitman, R. (eds) (2000) *The Foreign Policies of the European Union Member States*, Manchester: Manchester University Press.

Neuhold, H. and Sucharipa, E. (eds) (2003) *The CFSP/ESDP after Enlargement: A Bigger EU = A Stronger EU?*, Favorita Papers of the Diplomatic Academy, Vienna, No. 2/2003, Vienna.

Nuttall, S. (2000) *European Foreign Policy*, Oxford: Oxford University Press.

Owen, D. (1995) *Balkan Odyssey*, London: Cassell.

Pappas, S. and Vanhoonacker, S. (eds) (1996) *The European Union's Common Foreign and Security Policy*, Maastricht: European Institute of Public Administration.

Patten, C. (2005) *Not Quite the Diplomat*, London: Allen Lane.

Paulauskas, Kestutis (2006) *The Baltics: From Nation States to Member States*, EU Institute for Security Studies Occasional Paper No. 62.

Peterson, J. and Pollack, M. (eds) (2003) *Europe, America, Bush: Transatlantic Relations in the Twenty-First Century*, London: Routledge.

Peterson, J. and Sjursen, H. (eds) (1998) *A Common Foreign Policy for Europe? Competing Visions of the CFSP*, London: Routledge.

Philippart, E. and Winand, P. (eds) (2001) *Ever Closer Partnership: Policy-Making in US–EU Relations*, Brussels: PIE-Peter Lang.

Piening, C. (1997) *Global Europe: The European Union in World Affairs*, Boulder, Colo./London: Lynne Rienner.

Regelsberger, E. (2003) 'The Impact of EU Enlargement on CFSP Procedures and Policies – Some Mixed Results', in Neuhold, H. and Sucharipa, E. (eds) *The CFSP/ESDP After Enlargement: A Bigger EU = A Stronger EU?* Favorita Papers of the Diplomatic Academy, Vienna, No. 2/2003, Vienna.

Regelsberger, E., de Schoutheete de Tervarent, P. and Wessels, W. (eds) (1997) *Foreign Policy of the European Union: From EPC to CFSP and Beyond*, Boulder, Colo./London: Lynne Rienner.

Reiter, M. (2002) *Asia–Europe: Do They Meet?* Singapore: Asia Europe Foundation.

Rieber, R. and Monar, J. (eds) (1995) *Justice and Home Affairs in the European Union: The Development of the Third Pillar*, Bruges: College of Europe.

Rifkin, J. (2004) *The European Dream*, New York, Penguin.

Sageman, M. (2005) *Understanding Terror Networks*, Pennsylvania, Pa: University of Pennsylvania Press.

Schimmelfennig, F. (2004) *The EU, NATO and the Integration of Europe: Rules and Rhetoric*, Cambridge: Cambridge University Press.

Sjöstedt, G. (1977) *The External Role of the European Community*, Westmead: Saxon House.

Sloan, S. (2002) *NATO, the European Union and the Atlantic Community: The Transatlantic Bargain Reconsidered*, Lanham, Md: Rowman & Littlefield.

Smith, H. (2002) *European Union Foreign Policy: What It Is and What It Does*, London: Pluto Press.

Smith, K. (2003) *European Union Foreign Policy in a Changing World*, Cambridge: Polity Press.

Smith, K. (2004) *The Making of EU Foreign Policy: The Case of Eastern Europe*, 2nd edn, Basingstoke: Palgrave.

Smith, M. E. (2003) *Europe's Foreign and Security Policy: The Institutionalization of Cooperation*, Cambridge: Cambridge University Press.

Smith, R. (2005) *The Utility of Force*, London: Penguin.

Soetendorp, B. (1999) *Foreign Policy in the European Union*, London: Longman.

Telò, M. (2005) *Europe: A Civilian Power? European Union, Global Governance, World Order*, Basingstoke: Palgrave.

Tocci, N. (2005) 'The Challenges of the European Neighbourhood Policy – Does the ENP Respond to the EU's Post-Enlargement Challenges?', *The International Spectator*, vol. 40 no. 1.

von Dosenrode, S. and Stubkjaer, A. (2002) *The European Union and the Middle East*, London: Continuum.

Wallace, W. and Wallace, H. (2004) *Policy-making in the European Union*, 5th edn, Oxford: Oxford University Press.

Waltz, K. (1979) *Theory of International Politics*, London: Addison-Wesley.

Whitman, R. (1998) *From Civilian Power to Superpower? The International Identity of the European Union*, London: Macmillan.

Wiessala, G. (2002) *The European Union and Asian Countries*, London: Continuum.

Xenakis, D. and Chryssochoou, D. (2001) *The Emerging Euro-Mediterranean System*, Manchester: Manchester University Press.

Youngs, R. (2001) *The European Union and the Promotion of Democracy: Europe's Mediterranean and Asian Policies*, Oxford: Oxford University Press.

Zielonka, J. (ed.) (1998) *Paradoxes of European Foreign Policy*, The Hague: Kluwer Law International.

Zielonka, J. (ed.) (2002) *Europe Unbound: Enlarging and Reshaping the Boundaries of the European Union*, London: Routledge.

WEBSITES

There are many useful websites for students of EU foreign policy. The EU institutions can all be accessed via the europa server at http://www.europa.eu.int. This leads the reader to the Commission, Council and Parliament websites. The Commission websites most relevant for external relations include DG Relex, DG Trade, DG Development and DG Enlargement. A useful guide to the Commission's delegations is provided in the brochure *Taking Europe to the World: 50 Years of the European Commission's External Service*, Luxembourg: Office for Official Publications of the European Communities, 2004.

The ministries of foreign affairs of the member states usually have good information about the EU, albeit from their own national perspective.

Austria
Ministry for Foreign Affairs
http://www.bmaa.gv.at/view.php3?rid=1&LNG=en&version=

Belgium
Ministry of Foreign Affairs
http://www.diplobel.fgov.be/

Cyprus
Ministry of Foreign Affairs
http://www.mfa.gov.cy/mfa/mfa.nsf/mfa?OpenForm

Czech Republic
Ministry of Foreign Affairs
http://www.mzv.cz/wwwo/mzv/default.asp?amb=1&idj=2&trid=3

Denmark
Ministry of Foreign Affairs
http://www.um.dk/en

Estonia
Ministry of Foreign Affairs
http://www.vm.ee/

Finland
Ministry for Foreign Affairs of Finland
http://formin.finland.fi/english/

France
The Ministry of Foreign Affairs
http://www.france.diplomatie.fr/index.html

Germany
Federal Foreign Office
http://www.auswaertiges-amt.de/

Greece
The Ministry of Foreign Affairs
http://www.mfa.gr/

Hungary
http://www.meh.hu/

Ireland
The Department of Foreign Affairs
http://foreignaffairs.gov.ie/

Italy
Ministry of Foreign Affairs
http://www.esteri.it/

Latvia
Ministry of Foreign Affairs
http://www.mfa.gov.lv/

Lithuania
Ministry of Foreign Affairs
http://www.urm.lt/

Luxembourg
Ministry of Foreign Affairs
http://www.mae.lu/

Malta
Ministry of Foreign Affairs
http://www.foreign.gov.mt/

Netherlands
Ministry of Foreign Affairs
http://www.minbuza.nl/homepage.asp

Poland
Ministry of Foreign Affairs
http://www.msz.gov.pl/

Portugal
Ministry of Foreign Affairs
http://www.min-nestrangeiros.pt/mne/

Slovakia
Ministry of Foreign Affairs
http://www.foreign.gov.sk/En/index.html

Slovenia
Ministry of Foreign Affairs
http://www.foreign.gov.sk/En/index.html

Spain
Ministry of Foreign Affairs
http://www.mae.es/

Sweden
Ministry of Foreign Affairs
http://www.ud.se/

United Kingdom
Foreign and Commonwealth Office
http://www.fco.gov.uk/

THINK-TANKS

Many think-tanks cover the external relations of the EU, including:

Atlantic Council of the US
http://www.acus.org

CEPS – Centre for European Policy Studies
http://www.ceps.be

CSIS – Center for Strategic and International Studies
http://www.csis.org

DGAP – Deutsche Gesellschaft fuer Auswaertige Politik
http://www.dgap.org

ELIAMEP – Hellenic Foundation for European and Foreign Policy
http://www.eliamep.gr

EPC – The European Policy Centre
http://www.theepc.be

GMF – The German Marshall Fund
http://www.gmfus.org

IAI – Instituto Affari Internazionale
http://www.iai.it

IFRI – Institut français pour la recherche internationale
http://www.ifri.org

IRRI – Royal Institute for International Relations (Belgium)
http://www.irri-kiib.be

ISIS – International Security Information Service
http://www.isis-europe.org

The Royal Institute of International Affairs (Chatham House)
http://www.riia.org

SIPRI – Stockholm International Peace Research Institute
http://www.sipri.org

SWP – Stiftung Wissenschaft und Politik
http://www.swp-berlin.org

NGOs

Many NGOs lobby Brussels to promote or change policies. Some of the most important in external relations include:

Amnesty: http://www.amnesty.org
Conflict Prevention Partnership: http://www.conflictprevention.net
Crisis Group: http://www.crisisgroup.org
EPLO: http://www.eplo.org
Greenpeace: http://www.greenpeace.org/international
Human Rights Watch: http://www.hrw.org
International Alert: http://www.international-alert.org
Médecins sans Frontières: http://www.msf.org
Oxfam: http://www.oxfam.org/
Solidar: http://www.solidar.org

MEDIA

The media give rather poor coverage to external affairs, but among the most important written outlets are:

Agence Europe: http://www.agenceurope.com
All Africa: http://www.africanews.org/
Arabic News: http://www.arabicnews.com/
Asia Times Online: http://www.atimes.com/
BBC World Service: http://www.bbc.co.uk/worldservice/index.shtml
China Daily: http://www.chinadaily.net/
CNN Network: http://www.cnn.com
Corierre del Serra: http://www.corriere.it/
Economist: http://www.economist.com/
European Voice: http://www.european-voice.com
Financial Times: http://news.ft.com/home/europe
Frankfurter Allgemeine: http://www.faz.net/s/homepage.html

International Herald Tribune: http://www.iht.com/
Le Monde: http://www.lemonde.fr
El Pais: http://www.elpais.es/
Der Spiegel: http://www.spiegel.de

OTHER USEFUL WEBSITES

Acronym Finder: http://www.acronymfinder.com/
Asia-Pacific Economic Cooperation (APEC): http://www.apec.org/
Association of South-East Asian Nations (ASEAN): http://www.asean.or.id/
Carnegie Commission for Preventing Deadly Conflict: http://www.ccpdc.org/
Carter Centre: http://www.cartercenter.org
Conflict and Conflict Resolution Resources: http://www.cfcsc.dnd.ca/links/intrel/
    confli.html
Conflict Prevention Web: http://www.caii-dc.com/ghai/welcome.htm
Council of Europe: http://www.coe.fr/index.asp
European Platform for Conflict Prevention and Transformation: http://www.
    oneworld.org/euconflict/
European Union Internet Resources: http://www.lib.berkeley.edu/GSSI/eu.html
G8 Information Centre: http://www.g7.utoronto.ca/
Global Policy Forum: http://www.globalpolicy.org/
Heritage Foundation: http://www.heritage.org/
Institute of Development Studies: http://www.ids.ac.uk
International Atomic Energy Agency (IAEA): http://www.iaea.org.at
International Court of Justice (ICJ): http://www.icj-cij.org/
International Development Studies Network (IDSNet): http://www.idsnet.org
International Institute for Strategic Studies: http://www.iiss.org
International Institute for Sustainable Development: http://iisd1.iisd.ca/
International Monetary Fund (IMF): http://www.imf.org
International Organisations: http://www.uia.org/website.htm
International Relations and Security Network: http://www.isn.ethz.ch
North Atlantic Treaty Organisation (NATO): http://www.nato.int/
Organisation for Economic Co-operation and Development (OECD): http://www.
    oecd.org/
Organisation for Security and Co-operation in Europe (OSCE): http://www.osce.org/
Organisation of African Unity (OAU): http://www.oau-oua.org/
Organisation of Petroleum Exporting Countries (OPEC): http://www.opec.org
Rand Corporation: http://www.rand.org/
Soros Foundation: http://www.soros.org/
United Nations (UN): http://www.un.org/
United Nations Development Program: http://www.undp.org/
United States Institute for Peace: http://www.usip.org
Woodrow Wilson International Center for Scholars: http://wwics.si.edu
World Bank: http://www.worldbank.org
World Directory of Think Tanks: http://www.nira.go.jp/ice/tt-info/nwdtt99/
World Health Organisation (WHO): http://www.who.int/
World Trade Organisation (WTO): http://www.wto.org

Index